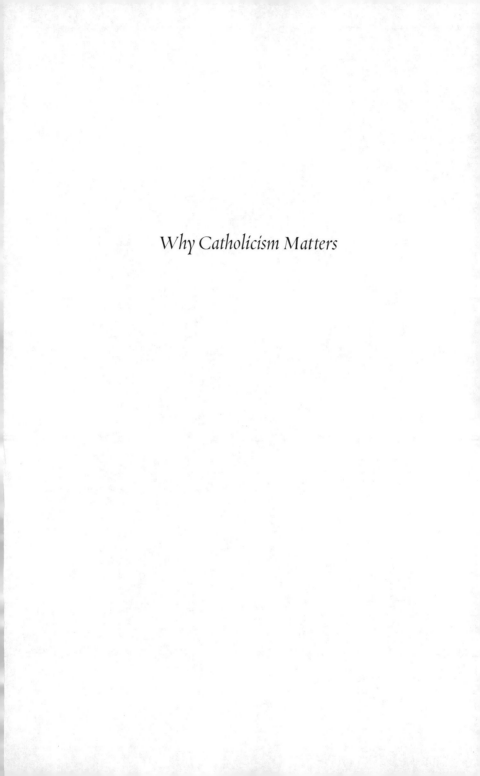

Why Catholicism Matters

Why Catholicism Matters

How Catholic Virtues Can
Reshape Society in the 21st Century

BILL DONOHUE

IMAGE

NEW YORK

Copyright © 2012, 2013 by Dr. William Donohue

All rights reserved.
Published in the United States by Image, an imprint of the Crown
Publishing Group, a division of Random House, Inc., New York.
www.crownpublishing.com

IMAGE is a registered trademark, and the "I" colophon is a trademark
of Random House, Inc.

Originally published in hardcover in slightly different form
in the United States by Image, an imprint of the Crown Publishing
Group, a division of Random House, Inc., New York, in 2012.

Cataloging-in-Publication Data is on file with the Library of Congress.

ISBN 978-0-307-88534-0
eISBN 978-0-307-88535-7

Jacket design by Laura Duffy

First Paperback Edition

For Father Philip K. Eichner, S.M.

Contents

Introduction 1

Prudence 39

Justice 97

Fortitude 157

Temperance 217

For Discussion 278

Acknowledgments 281

Notes 282

INTRODUCTION

The quest for the good society has intrigued philosophers down through the ages. It has also been the object of radical pursuit on the part of activists and revolutionaries. It is hardly an exaggeration to say that almost all of these efforts have been an utter failure. Most of them failed because their ideas were inherently flawed. Others failed because their ideas, however practical and endearing, never took root; they were therefore destined for a short life. The few exceptions, such as the efforts of the Founding Fathers, were confined to the political sphere; in their case, the crafting of a government providing for liberty, while stunning, left most aspects of the good society unaddressed.

If there is one institution that embodies the right recipe for the makings of the good society it is the Roman Catholic Church. Its teachings, especially those that have a public impact, are as well suited to answering today's social problems as they were two thousand years ago. If only they were followed. But if the Church's teachers, namely the clergy, have often had a hard time following its teachings, not only can we expect somewhat less from among the faithful, but we cannot be surprised to learn that no society has ever succeeded in implementing them. That, however, is no excuse for not trying.

It is more important now than ever before that we accept

the challenge that Catholicism poses. The conditions in the third millennium are not auspicious. Not only do war, ecological disaster, poverty, and illness threaten to destroy civilization, the West seems to have lost its moral compass. All of which means that we must make some hard choices. Not only is Europe, once the bastion of economic and scientific achievement, sliding backward, it is morally deracinated; regrettably, it has rejected its own glorious heritage in the name of multiculturalism. Although there are signs that a reality check has been delivered, for example, the heads of state in England, France, and Germany have become vocal critics of multiculturalism, the preoccupation with radical individualism continues, and the net losers are the people who have lost how community binds them.

Matters are not much better in North America, where social solidarity has waned and moral anarchy is cresting. It is hardly controversial to note that Canada and the United States suffer from many of the same economic, social, and cultural conditions that plague Europe. Enter the Catholic Church. Its teachings, its rich heritage, and its enormous individual and collective contributions provide an opportunity to rebound, and God knows the entire planet needs a moral reboot. In essence, this book is an attempt to persuade the reader to give Catholicism a chance.

There are many visions of the good society, but it is hard to improve on the one found in the Preamble to the U.S. Constitution. It is a vision of a society where justice, domestic tranquility, the common defense of the people, their general welfare, and the blessings of liberty reign supreme. It may be other things as well, but it most assuredly envisions these conditions.

If the Catholic Church has the answer, then there must be something that makes it different from other religious, as well as secular, institutions. There are many differences, some of which are theological: the revelation of One God in three persons was certainly revolutionary, and the divine connection between God and every human person is an important element of Christianity. The legacy of Christianity would not have been possible without the Church's triumph over paganism, and without this victory—called by sociologist Robert Nisbet "the greatest psychic revolution in the history of Western culture"—the world would be a different place today.[1] "For had this revolution never occurred," writes Nisbet, "had the Christians been defeated by indigenous Greco-Roman gods, by gods imported from the East, or by both, the West would have known only a fraction of the social, economic, cultural, and intellectual history that has been a continuous flow from the earliest centuries of Christianity."[2]

What made the "psychic revolution" a success is the heart and soul of Catholicism's central contribution to the modern world: the preeminent role it affords the faculty of reason, and the nobility of its goal, namely, the pursuit of truth. Absent an awareness of how these attributes constitute the nucleus of Catholic teachings—they are its most defining markers—all the good that the Catholic Church has done is impossible to appreciate.

As already indicated, if the quest for the good society is to succeed, it cannot do so by resting on righteous teachings; the teachings must be institutionally anchored. The Catholic Church wins on this score hands-down. Indeed, any institution that has spanned almost two millennia, amidst internal discord and external oppression, must be an organizational genius. That genius lies in a structure that is at once both hierarchical and communal. Without a formal hierarchical structure, it would be impossible for the Church to maintain a global organization; but the Church has the pope, who is assisted in this role by the Magisterium, the official teaching body of the Church, that is, the pope in communion with the bishops. But if the Church were simply a top-down structure, it would never last. "The communal foundations were established early on," notes Nisbet, and by that he means "the multiplicity of small, cohesive, family-like communities within which the Good News was assimilated and passed on to succeeding generations."[3]

If the early Church was made of autonomous tiny communities, today's Church is enriched by hundreds of thousands of parishes throughout the world. There is a famous saying in American politics, attributable to former House Speaker Tip O'Neill, that all politics is local. It can also be said that in the Catholic Church, all religion is local. To be sure, Catholics in every nation recognize the authority of the pope as the leader of their world body, but what they identify with most is their own parish. There is no other institution on the face of the earth that can match the Catholic Church's unique blend of hierarchical and communal attributes. These attributes not only play an integral role in determining its success, they account for why Catholics are able to ride out scandals that touch the hierarchy.

To give but one example of how the organizational apparatus of the Catholic Church is a plus, consider what our society would look like today without the university.

The University

The towering figures in ancient Greece and Rome bequeathed to us a stunning array of scholarship, but they never created a single university. That work was accomplished by the Catholic Church. It was in the monasteries, dating back to the first millennium, that the university was first born. The contribution that Irish monasticism made in preserving the great works of the ancient world was particularly impressive, and in this regard the evangelizing work of Saint Patrick was seminal. Were it not for this Irish-Christian effort, the barbarian stamp on Western civilization would have been hard to defeat. Credit is due to the Irish monks who attracted students from many parts of Europe who were eager to learn, and to a subset among them who traveled to the continent founding monasteries in the great cities of Europe. Had they not prevailed, it is difficult to see how classical Greek and Roman literature would have been able to survive.

The Catholic university was not a place for meditation, or for the exclusive study of theology; it was a venue for creative thinking. It featured a curriculum consisting of disciplines that roughly approximate what we call the liberal arts today. Students learned from Aristotle and Cicero, drawing on their philosophical genius as a bedrock for Christian thought. Canon law was, of course, studied, but so was civil law. Most important, the papacy played a central role: were it not for several popes who intervened against those who sought to deny academic freedom, the course of learning in the time to come would have been stifled. One of the first universities in history, the University of Paris, flourished because of Pope Gregory

IX: he blocked attempts by ecclesiastical authorities to compromise the autonomy of this citadel of higher education.

Historian Thomas E. Woods, Jr. points to another significant element in the role of the Catholic Church in higher education, and that is its unyielding devotion to the study of logic. From the beginning, Catholic education at the highest levels was anything but rote learning. "The medieval study of logic," writes Woods, "provides additional testimony to the medievals' commitment to rational thought."[4] And since rational thought was the vehicle by which truth was ascertained, it is easy to see how religious and secular ideas were seen as complimentary in nature. In this environment serious ideas could be developed.

It is precisely this juxtaposition of the religious and the secular that accounts for the towering achievements of the Catholic Church in so many areas. The Church's contributions to art, architecture, and music, to name but three examples, are not fathomable without reference to the premium placed on reason—reason in service to the Divine. The two are integrally bound.

Art

The artistic explosion that marks the Renaissance would not have been possible without the deeply religious convictions of the artists, and the patronage of many popes. Leonardo da Vinci, Michelangelo, and Raphael may be known mostly for their masterpieces, but to really understand their genius we need to acknowledge their Christian faith.

While Leonardo's *Mona Lisa* is one of the most popular pictures in the world, his most important work may very well be *The Last Supper*. With the hands of the Lord extended and His head bowed, it anticipates a sadness of what is yet to come—His crucifixion. Everyone agrees that one of the greatest sculptures the world has ever known is Michelangelo's *Pietà*. James J. Walsh, an early-twentieth-century scholar, said it best when he wrote, "Only a man with deep belief in the doctrine that Mary was the Mother of God could have made this wonderful group in which the dead Savior taken down from the cross is lying across His Mother's knee."[5] Similarly, Raphael's Madonnas, most especially his *Sistine Madonna*, could not have been produced absent a sincere devotion to Our Blessed Mother. Much the same could be said about Spanish artists such as Murillo and Velázquez; they also gave us some of the greatest paintings of the Madonna. In the Low Countries, the Van Eycks, who did much to advance oil painting, did their greatest work on religious subjects.

While these works of art are, at bottom, a tribute to Catholicism, many of the artists sought to do more than give glory to God; their depiction of sorrow, for instance, is very much a Christian theme. When we think of suffering we think of the Cross, but when we think of the portrayal of suffering, no artistic contribution rivals the *Pietà*; it is the ultimate expression. Throughout the ages, the Christian belief in the power and redemptive value of suffering has been captured many times in art, often in a very personal way, and this is still true today. The much heralded writer Jack Kerouac found relief from his maladies, which included alcoholism and depression, by immersing himself in the story of the Crucifixion and the Resurrection. Douglas Brinkley, the editor of Kerouac's journals, says that when Kerouac "rediscovered his Catholic heritage, he embraced the iconography, drawing crucifixes and rosaries in his notebooks."[6]

Why, after all these years, do so many learned men and women—most of whom are not Catholic—continue to admire Renaissance art, seeing in these religious representations something of eternal beauty? Without question, much of the admiration is situationally based: in contrast to what passes as art today—much of it sophomoric, if not a fraud—Renaissance works belong in a veritable Hall of Fame. Andy Warhol's quip, "Art is what you can get away with," is an unfortunate truism, one that accurately describes the contemporary scene. But this line of reasoning has absolutely no explanatory power in understanding Botticelli. The really great works of art are not celebrated because they are "original"—original contributions are readily available in the asylum; they are loved because they speak to what is true and beautiful.

Architecture

According to Walsh, "The greatest contribution that the Church has made to civilization, that is to the human cult of the beautiful, is in architecture."[7] (Notice his association of civilization with the nurturance of beauty, a notion that is regrettably quaint today.) He had in mind the early basilicas, such as Saint Lawrence outside the walls of Rome, as well as the three greatest Christian buildings of all time: Hagia Sophia in Constantinople, the Cathedral of Chartres, and St. Peter's.

After the Romanesque age came the development of the Gothic cathedrals, some of the most cherished treasures in the world. For Pope Benedict XVI, the cathedral is not only "the true glory of the Christian Middle Ages"; it represents "one of the loftiest expressions of universal civilization."[8] Speaking of the Gothic cathedral, Benedict notes, "The upward thrust was intended as an invitation to prayer and at the same time was itself a prayer"; the soaring cathedral sought "to express in its architectural lines the soul's longing for God."[9]

The creation of stained-glass windows during this period greatly impressed philosopher Will Durant. "When Gothic architecture reduced the strain on walls and made space for larger windows, the abundant light thereby admitted into the church allowed—indeed, demanded—the coloring of the panes," he wrote.[10] Picking up on the same observation, Benedict sees something spiritual: "A cascade of light poured through the stained-glass upon the faithful to tell them the story of salvation and to involve them in this story."[11] Charles David Eldridge, who, like Walsh, chronicled the Church's achievements during the 1920s, looked at the upward thrust of the "pointed gables, high arches [and] lofty spires," finding that "they blend earth's beauty with heaven's glory, and reveal to the race the reality of the spiritual and grandeur of the eternal."[12] That such incredible feats are not even attempted today is a telling sociological commentary.

Music

As with art and architecture, the history of Church music shows how strongly it is tied to the development of Christianity. Even at the Last Supper, psalms were sung. Those who spread the Gospel did so not merely by teaching, but by adopting local melodic strains to the liturgy. Sensing the need to standardize the liturgy, monks facilitated the process by developing musical notation—they were the first to do so— thus making it possible for a universal church to spread. In the sixth century, Gregorian chant took hold, a genre known for its single melody and spiritually uplifting qualities; it was the official music of the Church for six centuries. Mozart once said that he would gladly trade all his work for the right to declare himself the composer of Gregorian music.

Once the Church came to accept polyphony, the way was clear to create music suitable for the Mass. No one succeeded more than Palestrina, the greatest musician of the Renaissance. He was appointed musical director of the Julian Chapel in the Vatican in 1551, and it was through his contribution that sacred music reached new heights. By contrast, the Masses that Mozart, Joseph Haydn, and Beethoven later gave us were profound musical accomplishments, but their theatrical elements rendered them unsuitable for liturgical purposes. Nonetheless, works such as Beethoven's *Missa Solemnis* continue to inspire.

Even today Catholicism continues to play a role in the life of great musicians. Jazz giant Dave Brubeck was raised as a Protestant, but there was nothing devout about his upbringing. That all changed when he was asked by a Catholic publisher, Our Sunday Visitor, to offer a composition to accompany the Mass. Once the work was completed, a Catholic priest friend commented how much he loved the music, but he was not too pleased that the Our Father had been omitted. Brubeck replied that he could not figure out a way to include the Our Father without interrupting the musical flow. Then, while on vacation in the Caribbean with his family, the great improvisor dreamed the entire Lord's Prayer with chorus and orchestra. "I jumped out of bed and wrote down what I had heard as accurately as I could remember," Brubeck recalls. "Because of this event, I decided that I might as well join the Catholic Church because someone somewhere was pulling me toward that end."[13]

Economic and Scientific Achievements

If the artistic achievements of the Catholic Church are legion, much the same can be said about its role in education. Historians have come to understand that without the core role that the Catholic Church played during the Middle Ages in starting and sustaining universities, much of the creativity that led to genuine improvements in daily life would not have been possible. The monasteries, in particular, were a catalyst to economic well-being and prosperity. To take one example, it is hard to conceive how agriculture would have progressed without the advances made by the Benedictine monks; they were the unparalleled experts of cultivating the wilderness and introducing crops during medieval times.

Owing to the influence of sociologist Max Weber, it is often assumed that Protestantism gave rise to capitalism and the development of the modern world, but as Catholic theologian Michael Novak says, "Today's historians find capitalism much earlier than that in rural areas, where monasteries, especially those of the Cistercians, began to rationalize economic life."[14] The evidence supports Novak's contention that "the Catholic Church was the main locus for the first flowering of capitalism." Sociologist Randall Collins says of the Cistercians, "They had the Protestant ethic without Protestantism."[15]

Social scientist Charles Murray has examined these advances and is able to tally approximately four thousand first-time accomplishments. What is perhaps most astonishing about his findings is that almost all—nearly 100 percent—of the scientific and technological breakthroughs in history originated in Europe or North America.[16] After much reflection, Murray came to a conclusion that he did not anticipate when he first began his research, namely, that the key to understanding this phenomenon is Christianity.

Murray points to the critical role that Thomas Aquinas played in combining Aristotelian thought with Catholic teachings. "What Aquinas did," Murray notes, "was to say that creating beauty is pleasing to God, that discovering the workings of his universe is pleasing to God, and glorifies God, and that by doing these things you are fulfilling your role as a Christian. When you combine that with the rediscovery of the Greek legacy at about that same time, you just got a huge explosion of creativity."[17]

Of course, many of the achievements that Murray cites are traceable to the Scientific Revolution, a phenomenon that would not have taken place without the pivotal role played by the Catholic Church. Although historians look to the sixteenth century as the time when this revolution took place, sociologists such as Rodney Stark trace its origins to the eleventh century.[18] It was then that Catholic scholars began their important work. David Klinghoffer, who writes from a Jewish perspective, similarly notes, "The origins of modern science, from about 1300 onward, were overwhelmingly religious."[19] He cites scientists from Copernicus to Kepler, along with Boyle, Linnaeus, Faraday, Kelvin, and Rutherford, as scientists who sought to understand God through His creation. From this historical perspective, it seems rather absurd to hear it said today that there has always been a disconnect between science and religion. Indeed, the connection could not be stronger.

Stark emphasizes that "[f]rom the start, the medieval Christian university was a place created and run by scholars devoted entirely to knowledge." Furthermore, "it was in these universities that European Christians began to establish science."[20] He offers by way of example the field of physiology based on human dissections. It was not the Greeks, Romans, Muslims, or Chinese, Stark says, who were responsible for this contribution; it was the Christian scholastics. But of all the areas of science that Catholic scholars supported in the universities, none tops astronomy. The Catholic scholars were so committed to this field that they designed the great cathedrals in Bologna, Florence, Paris, and Rome as solar observatories.

Copernicus, a Catholic priest, pioneered astronomy. Galileo, of course, is remembered today as someone who was censored by the Catholic Church, but this reading of events is misleading. Not only did he never spend a single day in prison, but he was never tortured as some revisionist authors have said. He spent his time under "house arrest" in an apartment in a Vatican palace, with a servant. More important, his work was initially praised by the Catholic Church: Pope Urban VIII bestowed on him many gifts and medals.

Galileo did not get into trouble because of his ideas; after all, his ideas were taken from Copernicus, who was never punished (on the contrary, Copernicus's theory found a receptive audience with Pope Clement VII). Galileo's towering ego was what got the best of him; he made unverified claims that led even the scientists of his day to wince. Indeed, Father Roger Boscovich continued to explore Copernican ideas at the same time that Galileo was charged with heresy, without attracting a bit of opposition. Had Galileo not presented his hypothesis as fact—that was the heresy—he would have escaped trouble. In any event, a century later all of Galileo's works were published, and in 1741 Pope Benedict XIV granted them an imprimatur.

The Church's role in preserving the university involved more than academic accomplishments. British scientist James Hannam writes that "[t]he main scientific *institution* of the Middle Ages was the university."[21] That the Catholic Church, responsible for the creation of universities, has not received fair credit for this achievement is indisputable. Hannam correctly notes that "most of the stories about how the Church held back science are myths that arose after the Middle Ages." Moreover, it was from the Christian ethos that scientists such as Kepler and Copernicus derived their scientific ideas.

It is no wonder that Jesuit brother Guy Consolmagno, a research astronomer and planetary scientist at the Vatican Observatory, maintains that not only is there no conflict between science and religion, but "[s]cience grew out of religion." He makes the cogent point that "[t]here is nothing in the Bible opposing evolution, but there is something in the Bible against astrology."[22]

Further proof that the alleged conflict between science and Christianity is a myth is demonstrated in the scientific heroics of Georges Lemaître. A Belgian priest, he is known as the father of the "Big Bang" theory. In the late 1920s and early 1930s he crafted his argument that the universe consisted initially of a single particle—what he dubbed the "primeval atom"—which disintegrated in an explosion, giving rise to the physical universe.[23] In January 1933 Einstein, standing with Lemaître in California, said of the priest's work, "This is the most beautiful and satisfactory explanation of creation to which I have ever listened."[24] The *New York Times* commented on this historic moment, saying, "His view is interesting and important not because he is a Catholic priest, not because he is one of the leading mathematical physicists of our time, but because he is both."[25]

All the evidence suggests that there is something unique about Christianity and its relation to modernity. "While the other world religions emphasized mystery and intuition," writes Stark, "Christianity alone embraced reason and logic as the primary guide to religious truth." That's because, as Stark asserts, "the church fathers taught that reason was the supreme gift from God and the means to *progressively increase* their understanding of Scripture and revelation. Consequently, Christianity was oriented to the future, while the other major religions asserted the superiority of the past"[26] (his italics).

Stark's observation is key. The idea that progress can be made is predicated on a mind-set that is future oriented; a people whose collective psychological makeup is oriented toward the past or the present are incapable of making progress. By providing for a future orientation, Catholicism allowed for the idea of progress to take root. Stark hardly exaggerates when he concludes, "Christianity created Western civilization. Had the followers of Jesus remained an obscure Jewish sect, most of you would not have learned to read and the rest of you would be reading from handcopied scrolls."[27]

Focus on the Other

Achievements in science and technology, however noteworthy, do not alone reveal why Catholicism matters. For a fuller appreciation we must turn to the domain of Catholic social teaching, which is characterized by a richness that is impressive, and which yields an equally consequential list of accomplishments. Most important, Catholic social thought is brilliant, and it is the best prescription for realizing the good society, as well as a great resource for encouraging the development of excellence in the twenty-first century.

The comprehensiveness of Catholic social teaching encompasses the political, economic, social, and cultural segments of society. Unlike so many other religious and secular organizations, the Church promulgates teachings that are not uniformly liberal or conservative; its crossover qualities make it all the more appealing. The Church is generally liberal on economic issues, and generally conservative on cultural issues. It is certainly respectful of democratic government, but it understands that even in the best of institutional arrangements, injustice may flourish. Its penchant for fairness leads it to support programs that ameliorate the conditions of the poor, but the Church is not automatically committed to statist, or governmental, reforms. The Church believes in freedom of choice, but it does not approve of everything done in the name of liberty. However, that does not mean that it equivocates; it is decisive, yet discerning.

Catholic social thought has a natural teleology, or ultimate purpose, that not only guides its teachings but drives them. In a nutshell, it is the Church's "focus on the other" that best explains why it does what it does. Another way of putting it is to say that the Catholic Church's teachings lean instinctively toward serving others and away from a preoccupation with one's self. Its orientation is communal, not individualistic, although this is not to say that it does not value the rights of the individual. It is just to say that the Church does not begin with a concern for what satisfies the individual; rather it begins with a concern for what serves the needs of the good society.

This teleological orientation is manifested in many ways. Take loneliness. From a Catholic perspective, this is a serious problem, because it is not in God's design that humans should be isolated, functioning as strangers. Pope Benedict

XVI, in his first encyclical, went so far as to say that "[o]ne of the deepest forms of poverty a person can experience is isolation."[28] His use of the word *poverty* is instructive: it signifies, in Catholic thought, not simply an absence of material well-being, but of social well-being. If all of us were able to "focus on the other," there would be no isolation, no social poverty of any kind.

How can we craft a society that pushes us to be our neighbor's keeper? Again, Benedict offers us wisdom. He teaches that "authentic service requires sacrifice and self-discipline, which in turn must be cultivated through self-denial, temperance, and a moderate use of the world's goods."

It would be hard to say something more radical than this in today's world. Indeed, the idea that we need to deny ourselves anything is likely to be scorned and mocked; never mind that it needs to be seen as requisite for serving others. But the Holy Father is right: how else would it be possible for individuals to make the kinds of sacrifices that are necessary if the needs of others are to be served? Putting others first is not a natural tendency, which is why the habit needs to be cultivated. And this is not likely to happen in an environment where temperance is seen as a hindrance.

Notice, too, that the pope links self-denial to a moderate use of the world's goods. One of the greatest strengths of Catholic social thought is the extent to which it sees core values as interconnected. Here is another example, also taken from Benedict. "If we wish to build true peace, how can we separate or even set at odds the protection of the environment and the protection of human life, including the life of the unborn?"[29] In a speech he gave in 2010 to ambassadors from

178 countries that have diplomatic relations with the Vatican, he linked war, hunger, environmental degradation, and the world financial crisis as manifestations of selfishness.[30] He is correct: if we had set our sights on others, the worst excesses could have been avoided.

The social teachings of the Catholic Church would not contribute to the good society unless they were based on an accurate conception of human nature. Indeed, this one issue—getting human nature right—is the do-or-die of all philosophical and social teachings. Getting it wrong means that all the teachings are infected, rendering their societal usefulness nil. Getting it right is not a sufficient condition for contributing to the good society, but it is a necessary one. The Founding Fathers, for example, also got human nature right; that is why the Constitution delivers. But their reach was limited in scope. The Church's reach is far-ranging, extending to every aspect of the human condition, from the needs of the individual to the requisites of society.

Human Nature

"If men were angels," James Madison wrote, "no government would be necessary." He was right, and the government the Founders crafted was based on this understanding. Absent government, the weak would perish at the hands of the stronger. But it is not enough to conclude that government is necessary; a government that does not institutionally block dictatorial impulses can deliver more evil than anarchy. That is why the Founders gave us a horizontal balance of powers at the federal level, dividing powers between the executive, legislative, and judicial branches. It also explains why they gave us a vertical federalist system, one that allows for federal, state, and local government responsibilities. The system works because it takes for granted that too much power in the hands of any single source spells the death of liberty; it also takes into consideration man's nature.

If the American Revolution was a success because the leaders who went on to build the country had a proper understanding of human nature, the French Revolution was a failure because the rebels got it wrong from the get-go. Jean-Jacques Rousseau, the intellectual father of the French Revolution, believed that "man is born free" but is "everywhere in chains." In other words, man is basically good, and all the evil we see in society is based on corrupt social institutions that have distorted man's nature. Such a view whets the appetite of those who believe that once they get control of the command center—namely, the government—they can create institutions that will allow man's original goodness to flourish once again. The architects of the French Revolution believed this moonshine, and the result was the creation of the most despotic regime to date, which obliterated religious liberty, savaging Catholics and the Catholic Church alike.

The Catholic Church offers the best hope of realizing the good society partly because it understands that man is inherently flawed and in need of redemption. Accordingly, the idea that man is, at base, a noble savage, and that human perfectibility is possible here on earth, is properly regarded as preposterous. Saint Augustine, referencing Genesis, taught that man entered the world in a state of sin. What we call original sin is, in fact, at the heart of the Catholic conception of man's nature. It is also the predicate of the Ten Commandments.

"Thou Shalt Not" would not have been uttered if man were sinless; we are commanded by God not to disrespect Him. Similarly, we are obliged not to dishonor our mother and our father; or to engage in murder or adultery; or to steal from or disrespect our neighbors; or to covet that which does not belong to us. The underlying idea is that if we were left to our own impulses, we would naturally incline toward these offenses. Hence the necessity of the commandments.

You don't have to be Catholic to understand how deeply important it is to be right about human nature. Harry Jaffa, a prominent scholar, put it this way: "Regarding the question of human nature evolving," he said, "there is no evidence that human beings as possessed of certain faculties and powers have changed since the beginning of recorded history."[31] Another writer who got it right was William Golding, author of *Lord of the Flies*. He surely understood what man was capable of, and what he shows us is not a pretty sight. Not surprisingly, the novelist believed in original sin.[32] He maintained that civilization was a good thing, for if man didn't learn to put a harness on his appetites, his nature was capable of monstrous deeds. Harvard professor Steven Pinker is not a man of faith, but that hasn't stopped him from concluding that "the *denial* of human nature can be *more* dangerous than people think" (his italics).[33] The Catholic Catechism says the same thing: "Ignorance of the fact that man has a wounded nature inclined to evil gives rise to serious errors in the areas of education, politics, social action, and morals."

While many academics in the social sciences and humanities

continue to believe that there is no such thing as human nature, believing instead that all that exists is a social construction—a creation of mankind—once we get beyond ideology and look at the evidence, we see something very different. What we find are hundreds of examples of human traits that are found in virtually every society in recorded history. These "human universals" underscore the Catholic understanding of man and society. More important, they explain why Catholic social teaching is a realistic recipe for the creation of the good society.

Owing in particular to the discipline of anthropology, social scientists have had a hard time shaking off the concept of cultural relativism, that is, the idea that the cultures vary so widely that the idea of a common core of human traits seems like nonsense. But these ideas are changing. "We may now legitimately conclude that the undeniable existence of so many universals is a final and firm refutation of the cultural relativism so confidently and misleadingly preached to millions of students for the past century,"[34] writes Canadian social scientist William D. Gairdner. We have known for a very long time that all humans, of all ages, crave affection and recognition. We know from the work of psychologist Jonathan Haidt, also, that loyalty to the in-group; respect for authority and hierarchy; a sense of purity, reciprocity, and fairness; as well as measures that provide for safety form a core part of all moral systems.[35] But it is the work of Donald E. Brown that has proved most persuasive.

Two decades ago, Brown tallied over three hundred human universals, traits that are found in every known society.[36]

Inequality is ubiquitous: hierarchy, authority, status differentiation, age, sex, social roles, economic inequality, nepotism, and ethnocentrism are commonplace. So is the distinction between the sacred and the profane. Man, as Aristotle taught, is indeed a social animal, and true to form we know of no human society without such features as a moral consensus, bonding, marriage, the family, mother-child attachment, in-group affiliations, and so on. Such traits as norms, values, socialization, social institutions, and sanctions are found everywhere, as are such sentiments as jealousy, envy, modesty, shame, guilt, grief, and the like. And yes, violence exists universally. Those who fancy that pre-literate man was not violent are monumentally wrong; the most barbaric practices imaginable—cannibalism, torture, wife beating—were staples of such societies.[37]

It is not hard for Catholics, accepting as they are of the doctrine of original sin, to understand that man is capable of great evil. Nor do they find it difficult to respect the natural authority that inheres in mothers and fathers. Values, ideas of right and wrong, and norms—the boundary rules—make sense, as do their enforcement, namely the use of sanctions. Sentiments, ranging from the affectionate to the venal, are part of what makes us human. It is because there is nothing in Catholic social thought that contradicts any of these behavioral truisms that the reach of these teachings is so wide; Catholic social teachings have application everywhere.

If Catholic social thought meshes nicely with the needs of the individual and society, offering a realistic approach to the attainment of the good society, in order for these teachings to be efficacious they must offer concrete guidance. It is not good enough to say that we must thwart those behaviors proscribed by the Ten Commandments; we need to know what to prescribe. That's where virtue comes in. In other words, the Ten Commandments tell us what not to do; virtue tells us what to do. To secure the proper answer, we need only turn to the cardinal virtues of the Catholic Church.

Cardinal Virtues

Positive psychology deals with the noble qualities of the human condition, and its practitioners have outlined a set of characterological strengths that tap these qualities. After combing the anthropological and psychological literature—looking for common characteristics—Martin Seligman and Chris Peterson seized on what they call six high-level virtues: wisdom, courage, humanity, justice, temperance, and transcendence.[38] Catholics, of course, know justice and temperance as two of the cardinal virtues; what the psychologists call wisdom roughly corresponds to prudence, and courage is another word for fortitude (humanity and transcendence speak to what Catholics call the theological virtues of faith, hope, and charity).

There is nothing inherently religious, then, about the cardinal virtues, and indeed Plato and Cicero pointed to these four virtues as contributing to the heart and soul of the good society, long before Saints Augustine, Gregory the Great, and Thomas Aquinas gave these virtues a Christian cast. But the Catholic Church further defined and promoted them.

"Simply put," says Catholic theologian William C. Mattison III, "a virtue is a good habit."[39] Habits, naturally, are born of practice, and it is a strength of the Catholic faith that teaches people how to cultivate good habits. The obverse of virtue is vice, and it, too, can be habit-forming. Worse, it can be cultivated. Here's a quick example. It is not by accident that some neighborhoods are relatively crime-free while others are crime-ridden: much depends on the kinds of characterological traits that are nourished in homes and in the community. Where discipline is not ingrained, trouble follows.

Left to our own selfish interests, many of us, perhaps most of us, would live a life of vice. But we know, almost instinctively, that such a life is not really a happy one. So we opt for virtue. But virtue does not come easy; the apprenticeship is demanding. It is up to the family, more than any other source, to inculcate virtuous behavior in children. Teachers matter, as do the clergy, but it takes a father and a mother to do the job best. Virtuous behavior cannot be ordered into being; it must be carefully and consistently crafted, making use of positive as well as punitive sanctions to get the job done. There is much in Catholic social teachings to consult as a guide along the way, and there is no better place to begin than with the cardinal virtues.

Although each of the cardinal virtues has its own distinctive qualities, these virtues cannot be viewed discretely as if they were independent of each other. On the contrary, it is the extent to which they are interrelated that makes them so potent. But if there is one virtue that directs the rest, it is prudence.

Prudence

Aquinas saw prudence as "right reason in action." To know what is right takes discernment, something that presupposes a mature conscience. To know what is the right thing to do also takes practice. It is from experience that we are able to weigh the options before us and arrive at the right answer. Contrary to what some impute, prudence does not mean being cautious (although there are times when it may make sense to be so); being prudent means doing what is right, and that may mean anything but playing it safe. In fact, there are times when it may mean taking a calculated risk. In any event, doing what is right is not something we can learn by reading some ethical handbook. What is right is something we know through reason, and that is why conscience and prudence are inseparable.

Saint Thomas taught us that the faculty of reason allows us to size up what choices are available to us in any given situation. After we deliberate, we need to choose. Finally, we need to act. None of this happens mechanistically, and for prudence to be practiced, all three conditions must be met. If we don't deliberate, we are bound to act randomly. But it is not enough to stop there; pondering gets us nowhere. We must select a course of action. And if after deliberation and judgment we do not act, then we have failed to do what prudence demands; there is no virtue in knowing what we should do and then opting for doing nothing.

To see why prudence is the chief virtue that informs the other three, consider the following. Imagine deciding what is the just thing to do without acting prudently. For instance, parents and teachers cannot possibly act justly when dealing with a troubled child without also acting prudently; they need to know exactly what buttons to push if they are to succeed. Similarly, fortitude without prudence is foolhardiness; a policeman who acts impulsively by charging into a compound without backup is acting recklessly. Acting temperately makes sense, but there is no virtue in becoming a neurotic. In short, prudence calibrates; it is the measure of the other cardinal virtues. Furthermore, acting imprudently kills the chances of acting justly, courageously, and temperately.

Justice

Justice is the second cardinal virtue, and it is noted as much for what it is as for what it is not; it is not about us. It is about others. To be precise, it is about giving others what they are due. Fairness and the common good are what justice is all about. This "focus on the other" approach to human relations is quintessentially Catholic, and it takes on special meaning when the virtue of justice is exercised. For justice to take hold, not only must we cast our eyes away from ourselves; we must invoke prudence to know what is the just course of action; then we can commit ourselves to act.

Love means "focusing on the other" as well. But love is specifically oriented toward someone we have a personal relationship with, someone to whom we are close, a person with whom we can share affection. Justice, on the other hand, is none of these things: it is oriented toward strangers, toward people we will never meet. As such, it is predicated on a strong commitment to doing what is right. But if a just society is to take hold, it is not enough for some individuals to act justly toward others; justice must be institutionalized. Just laws respect the rights of others, and a just verdict in the courtroom is one that treats others the way we would want to be treated ourselves. In this regard, the Catholic contribution to law, especially international law, is significant.

Canon law, developed in the Middle Ages based on principles of Roman law, became the model for civil law. It was the emergence of ecclesiastical courts after Pope Gregory VII, as Michael P. Foley has noted, that triggered imitation in the civil courts.[40] Similarly, Christianity was the foundation for the promulgation of the common law. Many of the barbaric practices that were associated with meting out justice—ordeals by fire and water—were superseded by more civilized approaches found in ecclesiastical courts. The concept of due process, a central tenet in Western law, owes much to the Catholic Church. When someone was put forward for beatification or canonization, the Church instituted a "devil's advocate" system: objections were intentionally raised, putting the onus on the candidate's postulator. Our adversarial system of justice, played out in the courtroom, was established based on this kind of exchange between the plaintiff and the defense.

There are times when acting justly may require something other than giving others their due. It may require violence. Self-defense is not a taboo in Catholic social teaching, nor is taking the life of another in war, provided that certain conditions are met. Saint Augustine gave us the concept of the "just war" because there are times when opting for pacificism may be more destructive to the ends of justice than taking up arms.

Many years ago when I was teaching at a college, I listened to a visiting professor lecture to a mostly Catholic faculty on the merits of pacifism. He cited the tradition of the Quakers as exemplary and chided the audience for its affiliation with a religion that justifies war in some instances. Looking at the faces in the room, it seemed as though he was getting his point across. But when I informed him that the only reason that any of us was alive today was owing to the fact that pacifism had been rejected as a just option during World War II, he looked troubled; the audience reacted as if they had been slapped across the face. In essence, decent people everywhere want peace, but there are times when practicing pacifism undermines the prospects for achieving it; sometimes collective self-defense is necessary to win the peace.

Saint Augustine, of course, was no warmonger. He wanted peace, but he also knew that there were times when we had to fight in order to achieve peace. He laid down several criteria for war, among them that the cause must be just; that there must be a probability of success; that the means used must be proportionate to the desired outcome; and that force should be invoked only as a last resort. There are related conditions as well, such as never intentionally killing noncombatants; in fact, the intentional killing of civilians is the definition of terrorism.

Justice is often confused with treating others equally. In law, of course, there can be no justice without treating everyone equally, but there are times when injustice is created if everyone is treated equally. A teacher who awards the same grade to every student, independent of performance, is acting unjustly. The same would be true if we gave everyone who competed in the Olympics a gold medal simply for trying. Justice, then, is not analogous to equality, although there are times when treating everyone equally (such as allowing everyone only one vote) is the just thing to do. Justice is about equity, and equity is about fairness. Equality is about sameness.

Serving the common good is what animates justice. This can mean many things, but in Catholic social thought it largely means providing for those in need. Father Benedict Groeschel reminds us that charity and kindness to the poor, while admirable, should not be our primary impulse. Justice, he says, should implore us to act with generosity toward the indigent. "We owe it," he argues.[41] He is speaking, naturally, from a long Christian tradition—beginning with Jesus—that commands us to do right by the dispossessed. Yes, "we owe it" to the least among us. It is not an option, not for Christians anyway.

Fortitude

Knowing what to do and acting in a just manner are necessary virtues in the good society, but getting the job done often requires courage. That's where the virtue of fortitude comes in; it fires us, propelling us to do our duty.

We often think of fortitude as bravery, such as when a soldier lays down his life for a just cause. That certainly would qualify. But there are other instances, more mundane, that also meet the test. The sick and dying need fortitude just to face their condition, as do their loved ones (they often suffer more, needing plenty of courage not to give up). Going against the grain requires fortitude as well, as in standing up for what is right when it is not popular to do so. The opposite of fortitude, cowardice, has nothing to recommend it, although it may temporarily appeal to those looking for an easy way out. Fortitude, then, is something that needs to be nourished in everyone. We never know when and where we may be required to draw on it; we also have a vested interest in seeing to it that others possess it as well.

Fortitude is most in evidence in life and death situations. Pope John Paul II risked his life when he attended seminary in Poland during World War II; had the Nazis found him, he might have been killed. Priests and nuns who hid Jews in convents and seminaries in Italy during the Holocaust could not have carried out their heroic acts without the courage instilled in them by their training. Similarly, Catholic doctors and nurses who refuse to perform or assist in abortions—often risking reprisal—are walking examples of courage in action. More and more common is the expectation that health care personnel will approve of, if not facilitate, the death of the terminally ill. Students in medical schools who say no to such instruction need the courage to resist.

Of course, one does not have to be a Christian to know the virtue of fortitude—other religious and secular traditions reserve a special place for it as well. "But the Christian understanding of the model of fortitude is different," says Mattison, "due to the different Christian view of what is most important in life." For Christians, he says, "it is the martyr, not the soldier on the battlefield, who is the model of fortitude. A *martyr* is someone who is killed for his faith" (his italics).[42] Saints Peter and Paul come quickly to mind. What made their martyrdom count was not their willingness to suffer; it was, as Saint Augustine instructs, the nobility of their cause. But fortitude separated from prudence and justice yields ignoble results. The daredevil may entertain us, but his antics are not the fruit of virtue.

Fortitude is not like a switch that can be turned on and off. The Catechism says it best: "Fortitude is the moral virtue that ensures firmness in difficulties and constancy in the pursuit of the good." Constancy. Without it, forget it. But not constancy for its own sake, constancy "in the pursuit of the good." This makes such great sense that it is hard to conceive of the good society without the exercise of fortitude. Indeed, when cowardice is exercised, the prospects of evil winning out grow commensurately.

Temperance

Evil can also triumph when moral destitution becomes the norm. Put plainly, the good society cannot be achieved without the willingness of citizens to shun a life of recklessness. To the extent that restraint is treated as a dirty word, the likelihood that there will be a good society to live in dwindle. Temperance is a cardinal virtue precisely because its absence spells personal disaster and social chaos. Not for nothing are we told in the Old Testament to restrain our appetites. Ditto in the New Testament when we are called to practice moderation. What may come naturally to us—living a life of debauchery—admittedly has a sensory appeal, but it makes no practical sense to live that way on a daily basis. Nor does it make any sense to want to live in a society were immorality thrives.

The other three cardinal virtues "focus on the other," but not temperance; its focus is inward, on us. Contrary to what some may believe, acting temperately is not analogous to stifling desire or eschewing pleasure. It is about moderation. Alcohol is not in itself bad—did not Jesus make more wine? What is bad is unrestrained use. Sex is good, Saint Thomas told us, provided it is used constructively by married men and women. In fact, Saint Thomas even went so far as to say that those who flip the other way—those who seek to shut down and repress all sexual feelings—are guilty of a moral defect. So yes, seeking pleasure for pleasure's sake is not acting temperately, but it is also not necessary to live in a state of total denial. Temperance is meant to regulate our desires, not suppress them.

It is not an excess of purity, however, that is among our biggest social problems these days. Quite the opposite—it is the unheralded, nonstop celebration of narcissism, and its cousin, hedonism, that threaten to undermine civil society. Intemperance is not the exception to the rule, it is the norm. The consequences are all around us, and the social debris is not a pretty sight. Obesity, alcoholism, drug abuse, out-of-wedlock pregnancies, abortion, sexually transmitted diseases—all are a function of excess. Indeed, it sometimes seems as though we have declared war on moderation.

Josef Pieper, who wrote a masterful book on the cardinal

virtues, was right to say that temperance is liberating.[43] From the perspective of today's moral code, however, such a notion makes no sense. Think about it. It is simply not possible for individuals to master themselves and be all that they can be without acting temperately. We know of not a single Olympic gold medal winner who has ever won because of sheer talent. It takes work, and lots of it. And work doesn't come easy; it requires great self-discipline, an attribute that must be nurtured over and over again. Tough as the grind is, it has its rewards: not because you'll win (most who compete lose), but because of the genuine feeling of accomplishment you get by pushing to be the best. The real race in life is achieving what we know we are capable of, not anything else.

As with all the virtues, the model of temperance is Jesus. Father Groeschel asks us to consider "the humble life of our Lord Jesus Christ and what He chose for Himself. He chose to be born in a little hamlet in a rural part of an occupied country. He lived His whole life in poverty, and He died the death of a poor man. Crucifixion was reserved for the poor and helpless."[44] The point is not that we must aspire to the lifestyle of Jesus, but that we shall try to learn from His humbleness and seek to acquire the virtue of temperance and make it part of our everyday life. That's quite a challenge, but the rewards are many.

Virtue and the Good Society

Think what society would look like if vice, not virtue, ruled the day. Consider the seven capital sins as representative of vice:

pride, covetousness, lust, anger, gluttony, envy, and sloth. A society replete with these capital sins is a society no rational person would ever elect to live in. This proves the point that reason leads us to choose virtue over vice. The virtues are to be used to conquer the vices: prudence is the natural antidote to pride; justice works against covetousness and envy; fortitude checks anger and sloth; and temperance is the answer to lust and gluttony.

The cardinal virtues can be applied in many different areas of life, and that is why different authors who write about them choose different matters to discuss. Much depends on the author's interest and expertise. So what follows is nothing more than some ways of conceptualizing how prudence, justice, fortitude, and temperance can be applied to some important social issues.

Prudence, the king of all virtues, is relevant to many topics, but there is one that is so central to the good society that it jumps right to the front of the line—freedom. Unfortunately, many who employ the word distort its real meaning. It is for this reason that Catholics, as well as non-Catholics, need to gain a better appreciation for what Catholicism has to say about this subject. The idea of natural rights and their universal application—from conception to natural death—is noble. Freedom means choices, but to realize the proper choices we need to draw on prudence.

A society without justice cannot be considered good, whatever else it may be. The "focus on the other" in the discussion of the virtue of justice speaks to the seminal teachings of the Catholic Church and the yeoman works of the faithful; it is a record of vast accomplishment. Economic justice is more than a slogan in the Catholic portfolio; it is a concept that comes to life in the works of many encyclicals. Moreover, serving the dispossessed is a hallmark of Catholic justice, and the enormous contributions made by priests and nuns, in particular, deserve wide recognition. Welcoming the stranger is not a popular cause these days, but for the Catholic Church it is a cause always worth pursuing.

No religion is better known for its martyrs (at least those who die for a just cause) than Roman Catholicism, and that is why this history needs to be acknowledged. Not as well known, however, have been the courageous efforts of Catholics from the pope to the laity to fight totalitarianism. Fighting fascism on one front and communism on the other—sometimes simultaneously—constitutes a chapter in history that demonstrated pure courage in action. The heroics of Pope Pius XII in undermining Hitler, and in doing what he could to save Jews, took real fortitude. Similarly, the efforts of Pope John Paul II to bring down the Soviet Union deserve much recognition. More recently, Pope Benedict XVI has joined today's battle against radical Islam by addressing this issue head-on as no other leaders have.

Survey data continually show how worried the people of North America and Europe are about the moral direction of their society. Unfortunately, their concerns are not matched by a determination to take the initiative to stem the tide. The good news is that we are not without a prescription: Catholic social teachings have much to say about the virtue of temperance. The problems besetting society today have much to do with the dissolution of marriages and families, and we are dreaming if we think this situation will repair itself without hard work. In fact, the shaky status of marriage and the family is being challenged with greater ferocity today than ever before, as witnessed in attempts to cast marriage between a man and a woman as deserving of no special status.

The good society lies in waiting, but the right recipe has been around for two thousand years. The more we learn about the inspiring record of Catholic social teachings and their application to real-life problems, the more likely it is that all of us will see how unfounded the negative stereotypes of Catholicism really are. But first we need to be educated about the glorious record of these teachings. Then we will know why Catholicism matters.

Prudence

P RUDENCE being the most senior of the cardinal virtues, it is perhaps the most widely applied virtue. Almost every human action, if it is ordered to doing what is right, relies on this virtue. Without question, this would include the quest for freedom.

No discussion of freedom can ignore the issues of natural law and natural rights, subjects that have long been central to Catholic scholarship; they provide a good platform to discuss related matters. Freedom means more than individual rights, and on this score the contributions of the Catholic Church are impressive. While a discussion of "rightful freedom" might fall on deaf ears these days, it is important to understand the value of rightful freedom in making prudential judgments. Similarly, the idea of severing freedom from morality, while much in vogue, is something that the Catholic Church has long opposed, and for good reason: the most vulnerable among us pay the biggest price when the two attributes are treated as discrete entities. The subject of slavery, of course, deserves extended treatment, as does the Church's reaction to it.

Human rights, while critical to the makings of the good society, are, by themselves, inadequate. More is needed—the society must recognize the importance of human dignity. When human life is treated as a commodity, as a throwaway item, certain consequences follow, none of which is noble. The intentional killing of innocent human beings, whether at the beginning or the end of life, affects more than the victim; it affects the conscience and soul of society.

Natural Rights and Natural Law

Fareed Zakaria notes that "Greece was not the birthplace of liberty as we know it. Liberty in the modern world is first and foremost the freedom of the individual from arbitrary authority, which has meant, for most of history, from brute power of the state." Zakaria puts his finger on how this first evolved: "The Catholic Church was the first major institution in history that was independent of temporal authority and willing to challenge it. By doing this it cracked the edifice of state power, and in nooks and crannies individual liberty began to grow." For this reason, he concludes that "the rise of the Christian Church is, in my view, the first important source of liberty in the West—and hence the world."[1]

Even a cursory look at Eastern civilizations yields not even a glimpse of how the concept of freedom would ultimately take root in society, so completely foreign has this idea been. In fact, it wasn't until the nineteenth century, as Harvard sociologist Orlando Patterson points out, that the Chinese and Japanese even had a word to describe freedom.[2] As another sociologist, Rodney Stark, has pointed out, among "the world's faiths, only Christianity has devoted serious and sustained attention to human rights as opposed to human duties."[3] Where in Islam, Hinduism, and Buddhism, for example, is there a record of the development of freedom? No, to learn of this we must look to the Christian West.

Not only are freedom and Christianity compatible, then; it is difficult to understand the former without the latter. The results of the joining of freedom with Christianity are without equal. "Individually liberating, socially energizing, and culturally generative," Patterson writes, "freedom is undeniably the source of Western intellectual mastery, the engine of its extraordinary creativity, and the open secret of the triumph of Western culture, in one form or another, over the other cultures of mankind."[4] The Jamaican scholar is neither exaggerating nor being a braggart; he is simply telling the truth. Christianity is the one religion that places freedom at its doctrinal core. It is this kind of exceptionalism that makes Roman Catholicism so endearing.

Michael Gerson, an Evangelical and former presidential speech writer, takes a sober look at the achievements of the Roman Catholic Church and comes away impressed. "An institution accused of superstition is now the world's most steadfast defender of rationality and human rights," he says. He pointedly asks, "It has not always lived up to its own standards, but where would those standards come from without it?"[5] The standards of rationality and human rights that he speaks of found expression in the United Nations Universal Declaration of Human Rights. Freedom of conscience and religion, for example, did not spring from secular thought. Nor did the idea that human beings are equal in the eyes of God and should be seen as equal in law. Nor did the idea that every human possesses equal dignity and worth. These ideas are all traceable to Christianity.

The 1948 UN Universal Declaration of Human Rights begins by recognizing "the inherent dignity" and "equal and inalienable rights of all members of the human family."[6] Such ideas were recorded in papal encyclicals such as *Rerum Novarum* in 1891 and *Quadragesimo Anno* in 1931: these Church documents addressed the "inherent dignity" and "worth of the human family" long before there was a push for an international bill of rights. And seven years before the UN document was approved, Pope Pius XII used a radio address to push for such a universal statement. In the early 1960s Pope John XXIII was so impressed with the principles laid out in the document that he hailed it as "an act of the highest importance." No wonder that when Pope John Paul II went before the international body in 1979, he called the post-war document "one of the highest expressions of the human conscience of our time." It is for reasons like these that former U.S. ambassador to the Vatican and Harvard law professor Mary Ann Glendon has written that "the Church has emerged as, intellectually and institutionally, the single most influential champion of the whole, interconnected, body of principles in the Universal Declaration."[7]

As important as the UN document is, it lacks something critical: an unshakable foundation. Catholic theologian Thomas D. Williams writes, "Unless human rights have an objective foundation, they are little more than a verbal fiction."[8] What he is getting at was understood by Pope John Paul II, who, although admiring of the UN Declaration, nonetheless complained that it "does not present *the anthropological and ethical foundations of the human rights* which it proclaims" (his italics).[9]

In other words, it was not grounded in something as concrete and overarching as natural rights and natural law.

Anyone can assert that he has rights, but no one is obliged to respect them, unless, of course, there is something binding. That something binding cannot, however, be merely in the form of a contract. Contracts are revocable. For rights to have meaning, they must have a firm basis. This is not a problem in Catholic thought, but it most certainly is a real jam for unbelievers, as well as for the faithful of many religions. It is a staple of Catholic thought that human rights inhere in every human being as a gift from God. They are not awarded to us; they are natural to us. Made in the image and likeness of Jesus Christ, humans the world over—in every society throughout all of history—possess natural rights. Governments may proclaim certain individual rights, but in Catholic thought governments can never be the origin of such rights. Our rights are inalienable and irrevocable. If this sounds familiar, it should; it is the heart and soul of the Declaration of Independence.

There is a confluence between Catholic thought on the subject of liberty and the thinking of the men who founded America. While it is true that some of the Founders were Deists—men like Washington, Jefferson, Franklin, and Paine who doubted the inerrancy of Scripture and the divinity of Jesus—all of those who forged the new social order, whether they were religious or not, understood the need for religion in a free society. As Thomas S. Kidd has shown, those responsible for the American Revolution shared five religious principles: there was a Creator who made all men equal, endowed with the same rights; God sometimes made nations His providential instrument; the tendency to sin demanded strong social institutions; virtue had to be strongly inculcated in the populace; and religious liberty was a must.[10] Because they understood human nature and believed in God, the Founders were able to develop an understanding of liberty that was as timeless as it was fruitful. That is why their thinking, and the thinking of the Church Fathers on this subject, is so similar.

Natural rights have staying power because they are grounded in natural law. Natural law holds that all human beings are capable of understanding, through the faculty of reason, right from wrong. It further maintains that there are norms of behavior that are eternal and applicable to all human conditions, no matter how "advanced" or "primitive" the people are. Universal in nature, natural law is inscribed in the hearts and minds of men and women everywhere, and it is not subject to veto by government. To be sure, governments can legitimize wrongdoing—they can approve of the most horrendous and despicable acts of oppression—but they cannot erase what every human being knows in his heart of hearts is true.

The belief in natural law is hardly unique to Catholicism, although no belief system, religious or nonreligious, has a richer history of promulgating it. The Greeks knew natural law, and no one promoted it better than Aristotle, who is often known as the "father" of natural law. Although he never used the term *natural law,* he spoke of a "universal law" that meant the same thing. Indeed, he explicitly said that "Universal law is the law of nature." The Romans were also devotees of natural law, and in fact they incorporated elements of natural law into their own code of law. Cicero defined natural law as "true law," maintaining that it is "right reason in agreement with nature."[11] It is also "universal, consistent, [and] everlasting." Without the natural law the common good could not be realized, and it was the common good, he held, that was the object of government. Natural law was later embodied in the common law throughout the West, and was spelled out in the writings of Sir William Blackstone, the architect of common law.

Saint Thomas Aquinas gave natural law a Christian cast. He did not insist that the moral law be confined to believers; on the contrary, he said it was available to everyone through reason alone. But he thought that natural law was incomplete without a Christian understanding. He called the two great commandments—love of God and love of neighbor—the "first and common precepts of the natural law." He took this view from Jesus, of course, who cited the Old Testament texts to underscore the primacy of these commandments. Aquinas taught that the Ten Commandments, taken as a whole, were the embodiment of the natural law, but he also knew that while the first principles of the natural law were the same for everyone, there would be differences of opinion about the conclusions drawn from these principles. That's where prudence comes in.

Even something as clear as the Ten Commandments cannot be set on automatic pilot; that is, we still need to deliberate and conscientiously evaluate how to apply the principles that are embodied in them, and then relate them to specific situations. Aquinas knew this to be true, and it explains why he so highly valued the cardinal virtue of prudence; there is no substitute for right reason. In other words, adherence to natural law does not resolve all problems, although without it there can be no real prospects for liberty.

If the American experiment in liberty has been a success, and it must be so regarded when we compare our experience to that of other nations, then it is owing in no small part to our tradition of natural rights and natural law. When Jefferson wrote that "all men are created equal," and that they are "endowed by their Creator with certain unalienable rights," he was speaking the language of natural law and natural rights. When Washington proclaimed, "Of all the dispositions and habits which lead to political prosperity, Religion and Morality are indispensable supports,"[12] he was giving voice to these ideas. When Chief Justice John Jay, one of the authors of the Federalist Papers, argued that the legislature did not have the power to enforce laws that were "against all reason and justice," he was also expressing a belief in natural law.[13] But soon after these great Americans made their seminal contributions to freedom, the very idea of natural rights and natural law came under sharp attack.

Jeremy Bentham, the eighteenth-century English jurist, called natural rights "simple nonsense." More than that, he dubbed them "nonsense on stilts."[14] So what did he have to offer instead? Utilitarianism. He believed that serving the greatest good for the greatest number of people was a better index of morality than any fanciful notion of natural rights and natural law. This may sound good to those who are the winners, that is, those who are in the majority. But what exactly can we say about a society that can justify punishing those in the minority as long as in so doing it enhances the happiness of the majority? Once we cut the brakes that conscience affords, there is nothing left to stop the triumph of tyranny. If all we are left with is a calculation of which alternative promises the best outcome for the greatest number of people, it is a sure bet that some will lose their rights.

The idea that the only rights that exist are the ones that are posited, or given to us, by government is known as positivism. It is a legal theory that is widely held today, and its proponents cannot stomach natural law. In their own ways, intellectuals such as Freud, Darwin, and Marx were attracted to it, and it remains a popular idea among nonbelievers everywhere. Although it is morally flawed, it does sport a certain consistency: if there is no God, there are no commandments; if there is no body of ideas about right and wrong, then we are free to decide what qualifies as right and wrong; if there are no truths that are eternal and universal, then all we need to do is see what government posits, or decrees. Liberated from God and all the constraints that such a belief entails, the proponents of positivism think they are in the driver's seat, ready to write into law whatever they see fit. But history is not on their side, as even they had to admit when it came time to prosecute the Nazis at Nuremberg.

When the Nazis were put on trial for crimes against humanity, they justified their actions by citing their obedience to the law. They were not lying: they were in fact telling the truth—they did exactly what they were told to do. Yet still they were convicted. From a positivistic perspective, their convictions were unjust: if there is no morality except that which exists in law as posited by government, then the Nazis who gassed Jews can hardly be held culpable for following orders. But from a natural law perspective, the Nazis were as guilty as sin. They knew in their hearts that killing innocent persons was morally wrong. Indeed, it was on the basis of natural law that they were convicted. The German courts knew that justice could not be served by adhering to positivism; in the end, what they did was prudent. "The positive legislative act," one court said, "is intrinsically limited. It loses all obligatory power if it violates the generally recognized principles of international law or the natural law, or if the contradiction between the positive law and justice reaches such an intolerable degree that the law . . . must give way to justice."[15] Thus the Catholic natural law tradition was vindicated. So was prudence.

Slavery

Slavery strikes us today as something that is incomprehensible. Yet throughout most of history it was considered normal. It needs to be said, though, that slavery in the United States was unusual, if only because of its racial dimension. Slavery in most other instances was not racial; more typically it represented a situation in which one party was conscripted to serve another.

There is not a place on the face of the map that did not know slavery at one time or another. In most cases the practice was accepted as an everyday fact of life. The Hebrews, Greeks, and Roman saw nothing wrong with it, and neither did the Africans, Chinese, Japanese—the list is endless. Ancient Egyptian writings took note of slavery, as did the Code of Hammurabi. Aristotle thought it normal for slaves to obey their masters, and even Jesus never condemned slavery. Blacks in the United States owned slaves, as did whites, and slavery was not made illegal in some parts of Africa until the 1980s; it still exists in places like Mauritania and the Sudan, Muslims being the worst offenders. Yet today almost everyone knows slavery is wrong. Thanks in large measure to the Catholic Church.

The ubiquitous nature of slavery met its initial resistance in the West; Western civilization was the first civilization to condemn slavery. Christianity did not initially reject slavery, per se, but it did object to the maltreatment of slaves and insisted that certain humane conditions be afforded to them. By doing so, Christianity played the most important role of any religion or secular belief system in bringing about its demise. It was the belief that we are all God's children, that we are equal in the eyes of God, that ultimately triumphed. Without this judgment based on natural law, it would have taken much longer for the world to turn against slavery.

In antiquity, slavery was so common that Pope Pius I in the second century and Pope Callistus I in the third had been slaves. It wasn't until the fourth century that a Father rejected slavery, and that was Gregory of Nyssa, although it is fair to say that Saint Patrick (a former slave himself) was the first public person in history to condemn slavery. Both Saint Gregory of Nyssa and Saint Patrick taught that master-slave relationships were against nature, and nature's God. Several Church Councils in the fifth and sixth centuries registered criticism of the way slaves were treated, and pushed for reforms. Maltreatment of any kind was condemned, as were attempts to sever marital contracts between slaves. So although the Catholic Church, like every other institution in antiquity, was not unequivocally opposed to slavery, it set in motion a series of objections to slave conditions that made possible the eventual extinction of slavery. No matter, feudalism replaced slavery during the Middle Ages. Slavery made an ugly comeback with the discovery of the New World in 1492. But a hero came on the scene, someone who worked hard to undermine the resurgence of slavery. He was a Dominican priest named Bartolomé de las Casas, a true champion of Indian rights.[16]

Las Casas took after his father, who had sailed with Columbus on his second voyage; both father and son journeyed to Santo Domingo in 1502, like other Spaniards, because they wanted to make money. But Las Casas objected to the conditions under which the Indians lived. Indeed, he was horrified at the way his fellow Spaniards treated the Indians, and he found it impossible to reconcile such barbarism with Christian principles. It wasn't long before Las Casas joined the Dominicans, becoming the first priest to be ordained in the New World; he celebrated his first public Mass in 1512.

Las Casas was surely influenced by Antonio de Montesinos, another Dominican priest. In 1511 Montesinos spoke plainly to his Spanish parishioners: "Tell me, what right have you to enslave them? What authority did you use to make war against them who lived at peace on their territories, killing them cruelly with methods never before heard of? How can you oppress them and not care to feed or cure them, and work them to death to satisfy your greed?" After invoking these natural law principles, Montesinos asked, "And why don't you look after their spiritual health, so that they should come to know God, that they should be baptized, and that they should hear Mass and keep the holy days?"[17] The congregation did not take well to such a lecture and demanded that King Ferdinand recall Montesinos.

It wasn't long before Las Casas experienced his own epiphany. After reading a biblical passage about extracting wealth off the backs of others, he recalled what Father Montesinos had preached. When he visited an old friend, he stated his beliefs with exactitude: "Sir, I have decided it is impossible to be a devout Christian and own slaves," he said.[18] From that day forward, he spoke against slavery, winning the anger of his parishioners. He withstood a great deal of grief, but nothing stopped him from traveling to Cuba to call for the end of slavery. He went to Spain in 1515 and advised King Charles to abolish this exploitative system. Discouraged by his reception, Las Casas entered a monastery, where he wrote his classic, *History of the Indies.*

After ten years of reflection, Las Casas left the monastery and traveled to many parts of what we now call Central America, as well as to Mexico City, meeting with authorities and preaching against slavery. He wanted the Indians to convert, but not as a group as some priests wanted; he advocated converting the natives one by one. Most important, he grounded his objections to slavery in natural law. He maintained that all men were originally free, and that God did not want slavery. Pope Paul III formally adopted that same idea in 1537. The pope's decree, *Sublimis Deus,* was described by writer Gustavo Gutierrez as "the most important papal pronouncement on the human conditions of the Indians."[19] Pope Paul III later imposed penalties on those who worked to support slavery, calling upon Catholics to respect the Indians' God-given rights.

While slavery was still popular, its defense became all the more difficult. In 1541 Las Casas met with King Charles V, and the next year the king issued the New Laws, edicts that banned the enslavement of Indians. But the fight was not over, because widespread dissent broke out. Meanwhile, the pope made Las Casas the bishop of Chiapas in Guatemala in 1544.

With the issue of slavery still raging, Las Casas made his way back to Spain. It was there, in Valladolid, the capital of Castile, that a famous debate took place between Las Casas and a formidable priest, Juan Ginés de Sepúlveda in 1550. While admitting that Indians engaged in some barbaric practices, Las Casas defended the slaves and called attention to the barbarism of the Spaniards. He also put his adversary on the defensive: "The Indians never challenged the right of Christians to be Christians. They never attempted to seize our lands. They never displayed hatred toward Christ our Lord."[20] He pressed his case with precision, saying point-blank, "Slavery must be put to an end."[21] The debate lasted for weeks, and in the end nothing concrete was resolved. But the agenda had been set by Las Casas, and the cause of abolition had been joined with eloquence.

In 1537, Pope Paul III forbade slavery in the New World under penalty of excommunication. His condemnations were echoed by Pope Gregory XVI in 1839, but it was Pope Leo XIII in 1888 who proved to be the most decisive. After slavery was legally abolished, he called upon the bishops in Latin America to do everything they possibly could to see to it that the entire abuses attendant to slavery would finally end. He called the end of slavery a "happy event," one that concluded Christianity's long march to freedom.

Slavery in the United States

Catholics were a tiny, and unwelcome, minority in the United States during the heyday of slavery, so they were hardly in a position to register objections. Prudence dictated that the best they could do was to loosen the straps of slavery by calling for humane conditions. Brother Joseph Mobberly, an influential Jesuit, did just that, calling upon Catholic slaveowners to provide nourishment, religious instruction, and respect for marital relations. Because marriage was a sacrament, bishops in the Americas implored everyone to respect the right of slaves to marry and live together as one. As always, priests and religious preached that all people were equal in the sight of God, thus undercutting the basis upon which slavery was founded. No wonder that many historians credit Catholicism with having a built-in aversion to slavery, one that played out successfully in the end.

No one exemplified the natural law tradition better than Abraham Lincoln. In his famous 1858 debates with Stephen Douglas, he insisted that the Declaration of Independence employed the bedrock principles upon which the Constitution was inscribed.[22] "All men were created equal" allowed for no exceptions, he argued. He did not mean, of course, that all men and women were equal in terms of intellectual, artistic, and athletic abilities; what he meant was that all of us, regardless of our station in life, have rights that are inalienable. These rights were not given to us by government; rather they were rights we held because of our human status. It was incumbent upon government, then, to respect these rights.

Unlike some prominent defenders of slavery such as George

Fitzhugh, a sociologist who wrote that slavery was good for blacks because it prevented them from competing with whites in the marketplace, Douglas took the position that slavery should not be seen as a moral or religious issue; it was simply up to the people to decide what they wanted. This positivistic approach was well suited to justifying slavery based on the majority opinion and on purely utilitarian terms. It was also a moral nightmare for those on the short end of the stick. But this is exactly what is to be expected when moral relativism is enjoined: different strokes for different folks is a rationale to justify slavery. The tradition of natural law espoused by John Locke, and made evident by Jefferson in the Declaration of Independence, is morally far superior.

University of Dallas political scientist Thomas G. West acutely observes that the Declaration "is a striking example of government promotion of a particular theology."[23] What he means is that our founding document has four specific references to God. God is the author of the "laws of nature and nature's God"; He is the "Creator" who "endowed" us with inalienable rights; He is "the Supreme Judge of the world"; and He provides "the protection of Divine Providence." Try imagining how Lincoln could have prevailed over Douglas without this natural law tradition. Similarly, when William Henry Seward made his pitch for abolition, he appealed to a "higher"—that is, "natural"—law.

Those who fought slavery were not successful because they were right; they were successful because they were prudent. Lincoln knew that in order to save the Union, he had to walk carefully in making his case against slavery. Similarly, Judge John Noonan, an expert on how Catholic teaching on slavery developed, observes that had Jesus called for the abolition of slavery, it would have resulted in "an uprising like Spartacus's."[24] Prudently, He avoided such a calamity. Jesus, naturally, never justified slavery, and Saint Paul was quick to say that in Christ Jesus "there is neither slave nor free person." We know that Saint Paul did not think slavery was part of God's design, but prudence advised him not to champion its abolition. Nonetheless, it was not long before Saint Gregory of Nyssa condemned the practice outright.

The case against slavery would not have been possible without a vibrant return to Catholic natural law theory. But its power and validity hardly ended there. Supreme Court Justice Thurgood Marshall also referenced natural law when he spoke out against racial discrimination in the famous *Brown v. Board of Education* decision. He said that all men were created equal and that this "basic proposition" meant that all people "were endowed with certain natural rights."[25] Rev. Martin Luther King Jr. invoked natural law, arguing that "an individual who breaks a law that conscience tells him is unjust, and who willingly accepts the penalty of imprisonment in order to arouse the conscience of the community over its injustice, is in reality expressing the highest respect for the law."[26] Indeed, King sounded just like Saint Thomas Aquinas when he said that "a just law is a man-made code that squares with the moral law or the law of God."[27]

These great achievements, ranging from the abolition of slavery to the convictions at Nuremberg, could not have been possible without invoking natural rights and natural law. Moreover, these accomplishments could not have unfolded without the persistent contributions of the Catholic Church.

The Church was the first institution to give an intellectual home to the moral law and to human rights, and the world is much better as a result. Because they are rooted in the human condition, there laws and rights will never be dated, and by the looks of events in the third millennium, they will be consulted and cited again and again. Let's hope so.

Moral Relativism

Not only does the proper use of freedom liberate the individual who exercises it; it often has a positive effect on others. An artist who offers something beautiful and a screenwriter who makes us think are examples of freedom at its best. But in the hands of someone crude, what is portrayed on canvas and on the screen is not liberating; it is debilitating. Freedom by itself, then, tells us nothing; it has no moral content. We know whether to praise or condemn freedom by what someone does with it. When firefighters exercise their freedom, lives are saved; when arsonists exercise theirs, property is destroyed and people die. In other words, we cannot tell whether freedom is good or bad unless we know how it is used.

This may seem plain as day, but it is actually a very controversial idea. It is the Catholic idea of freedom, although one need not be Catholic to embrace it. Edmund Burke, the father of conservatism, was not Catholic, but he entertained the Catholic perspective. "The effect of liberty to individuals is that they may do as they please," the British statesman and orator said. He then prudently counseled, "[W]e ought to see what it will please them to do before we risk congratulations, which may soon be turned into complaints."[28] Burke nicely illustrates the importance of recognizing that it is the person who exercises freedom who determines its teleology, or final end. Put differently, freedom by itself has no ultimate purpose—all it means is that people are not stopped from doing what they want to do. That some people should be stopped from employing their rights is acknowledged by everyone who has ever encountered a reckless driver. Freedom's teleology, then, is determined by those who use it.

In today's world, there is great resistance to such a notion of freedom. Even the very suggestion that freedom needs to be prudently exercised is likely to be seen as burdensome. Yet without the exercise of prudence, the liberty to do as one chooses can literally negate freedom. Those who object to this reasoning completely reject natural law and therefore cannot accept any notion of freedom that ties its use to something proper. In the nihilistic play *Jerry Springer—The Opera*, a vulgar and assaultive performance, it is said at the end that "nothing is wrong and nothing is right."[29] Similarly, atheist writers such as P. Z. Myers maintain that "nothing must be held sacred."[30] While those who rail against any authority (except for when they are in command) are drawn to these ideas, it should be remembered that so was Hitler.

The Catholic Church offers a much more satisfying, and ultimately workable, perspective. It holds that there are moral absolutes, truths that are readily understood, and that the good society cannot be achieved without accepting these moral laws. The belief that "nothing is wrong and nothing is right" is so thoroughly foreign to Catholic thought as to be almost delusional. Yet this delusional belief is at the heart of moral relativism, whose proponents contend that each person is the best judge of right and wrong. The emphasis is on the autonomy of the individual, which is awarded an exalted status.

Moral relativism, so popular today, is an idea with a checkered past. It was popular for about a century in the ancient world before Plato and Aristotle made mincemeat of it. It re-emerged with a vengeance during the Enlightenment, and it is today celebrated by those associated with postmodernist thought. Without doubt, this viewpoint has triumphed the most in the dominant culture of Western nations; it is at the core of moral thinking throughout North America and Europe. The idea that each individual is the best arbiter of morality is seen as the definition of freedom.

From a sociological perspective, moral relativism is not only fanciful; it is rubbish. The very definition of society implies a moral consensus. And a moral consensus means that there is general agreement among individuals as to what constitutes right and wrong. Traffic lights and stop signs would have no force if everyone was free to decide whether to abide by them. Indeed, we operate on the principle that it does not matter what one thinks about traffic laws, and that is why the arresting police officer is unimpressed with excuses of a morally relative nature. Even those who worship at the altar of the unencumbered self find it hard to disagree with this position. The tragedy is that they still prefer to put prudence aside and insist that the principle of autonomy is superior to the perspective that operates based on moral absolutes.

One variant of moral relativism that has proven to be

very popular with social scientists is cultural relativism. By insisting that all cultures are morally equal, and that there is no valid way to rank cultures, the proponents of this idea have been able to justify just about anything. Ruth Benedict certainly tried. This influential anthropologist was so determined to promote the noble idea of tolerance for all peoples that she could not bring herself to condemn cannibalism.[31] Had she exercised prudence, the indispensable cardinal virtue, she would have realized that by pushing a good idea like tolerance to extremes, she was actually corrupting its value. Sadly, her prominent book on this subject, *Patterns of Culture*, appeared in 1934, just one year after Hitler came to power. In his own perverse way, he could have leaned on it for support.

The reference to Hitler is not being flip; it is being real. Consider what Dennis Prager, an observant Jew, has to say on the subject of moral absolutes: "Nazi, Communist, and Iraqi tortures are wrong not because they offend our taste, but because they violate an objective standard of good and evil to which all of us are responsible. Morality either exists, i.e., is absolute, or it is no more than a euphemism for personal taste."[32] Those who believe in cultural relativism, then, have no principled basis upon which to object to Hitler. From their perspective, he was simply doing what he thought was right. And he was: he sincerely believed that Jews were a cancer that had to be eliminated if Western civilization was to survive. But to those of us who are believers, as Prager is, there is such a thing as God and there is such a thing as natural law. Therefore, Hitler cannot be absolved of his monstrous crimes merely because he "felt" he was doing right. Surely he knew that it could not possibly be right to kill innocent people who had never harmed anyone else. He may have acted like a madman, but he knew exactly what he was doing.

Catholicism and Freedom

Some critics of Catholicism often point to condemnations of liberalism made by Pope Pius IX in his 1864 *Syllabus of Errors* as evidence of Catholicism's hostility to freedom. To be sure, Pius IX was critical of what he saw as the fruits of the French Revolution. There was much to condemn: the murder of the Catholic clergy and the plunder of Catholic property; the bloodstained attempts to wipe out any semblance of Catholicism; Napoleon's persecution of Pope Pius VII; and so forth. Indeed, the fruits of the French Revolution were so horrific that historians generally regard the government that came to power as the world's first totalitarian regime. It was these excesses, committed in the name of liberalism, that Pius IX saw as worthy of rebuke.

If Catholics were ill disposed to freedom, per se, then why did the newly inaugurated George Washington address Catholics as follows: "[Y]our fellow citizens will not forget the patriotic part which you took in the accomplishment of our revolution"?[33] Neither would the Frenchman Tocqueville have credited Catholics for their belief in moral truths, their independence of mind, and their bountiful virtues—all of which made them exemplary citizens. It is for reasons like these that Dennis McManus looks at the Catholic contribution to

America's founding and comes away impressed; he contends that the Catholic insistence on prudence, bringing wisdom to the debates over the Constitution, has proved to be lasting.[34]

Thomas D. Williams credits Pope Leo XIII for giving us the greatest exposition on freedom in the modern world. There had been many others before him who addressed the subject—Saint Augustine was famous for saying that people who abused freedom were nothing more than "slaves to sin"—but Leo XIII in the late nineteenth century built on these contributions and delivered in the encyclical *Rerum Novarum* "a veritable Magna Carta of rights."[35] Williams points to the rights of man, the family, the common good, workers, private property, leisure, a just wage, and freedom of association as the critical elements of freedom advanced by Leo XIII. All of these are positive examples of the exercise of freedom, quite unlike the open-ended ideas about freedom that some people promote. In an earlier encyclical, Leo explicitly said that no one has a natural right to do wrong, and that "liberty is to be regarded as legitimate in so far only as it affords greater facility for doing good, but no farther."[36]

Pope John XXIII was the first to use the term "human rights" in an encyclical; previously the concept had been referred to as "natural rights." In *Pacem in Terris*, he speaks of rights as being natural, God-given, and in accordance with our status as humans. It is from our personal dignity that our rights spring, and no government can legitimately abridge them. Like Aquinas, John XXIII also recognized that rights entail duties, and that the good society would insist on such a link. Important as his writings are, it is in the documents of Vatican II, the ecumenical council that bears his imprint, that we find the most widely cited Catholic contributions to the concept of liberty.

The Declaration on Religious Freedom, *Dignitatis Humanae*, means very little to those whose idea of liberty entails that religion and freedom be considered opposites; ditto for moral relativists. But if religion is the cradle of democracy, as Tocqueville nicely put it, then the prospects for freedom in this century will be dim unless we begin to appreciate the wisdom found in *Dignitatis Humanae*. This Vatican II document declares the centrality of religious liberty to freedom, properly understood. It grounds our rights in our nature, in our very dignity as human beings. The same theme is evident in the Pastoral Constitution on the Church in the Modern World, *Gaudium et Spes*. In addition, this document asserts that humans should have "ready access" to life's necessities, as well as "rightful freedom even in matters of religion."

In today's world, those who do not share the Catholic perspective, and most certainly those who explicitly reject it, find it hard to understand why anyone would speak of "*rightful* freedom." In their minds, there is only one freedom; freedom has no prescribed end. Besides, they ask, who is to say what freedom is right or wrong? But as we have seen, posing the question this way has all kinds of ramifications. If freedom isn't understood in terms of what it is to be used for, then what is there to stop its diminution in the hands of those who imprudently abuse it? For if freedom is meant to enhance the individual, and society, it must be prudently exercised. In recent years, no one has better captured the meaning of freedom, prudently understood, than Pope John Paul II.

Freedom and Morality

In 1859 John Stuart Mill wrote an essay, "On Liberty," that many regard as the most important commentary on the subject. Essentially he argued that everyone should be allowed to do whatever he wants to do, just so long as no one else is harmed. It sounds innocent enough, which explains its appeal. But what if we can't agree on what constitutes harm? And what if someone doesn't directly harm someone else but nonetheless lives a life of moral irresponsibility? Is it really just his business? When people act irresponsibly, someone else inevitably suffers. We don't live on an island all by ourselves; we live, as we were meant to live, with others in society. There is no escaping it. That is why theories of liberty that are fundamentally asocial are seriously flawed. In essence, there is more to liberty than rights.

Anyone, Catholic or not, who wants to read the most astute exposition on liberty ever written should consult *Veritatis Splendor*, an encyclical written by Pope John Paul II and released in 1993. Unlike "On Liberty" and the raging popularity of the mantra "I am the sole judge of my freedom," *Veritatis Splendor* establishes an indissoluble link between freedom and morality. In the mind of John Paul II, and according to the Catholic Catechism, freedom means *the right to do what we ought to do*. There is nothing more countercultural than this; it runs against the grain of everything Western civilization holds dear today. Typically our society today holds that freedom means the right to do whatever we want to do. Not only is this an amoral conception of freedom; but as our modus vivendi it is largely responsible for our contemporary personal and social disorders.

Freedom in Catholic thought has a natural teleology, one that is "focused on the other." As John Paul said elsewhere, freedom has an "inherently relational dimension,"[37] one that cannot be reconciled with the notion of freedom as a self-serving experience. Never understood in isolation from its consequences, freedom is a vehicle for realizing one's own abilities, as well as a natural partner in the workings of the good society. John Paul II knew this well, and regarded Jesus's call to "Come, follow me" as the greatest exaltation of freedom ever voiced. Those who follow Jesus would not only be impelled toward good acts; they would be liberated in the process. Freedom, in this construct, is something that benefits both the individual and society.

If freedom is inseparable from morality, then much can be gleaned by examining freedom's moral properties. John Paul II was emphatic when he said that the moral life has "an essential *'teleological' character*," owing to "the deliberate ordering of human acts to God, the supreme good and ultimate (*telos*) of man" (italics in original).[38] True freedom, then, must be seen in service to God's will. That it is seen these days as being given to us so that we can serve ourselves is not debatable. John Paul II is not without an explanation for this predicament. He sees acceptance of truth as an essential condition for authentic freedom: "You will know the truth, and the truth will set you free." This is more than good advice—it is a constitutive attribute of freedom. "Because there can be no freedom apart from or in opposition to the truth," the Polish pope advised, "the categorical—unyielding and uncompromising—defense of the absolutely essential demands of man's personal dignity must be considered the way and the condition for the very existence of freedom."[39]

From the viewpoint of those who prefer unconditional liberty, the right to do whatever one wants, John Paul's prescriptions seem dull and unsatisfying. But there is nothing prudent about seeking to have it all. It is not only immature; it is untenable. If everyone were to interpret freedom as autonomy, the result would ineluctably be a collision course: my right to do what I please will, at some point, necessarily come into conflict with your right to do what you please. What then? Prudence, on the other hand, counsels against "having it all," and respects a more limited, and therefore more realistic, interpretation of freedom. While those who favor what is called "ordered liberty" may not always credit prudence, this is exactly the virtue they are living.

Ordered liberty is a term often used to describe the kind of society envisioned by the Founders. It certainly resonates in Catholic thought. By saying that liberty must be ordered if it is to be achieved, its proponents are saying that unbridled liberty is the enemy of freedom. While it may seem paradoxical, liberty must be limited if it is to be realized. Edmund Burke knew this to be true, and so did those who have profited from it. To be exact, the most creative ages in history, as Robert Nisbet once commented, have been those in which men and women have been able to escape socially stultifying conditions *without* tearing up their social roots.

If freedom of action needs to be channeled in a positive way for true liberty to be achieved, and if the demands of ordered liberty require prudent interpretations, then the suggestion that the Ten Commandments are the bedrock of freedom should not shock anyone. Indeed, it is expository. So when John Paul writes, "Human freedom and God's law are not in opposition; on the contrary, they appeal to one another,"[40] what he says rings true. "The commandments," he instructs, "represent the basic condition for love of neighbor; at the same time they are proof of that love." Then he enjoins the debate forthrightly: "[The commandments] are the *first necessary step on the journey towards freedom*, its starting-point" (emphasis in original). He cites Saint Augustine at this juncture, recalling how Augustine said that to be free from "murder, adultery, fornication, theft, fraud, sacrilege, and so forth" was "the beginning of freedom."[41] Now contrast this with those who insist that sexual freedom is the end of liberty and the stage is set for the culture war.

Conscience

Those who believe in the reigning cultural idea of absolute freedom often smirk as they say that all along they thought that Catholics put a premium on conscience. Catholics do, but they also understand prudence, which is why their embrace of conscience rights is always qualified. It must be. Consider that all the great mass murderers and serial rapists had a conscience. That they acted in accordance with their conscience, then, tells us nothing about the morality of their actions. Jeffrey Dahmer, an infamous American criminal, killed his victims and then ate them for supper. He was following his conscience. Had he been guided by a "well-formed conscience," one anchored in the kinds of truths and moral absolutes found in the Ten Commandments, his conscience would have directed him to a different outcome.

John Paul II knew what would happen once natural law was abandoned. "Conscience," he admonished us, "is no longer considered a primordial reality as an act of a person's intelligence, the function of which is to apply the universal knowledge of the good in a specific situation and thus to express a judgment about the right conduct to be chosen here and now." The consequences are obvious. "Instead," he said, "there is a tendency to grant to the individual conscience the prerogative of independently determining the criteria of good and evil and then acting accordingly."[42] The free-ranging conscience, unhinged from a moral foundation, is one that is capable of justifying virtually any monstrosity.

Conscience plays its proper role when it is well formed. Think of it this way. Who excels the most at musical talent: the one who masters the master composers, or the one who merely improvises? Improvisation is fine, but for musical talent to be creative, the musician must embellish and build on the works of others. Otherwise the sounds produced may resemble those of inmates in the asylum who think themselves talented when they run a hammer along a radiator. The same thing is true when applied to the forming of our conscience. An unfettered conscience that consults no authority is not likely to render right judgments. But a well-formed conscience, one that consults morally authoritative sources and is oriented toward a "focus on the other," is exactly the kind of tool that can minimize injustice. A good conscience, John Paul understands, is one that seeks the truth.

False Conceptions of Freedom

If there are no moral absolutes, then what is seen as evil by some may be seen as less so by others, maybe even seen as ennobling. But in Catholic thought, as taught by John Paul II, there are such things as murder, genocide, rape, slavery, torture, racism, and the like that can never be justified. Above all, the right to life must be seen as an absolute. He mentions "homicide, genocide, abortion, euthanasia, and voluntary suicide" as being hostile to life. There are other behaviors that are similarly immoral. Such things as mutilation, subhuman conditions, arbitrary imprisonment, deportation, prostitution, and trafficking in women and children, as well as mistreatment of workers—all are worthy of condemnation.

Perhaps the most telling question to ask is: Which society would any rational person in the third millennium choose to live in? One that denies the existence of any universal standard of right and wrong? Or one that affirms the existence of such a standard? If the answer seems obvious, then it remains to be explained why so many prefer the moral relativism of our age to the Catholic understanding of freedom and morality. From the point of view of prudence, moral relativism makes no sense. But when irrationality kicks in, when the emotional appeal of doing whatever one chooses to do becomes the paramount motivator, the case for moral absolutes is lost. From a Catholic perspective, this tendency is not hard to understand because Catholicism accepts temptation and selfish ambitions as part of the human condition.

Pope Benedict XVI knows why false conceptions of freedom are attractive these days, and he places part of the blame on those who trumpet the merits of agnosticism and atheism. He warns that "ideological rejection of God and an atheism of indifference, oblivious to the Creator and at risk of becoming equally oblivious to human values, constitute some of the chief obstacles to development today." With force he states, *"A humanism which excludes God is an inhuman humanism"* (his italics).[43] In striking relief, he counsels, "The greatest liberty is to say 'yes,' to conform with the will of God."[44] In other words, our "focus on God" enables us to "focus on the other," thus allowing us to experience what real freedom has to offer. This may be a hard sell for nonbelievers, but their vision of freedom won't produce what they think they're looking for; they're building a prison of narcissism.

Many of those who reject God look to science as a guidepost for human freedom. For Benedict XVI this view is mistaken: "Such an expectation asks too much of science; this kind of hope is deceptive." He does not fail to appreciate the benefits that science can afford; it's just that science "can also destroy mankind and the world unless it is steered by forces that lie outside it."[45] Just as a knife can save a patient in the hands of a skilled surgeon; it can also be a lethal weapon in the hands of an evil man. We are free to choose what to do, but not all choices result in freedom. To get the right result, we must resort to reason, to prudence, and we must orient our behavior toward what is good. Again, this does not sit well with those who prefer a secular approach to freedom, but it works, meaning that it serves the good society. Accepting this vision, however, means setting our sights beyond the interests of the individual.

Benedict XVI is adamant about tying rights to responsibilities. Again, this is not a popular idea today. Try telling a young person who has been persistently taught that his rights are paramount that before he can be awarded more rights he must first demonstrate a sense of responsibility. Yet not to require him to do so is to ask for trouble. When someone abuses his rights, someone else's rights are abridged. It cannot be otherwise. Therefore, in the interests of the good society, it behooves all of us to pay heed to what Benedict XVI advises. In his encyclical *Caritas in Veritate* he states that "individual rights, when detached from a framework of duties which grants them their full meaning, can run wild, leading to an escalation of demands which is effectively unlimited and indiscriminate. An overemphasis on rights leads to a disregard for duties."[46] Any honest teacher, regardless of religious conviction, will find it hard not to agree with this verity.

The first freedom is freedom of conscience; it is inseparable from freedom of religion. "Religious freedom expresses what is unique about the human person," Benedict XVI said in his World Day of Peace address of 2010, "for it allows us to direct our personal and social life to God, in whose light the identity, meaning, and purpose of the person is fully understood."[47] Benedict implores us to give priority to religious liberty by accepting our public responsibilities. Translated, this means that we have a duty to give witness to our religious liberties by participating in the public square. Benedict drove this point home in 2012 when he met with U.S. bishops on their "Ad Limina" visit. "The legitimate separation of Church and State cannot be taken to mean that the Church must be silent on certain issues."[48]

Along with our right to religious liberty comes the responsibility of proclaiming—not thrusting forward or crassly proselytizing—our faith in the public square. It is right to have nativity scenes in places other than our front yards; it is right to have voluntary prayers in the public forum; it is right to have student clubs that serve people of faith; it is right to acknowledge God on our coins and in our pledges of fidelity to nation. What is not right is to privatize religion, treating it as if it were a communicable disease. While religious chauvinism is no virtue, the censorship of religion in the public square is inimical to the cause of freedom. Prudence dictates that there needs to be a middle ground.

No scholar has a more brilliant record of challenging the problems inherent in postmodernist thought than does Pope Benedict XVI. The idea that there are no objective truths, that everything that exists is nothing more than a social construction—a man-made social artifact—is the defining tenet of postmodernist thought. But Benedict knows that it is also its Achilles' heel. If all that exists is a matter of whim, or social invention, then nothing has any meaning. Those who believe there is no objective truth deny that there is any inherent meaning to such human categories as race, ethnicity, sex, motherhood and fatherhood; these constructs are mere manifestations of the nomenclature that some have succeeded in designing. That being the case, there is no room for God;

He is just another chimera. And if there is no God, then, as Nietzsche understood, there is no objective standard of right and wrong.

It is this view, fiercely held today by many intellectuals, that Benedict XVI directly confronts. It leads to, he says, a "dictatorship of relativism." What he means by this is the view that "recognizes nothing as definite and has as its ultimate measure only the self and its own desires."[49] Now it may be that postmodernist thinkers are guided by a noble effort to eliminate racism, sexism, and all forms of inequality and bigotry, but in the end they will have delivered a moral holocaust. If every moral perspective is considered equal, then whatever is superior risks being vetoed by its inferior competitor. Prudence, however, cautions against instituting moral equality as much as it rejects imposing a morally suspect ethos.

For Benedict XVI there is no freedom without truth. "Fidelity to man requires *fidelity to the truth*," he underscores, "which alone is the *guarantee of freedom* and of *the possibility of integral human development*" (italics in original).[50] Those who cast aside this insight must be prepared to offer a blueprint for the good society that does not recognize the link between freedom and truth. But what are we left with once we have discarded an objective measuring stick of morality? On what principled basis can we object to those who engage in antisocial behavior? Indeed, from the viewpoint of postmodernism, even the suggestion that some forms of behavior are antisocial is seen as a social construct having no universal validity.

Catholicism matters to the cause of freedom. It has played an indispensable role in the promotion of human rights, its teachings having been inscribed in declarations of liberty throughout the world. Before all other religious and secular belief systems recognized the evil of slavery, the Catholic Church took steps to thwart slavery's appeal, paving the way to its eventual extinction. Moreover, those guilty of genocide were denied their desire to vindicate their behavior by citing the positive law, and that is because judges found relief in the resurrection of natural law. Similarly, Catholic thought has done more to challenge the popularity of myopic visions of freedom than has any other belief system. The application of Catholic principles has borne much good fruit and promises to yield a greater harvest in the future. Prudence is what directed Catholic thinking in the pursuit of liberty, and prudence is what the world needs now more than ever.

Human Dignity

All discussions of human rights eventually turn to a more central concern, that of human dignity. In Catholic thought, people possess rights because rights naturally flow from the dignity that is inherent in the human person. Pope John XXIII wrote that "every human being is a person, that is, his nature is endowed with intelligence and free will." Furthermore, a person's rights, as well as his responsibilities, "are universal and inviolable so they cannot in any way be surrendered."[51] This may sound fairly uncontroversial, but it has proven to be the source of much debate.

To say that every human being is a person is to make a highly contentious statement. Some believe that humanness and personhood are two different categories. Those who hold to this conviction believe that although an embryo, or a fetus, is human, it is not fully so, and therefore it cannot qualify as a person. Some go so far as to deny human status to the embryo or fetus, making the argument that it is just a clump of cells. But given the reality of life as shown in a sonogram, serious commentators are unable able to entertain this fiction. For John XXIII, our rights are a reflection of our humanness, and since every human is already a person—the distinction is seen as more semantic than real—no government has a legitimate right to deny rights to any part of the human family.

Father Richard John Neuhaus had a gift of asking the right questions and then providing cogent responses. "Who belongs to the community for which we as a community accept responsibility, including the responsibility to protect, along with other natural rights, their right to life?" He answers that this is "a preeminently political question."[52] Don't misunderstand him; he does not for a moment discount the role played by bioethicists and others; he simply means that at the end of the day, agents of government will decide. Lawmakers, however, are not unaware of what shapes the popular consensus, and what is generally agreed to may reflect religious as well as secular values. Unfortunately, many attempts have been made to bar those of a religious persuasion from entering the conversation, although this censorial approach finds little public support; this tactic is usually adopted by intellectuals who are without faith, some of whom are downright disrespectful of the rights of the faithful.

Steven Pinker is a Harvard professor who rejects the very concept of human dignity. He regards the term *dignity* as "squishy" and relegates it to the bin of subjectivity. He prefers to make ethical judgments based on an ethic of personal autonomy. He is not unaware that his critics have raised a red flag about where this position leads to, yet he is dismissive. "Several essayists play the genocide card and claim that the horrors of the twentieth century are what you get when you fail to hold dignity sacrosanct," he says. "But one hardly needs the notion of 'dignity' to say why it is wrong to gas six million Jews or to send Russian dissidents to the gulag."[53] Yet his rejoinder is unsatisfactory, if for no other reason than it is not a rejoinder at all: he never explains on what basis a valid case can be made against genocide. Insisting on an ethic of personal autonomy isn't helpful. What can he say to those who maintain that it is their preference that Jews die?

Pope John Paul II reminds us of a principled basis for accepting the dignity of man, and it is anything but squishy; it is found in one of the two great commandments, "You shall love your neighbor as yourself." There's nothing subjective about that. "In this commandment we find a precise expression of *the singular dignity of the human person*," the pope stresses, "the only creature that God has wanted for its own sake."[54] The penultimate "focus on the other" prescription is found in this commandment, the effect of which is to divert our eyes away from ourselves. By doing so we are able to appreciate how equal all human beings are, equal in their inherent worth and equal before God. That they should be treated as such by law is indisputable.

If all humans are of equal worth, entitled to the same rights, then we should be able to find plenty of examples of this principle in Catholic teachings. We do. In 1983 Joseph Cardinal Bernardin gave an address at Fordham University,

"A Consistent Ethic of Life: An American-Catholic Dialogue."
He included something for everyone. He declared that Catholic thought was a "seamless garment" and that such things as abortion, the use of nuclear weapons, and the death penalty were unjustifiable. If we are serious about human rights and the dignity of all, he reasoned, we cannot make exceptions based on ideological interests. We must be consistent. This is an eminently defensible position, but in fairness to Bernardin's critics, it must be noted that although the Catholic Church is opposed to nuclear proliferation and the death penalty in almost all cases, it does not condemn them in the same absolute way it condemns the intentional killing of innocents.

Because abortion means the taking of innocent human life, no exceptions can be countenanced. Nations, like individuals, however, have a right to defend themselves from aggression, and there are occasions when going to war can be just. How do we decide? Prudence is the best guide. In general, Catholic teachings lean toward the use of nonviolent means.

Pope John Paul II showcased the Catholic presumption in favor of nonviolence when he considerably narrowed the conditions under which the use of the death penalty was legitimate. Allowing only for rare instances when the national security could not otherwise be protected, he essentially took capital punishment off the Catholic table. His leadership on this issue inspired a movement within the Catholic Church, the Community of Sant'Egidio, to consider a campaign in favor of a UN moratorium on the death penalty. The campaign succeeded in passing in the General Assembly, although its future adoption by member states remains problematic.

No matter, as Catholic journalist John Allen said, the vote for a moratorium was "a victory for the Catholic Church," so much so that the initiative is "difficult to imagine without the Catholic contribution."[55]

Embryonic Stem Cell Research

It is a biological truism that all of us started as an embryo. Had someone decided to do research on us when we were at that stage, we would never have been born. That's because it is impossible to do embryonic stem cell research without killing the embryo. Should this matter? It most certainly would have mattered to us had we been the subject of such research. What obligations, if any, do we have to those at the embryonic stage? From a Catholic perspective, the answer is straightforward: we must protect all innocent human life, from conception until natural death.

Most critics of the Catholic position say that embryos may be human but they lack the properties that qualify for full human status. So why don't they eat them? Sounds coarse, but why not? Leon Kass, an ethicist who writes from a Jewish perspective, offers this challenge to those who defend embryonic stem cell research. If the proponents of embryonic stem cell research were served human embryos as a delicacy, or as a "human caviar,"[56] would they partake? If not, why not? Because of a natural aversion to cannibalism? Does not that concede the point made by the Catholic Church?

Kass says that the human embryo "is not mere meat; it is not just stuff; it is not a 'thing.'" So what is it? The fertilized human egg, the zygote, and early embryonic stages, Kass informs, "are clearly alive." He describes exactly what he means: "They metabolize, respire, and respond to changes in the environment; they grow and divide." While it is not yet differentiated, the blastocyst [an embryo barely visible to the naked eye] "is an organic whole, self-developing, genetically unique and distinct from the egg and sperm whose union marked the beginning of its career as a discrete, unfolding being." Moreover, "after fertilization is complete, there exists a new individual, with its unique genetic identity, fully potent for the self-initiated development into a mature human being, if circumstances are cooperative."[57]

This is not Kass's opinion. It is not a theological belief. It is a scientific fact. People are still free, of course, to support embryonic stem cell research, but they are not free to make up their own facts. Prudence, of course, would argue that we should not support research that kills human life, even in the early stages. But, say the proponents of this kind of research, embryos are not deserving of the same respect as adults. Which begs the question: "Who else doesn't qualify?" The mentally or physically disabled? Princeton professor and noted Catholic author Robert P. George cuts to the chase: "One need not be *actually* or immediately conscious, reasoning, deliberating, making choices, etc., in order to be a human being who deserves full moral respect, for plainly we should accord people who are asleep or in reversible comas such respect" (his italics).[58] The consequences to society are ominous if we reject such common sense.

It is commonly said that the Catholic Church is opposed to stem cell research. It is not. It is opposed to embryonic stem cell research. It is not opposed to adult stem cell research, and that is because a human life doesn't have to be extinguished in order for the stem cells to be made available for research. Taking stem cells from an arm or leg, or even the placenta, is perfectly fine by Catholic lights. Not only that, but research is fast making moot the need for embryonic stem cell research.

Scientists are now able to make ordinary human skin cells that approximate the powers of embryonic stem cells. By directly reprogramming adult stem cells, scientists are able to skirt the ethical issues entailed with research on embryos. Researchers have found a way to "coax" adult cells to regress into an embryonic state, thus alleviating what had been the biggest obstacle to developing the cells into potential cures. Moreover, adult stem cells are much more controllable; that is, it is easier to direct them to become the desired cell type. Indeed, adult stem cells have saved hundreds of thousands of lives over the decades through bone marrow transplants, a routine treatment for people with leukemia, lymphoma, and other blood diseases. "That's really one of the great success stories of stem cell biology that gives us all hope," says Dr. David Scadden of Harvard.[59] Progress is being made so fast that Dr. Bernadine Healy, former director of the National Institutes of Health, says that embryonic stem cell research is a dead end and is already "obsolete."[60]

The prospects for making human cloning obsolete are not encouraging, and the pursuit of these techniques is more ominous than embryonic stem cell research ever was. The prospects are hair-raising. By taking from the cells of a donor, scientists are seeking to create an exact copy. But what happens when they fail? What do we do with defective organisms?

Flush them down the toilet? Pretend they are not human? What if those who wanted to acquire their own double change their minds? Do we auction off the unclaimed ones? Once they are born, how will society receive such persons? Will being cloned give rise to psychological problems? Some lesbian activists are already celebrating the day when males will "become obsolete." Is this what the good society looks like? Or would we be better off following the Catholic way, respecting human life as God's gift?

Much of the discussion about stem cell research and cloning is based on what might happen down the road. The same is not true of abortion. We've been down that road, and it is minefield.

Abortion

It would be hard to name an issue that has divided more Americans than abortion. The data show, however, that a majority of Americans now identify themselves as "pro-life," however marginally. This a result, it seems clear, of identifiable images of babies in the womb. The pictures don't lie. What we see are not elephants or seals. They are human beings, little boys and girls who have yet to make it to birth. The heart begins to beat with the child's own blood after three weeks, and the spinal column and nervous system are starting to form at the same time. After six weeks, brain waves are detectable and fingernails are forming. As the baby matures, we can see him move about, make facial expressions, open his eyes, and so forth. And yet right up until birth, these boys and girls are eligible to be killed. Not only that, they are killed in the name of freedom.

It is widely believed that the freedom being insisted upon emanates from the feminist community. Yet early feminists were strongly opposed to abortion. Most of the nineteenth-century feminists saw abortion as an evil that was condoned by men who were out to exploit women. Elizabeth Cady Stanton, who in 1848 organized the first women's rights convention, in Seneca Falls, New York, said abortion was just another case of women being treated like property, "and it was degrading to women that we should treat our children as property to be disposed of as we see fit."[61] Also taking this view was Susan B. Anthony, the heralded champion of women's rights. She saw what happened when men took advantage of women by promoting abortion, and she explained the consequences with passion: "It will burden her conscience in life, it will burden her soul in death; but, oh, thrice guilty is he . . . who drove her to the desperation which impelled her to the crime!"[62]

Today feminists identify abortion as a woman's right. But survey after survey shows that the greatest supporters of legalized abortion have long been single men—a statistic that would surprise neither Stanton nor Anthony. In fact, this was true before abortion was legalized in the United States in 1973, and it has remained true up to this day. Obviously, these guys are not closet feminists. Most, let's be honest, have the cash to rid themselves of their problem; alternatively, they can always charge it to their credit card.

What made the feminists of the 1960s reverse gears and become ardent supporters of abortion rights? It is often said that this change was owing to a genuine concern over the number of women who were dying each year as a result of illegal abortions. For example, it was said there were five thousand to ten thousand deaths a year owing to abortions prior to 1973. But this is a lie. We know it is a lie because the man who broadcasted it about at the time, Dr. Bernard Nathanson, a practicing abortionist, has admitted he lied. He has had more than one conversion since then: he quit his trade, adopted a pro-life position, and converted to Catholicism. By the way, the actual number of women who died the year before *Roe v. Wade* made abortion legal was thirty-nine; the figure is not in dispute.

The Catholic Church has never had to switch gears; it has never been anything but pro-life. Not that it was first in this regard: four hundred years before Christ, Hippocrates condemned abortion, and in the first century A.D. some physicians refused to prescribe drugs that would induce an abortion, so-called abortifacients. They maintained that it was the charge of doctors to "maintain and save what nature had engendered."[63] According to Pope John Paul II, this natural law position can be found more explicitly in the Didache, the most ancient nonbiblical Christian writing. "You shall not kill" was interpreted to mean, among other things, that "you shall not put a child to death by abortion nor kill it once it is born."[64] Indeed, in the first centuries after Christ, murdering a child, or anyone for that matter, was considered to be among the three most serious sins, along with apostasy and adultery.

John Paul II lists abortion, infanticide, and euthanasia as constituting "the death of true freedom." To recognize these actions as rights under the law, he says, "means to attribute to human freedom a *perverse and evil significance*: that of an absolute power over others and against others"[65] (his italics). Mother Teresa put it this way: "The greatest destroyer of peace is abortion because if a mother can kill her own child, what is left for me to kill you and you to kill me? There is nothing between."[66] All of this makes sense. It is a perversion of liberty to say one has the right to kill an innocent person, and it is a catastrophic strike against peace to wage war on defenseless babies in the womb. Even those who champion abortion rights know this is true.

To be sure, there are a few rabid fans of abortion rights who would reject what John Paul II and Mother Teresa have said. There are books that boast about how abortion liberates women, such as *Abortion: A Positive Decision*, written by women's study professor Patricia Lunneborg; *Abortion Is a Blessing* by atheist advocate Anne Nicol Gaylor; and a volume by French author Ginette Paris, *The Sacrament of Abortion*. But any fair-minded reader of their works can see how strained their argument is: they are not simply trying to justify the indefensible; they are heralding the killing as a positive good.

More commonly, we hear the refrain from abortion rights advocates that no one really likes abortion. One wonders what's not to like about it if the contention is that no one is hurt. In other words, what's holding back their enthusiasm? After all, no one says that a flu shot is the lesser of two evils; if we need one, we get one, and no one gives it a second thought. "Even in the midst of difficulties and uncertainties," writes John Paul II, "every person sincerely open to truth and goodness can, by the light of reason and the hidden action of grace, come to recognize in the natural law written in the heart the sacred value of human life from its very beginning until its end, and can affirm the right of every human being to have this primary good respected to the highest degree."[67]

There is plenty of evidence that John Paul is right about this, and the best evidence comes from those who support abortion rights. "An abortion kills the life of the baby after it has begun. It is dangerous to your life and health." I read those lines on television to Phil Donahue. Taking the bait, he asked, "Who said that?" I answered, "Planned Parenthood in 1963." Sitting next to me was a rather uncomfortable Gloria Feldt, president of Planned Parenthood. Obviously, biology didn't change; Planned Parenthood did.

Feminist Naomi Wolf goes a ways toward buttressing John Paul's contention that those who are open to the truth know that abortion is wrong. In an essay published in the *New York Times* she began by standing fast on abortion rights, but then she came clean: it was time for her to tell her side of things, and she admitted that abortion at any stage "involves the possibility of another life." Now let's just say that she has a point. Still, she hasn't exercised prudence. Put it this way: If you drove down a street full of children playing and saw a cardboard box in your path, would you not assume that kids might be playing in it, and therefore go around it? Wouldn't prudence direct us, then, to ban abortion for the very reason that there is the "possibility of another life"?

Many who argue that abortion doesn't mean the killing of an innocent human do so because it is convenient to deny the obvious. When Gloria Allred, a famous American feminist attorney, was asked on TV whether it would be better if there were no abortions, she held to the party line saying, "Not necessarily." But three years later when she took the side of a pregnant woman, Laci Peterson, who had been killed by her husband after naming her unborn baby Connor, Allred contended, "[T]he fact that there are two individuals who are dead here, Laci and Connor, that has to be the most important consideration of everything." That's right, two individuals were murdered, not just one.

Hillary Clinton upset some feminists in 2005 when she said, "We can all recognize that abortion in many ways represents a sad, even tragic choice to many, many women." She never said why. By contrast, we never think it is "sad" when we learn that a family member has to get a root canal. It may be unfortunate, but it is not "sad." Furthermore, the choice to undergo this dental procedure would never be deemed "tragic." Rev. Donna Schaper, a New York minister, admitted more recently that she once had an abortion. "I am not bragging, nor am I apologizing," she said. Then she really opened up. "I happen to agree that abortion is a form of murder," she said, confessing, "I know I murdered the life within me." Once again, John Paul was vindicated.

The Catholic Church's teachings on the sanctity of human life occasionally receive unwitting support from those who reject the Church's position. Consider the real-life case of Jenny, a forty-five-year-old woman who learned that after six years of paying fertility bills, she was pregnant with twins. But she and her husband wanted only one baby, so they decided to get rid of one of them. Her reasoning is brutally honest: "If I had conceived these twins naturally, I wouldn't have reduced this pregnancy, because you feel like if there's a natural order, then you don't want to disturb it. But we created this child in such an artificial manner—in a test tube, choosing an egg donor, having the embryo placed in me—and somehow, making a decision about how many to carry seemed to be just another choice. The pregnancy was all so consumerish to begin with, and this became yet another thing we could control."[68] Jenny is more right than she thinks; once the natural order is tampered with, life is cheapened.

One of the most unfair falsehoods in circulation concerning the Catholic Church is that it favors punishing women who have had an abortion. To begin with, as John Paul outlines in the encyclical *Evangelium Vitae* (*The Gospel of Life*), there are many parties to abortion besides the woman. He lists the father, the family, friends, doctors, nurses, legislators, health care administrators, international institutions, foundations and associations that push for abortion, and those who encourage sexual permissiveness.

The Holy Father is even more direct in his message to women who have had an abortion: "The Church is aware of the many factors which may have influenced your decision, and she does not doubt that in many cases it was a painful and even shattering decision. The wound in your heart may not yet have healed. Certainly what happened was and remains terribly wrong. But do not give in to discouragement and do not lose hope."[69] He further advises that women who have had an abortion reconcile themselves with God. These are not the words of a cold-hearted, unforgiving man.

It would be a mistake to assume that these are just words. The Catholic Church has a formal program devoted exclusively to help women who have had an abortion, Project

Rachel. It is so helpful in getting women to reconcile themselves and move on that even Planned Parenthood has been
known to advise Catholic women about this program. The
Sisters of Life, established by John Cardinal O'Connor of
New York, are also devoted to helping women recover from
an abortion. Cardinal O'Connor even invited a woman who
had had an abortion, and subsequently became thoroughly
pro-life, to speak at the end of Mass. In short, the Catholic
Church does not abandon women who have undergone an
abortion. It reaches out to them in hopes that they will never
make that choice again.

Abortion supporters still say that there are times when an
abortion is truly the lesser of two evils. Kay James is a Pres-
byterian and a black woman who tells an interesting story
that should give these people pause. "What would you say to
a woman who came to you for counseling and said, 'I have
four children, and I find myself pregnant for the fifth time.
My husband is an alcoholic who physically abuses me and the
children. He does not provide financially for the family or give
emotional support to me. I don't know how I'm going to take
care of the kids that I have.' What would you say to a woman
like that?" The most common response is to recommend an
abortion, while raising such questions as "What kind of life
could that child be expected to have?" This was just a setup.
James then reveals to the audience, "[T]hat situation was *mine*
and that woman was my mother. I was the fifth child who was
born on a kitchen table in Portsmouth, Virginia, into early
years of poverty."[70]

The mother of Kay James exercised prudence by not taking
the easy way out, and prudence should convince us that it is

not in the interests of the good society to allow one group of human beings to determine whether another group of human beings, however small, should forfeit their right to life because their prospects of living a happy life are not good. Who elected them to make this decision? And isn't it obvious that this may be a slippery slope that is not reversible? Who's next in line?

Euthanasia, Infanticide, and Animal Rights

Who is next has already been answered. In some of those Western nations that have few abortion restrictions, euthanasia has been legalized. In other nations local laws authorize doctor-assisted suicide. The most notorious person in the United States with regard to mercy killing is Jack Kevorkian, known as "Dr. Death." He was convicted of murder and sentenced to prison in 1999, having gotten off scot-free on many previous occasions.

At age thirty, Kevorkian was already making waves. He spoke widely in favor of killing by lethal injection condemned prisoners who gave their consent to be killed. He later upped the ante by advocating that prisoners who were sentenced to capital punishment give their consent to donate their organs, and that after their death their organ be auctioned off to the highest bidder. He also pushed for the use of blood from fresh corpses for transfusions. After he was once acquitted, he continued on his merry way, performing suicides in his own apartment, leaving bodies in the medical examiner's parking lot. In 1991, while on trial for murder, he managed to slip away and help a fifty-three-year-old woman with multiple sclerosis to die. It is estimated that at least half of the people helped to die were not terminally ill.

Not surprisingly, Kevorkian dismissed the Catholic teaching on the sanctity of life as nothing more than "a concept invented by the human mind."[71] Indeed, the Michigan physician hated the Catholic teaching on doctor-assisted suicide so much that he was driven near to paranoia. "The pope has his hands on our neck," he said. "He's wringing it. I think he has a grip on our government, and I know he has a grip on the Michigan Supreme Court."[72]

Kevorkian's record is not an anomaly. In Holland, studies have repeatedly found that the number of cases of involuntary doctor-assisted suicides surpasses the number of voluntary cases. That's what happens when prudence is pardoned. Prudence calls us to be wary of embarking on programs that facilitate suicide, for once we go down this road, it is easy to predict that there may be many involuntary candidates for death. So-called mercy killing carries with it the germs of unmerciful conduct. The handicapped and the families of the mentally disabled can testify to that. None of this is idle speculation: in 2005 it was revealed that Dutch doctors were publicly admitting that they had killed disabled newborn infants.

Looking back in history, the Catholic Church was the first to outlaw the killing of infants, although during antiquity infanticide was widely practiced. Unfortunately, acceptance of this hideous practice is gaining in elite circles today. Noble Prize winners Francis Crick and James Watson have supported infanticide, as did Humanist of the Year Joseph Fletcher. When he was in the Illinois Senate, Barack Obama argued that a child born alive as a result of a botched abortion was not entitled to medical treatment. Partial-birth abortion, a procedure whereby a doctor jams a pair of scissors into the head of a baby who is 80 percent born, is defended by many abortion rights enthusiasts.

No one has attracted more attention for his views on abortion and infanticide than has Princeton professor Peter Singer.

Singer is the "father" of animal rights; he is also an atheist and a proponent of selective infanticide. He says that some defective children should undergo a trial period after birth while a decision is being made about putting them to death, and that in any event parents should be allowed to exterminate their disabled babies. He believes that "killing a newborn baby is never equivalent to killing a person, that is, a being who wants to go on living."[73] Interestingly, he maintains that there is absolutely no moral difference between killing a baby in the mother's womb and killing a newborn. If it is legal to kill an unborn baby, Singer concludes, it should be legal to kill infants. Just don't forget to protect the turkeys.

This kind of outcome is exactly what we get when we abandon natural law principles—something that atheists are fond of doing—and instead substitute utilitarian logic. Life becomes a game of Russian roulette where the losers pay big-time. But under Catholic social teachings there are no losers because unborn babies and newborn babies are equally, and prudently, protected. For the record, the Catholic Church, beginning with Saint Francis of Assisi, has a long history of advocating animal welfare. But the idea that animals have rights is absurd: animals cannot be held morally responsible for their behavior, thus vitiating their ability to exercise rights.

To show how far we've drifted, consider that Singer is leading the Great Ape Project, a movement to give chimps, bonobos, gorillas, and orangutans some of the same rights as humans. He is also of the opinion that bestiality is not necessarily a bad thing: he argues that "sex with animals does not always involve cruelty," and that "mutually satisfying activities" of a sexual nature should be respected.

All of these ideas—euthanasia, infanticide, treating animals as humans, bestiality—are contrary to Catholic teachings because they cheapen our God-given nature, violate our human dignity, and violate the natural law. Not unimportantly, the beings who are the target of these activities typically have not given their consent. As we have seen, what starts as voluntary euthanasia inevitably slides into involuntary euthanasia; the mentally and physically impaired cannot adequately fend for themselves; newborns are vulnerable to exploitation; animals cannot consent. The good society, one where prudence is employed in public decision making, cannot possibly treat these "freedoms" as anything but perversions of liberty.

John Paul II anticipated objections to Catholic thought by weighing the subject of voluntary euthanasia. His conclusion is that "any state which made such a request legitimate and authorized it to be carried out would be legalizing a case of suicide-murder, contrary to the fundamental principles of absolute respect for life and of the protection of every innocent life." His next sentence will be understood by anyone who values prudence: "In this way the state contributes to lessening respect for life and opens the door to ways of acting which are destructive of trust in relations between people."[74] No nation has had a more disturbing experience of what happens when the door to the culture of death is opened than Germany.

Germany's Legacy and Catholicism's Vindication

Between the First and Second World Wars, a small but influential book was written by two distinguished Germans: a jurist named Karl Binding and a psychiatrist, Alfred Erich Hoche. Roughly translated it was called, *The Permission to Destroy Life Unworthy of Life.* The authors justified the acceleration of death not as murder, but as "in truth a pure act of healing." They pushed for the legalization of doctor-assisted suicide, saying it would be a good way to get rid of "dead-weight characters" such as the mentally enfeebled. Hitler put their ideas into practice in the 1930s. It is important to recognize that the development of such pernicious ideas was not rooted in anti-Semitism. Indeed, the Nazi euthanasia program was seen as being such a benefit to society that it was considered "a philanthropic act," a perk that was unavailable to Jews!

Hitler's own physician, Dr. Karl Brandt, played a major role in the euthanasia program.[75] A Nazi party member, Brandt was an advocate of abortion and euthanasia for infants with disabilities. Pope Pius XII condemned such practices as "incompatible with natural and divine law," but the anti-Catholic Nazis would not listen. The euthanasia program was just the beginning for the Nazis, and as they became inured to the practice, the killing of innocents—like Jews—perhaps didn't seem so much worse; it could be rationalized as being in the best interests of everyone. It is estimated that

275,000 patients in hospitals and psychiatric institutions met their death under the Nazi euthanasia program. Mercy killing clearly paved the way for the Holocaust.

Germany has learned a lot. Today that country has the most restrictive laws in the West on abortion, euthanasia, embryonic stem cell research, cloning, human experimentation, genetic engineering, in vitro fertilization, and surrogate motherhood. Moreover, Peter Singer has been told that he is not welcome to speak there.

In every sense of the word, everything that happened in Germany under Hitler is so sad. It would have been avoidable had natural rights and natural law been respected. Instead, utilitarian principles and positive law were operating. Every innocent person, from the unborn to the "defective," would have lived had respect for human dignity held sway. All six million Jews would have survived if they had been seen as moral equals in the eyes of God. Unfortunately, the Nazi regime saw the Catholic Church as the enemy.

After the war, the Nazis who carried out the Holocaust were found guilty because natural law was invoked. The good news is that today the state of Germany more closely approximates the teachings of the Catholic Church on life and death, making it the safest place in Europe for the vulnerable.

Human rights, human dignity, freedom tied to morality, a consistent ethic of life—these are the staples of Catholic teachings that promote true freedom. When these teachings are implemented, it is not possible to wind up with a culture of death. Quite the contrary, when these tenets are prudently applied, they encourage a culture of life. They also demonstrate why Catholicism matters.

JUSTICE

I F there is to be justice on earth, then those in a position to help the victims of injustice must be held accountable. Despite some obvious shortcomings, the Catholic Church has done more than any other religious or secular institution to deliver justice to the poor and oppressed. The Church's teachings on this subject are profound, but it is the behavior of so many of the faithful that really makes the difference.

To appreciate how the Catholic Church has reached out to the needy, it is helpful to contrast the Church's efforts with government programs. As we shall see, this is not a race the secular bureaucrats want to enter: comparing the efforts of policy makers with those of nuns, to take one example, yields a skewed outcome. Indeed, the contributions that nuns have made to serving the dispossessed is one of the proudest chapters in the history of the Catholic Church. Academic excellence is another staple in the Catholic arsenal, and no segment of society has benefitted more from parochial schools than those at the bottom of the socioeconomic scale. Reaching out to the "stranger," whether by serving him in foreign lands or by welcoming him as the latest immigrant, is another subject that will concern us in this chapter. Putting all of this together makes for a story that is as endearing as it is instructive.

Teachings and Practice

Some variant of the Golden Rule injunction "Do unto others as you would have them do unto you" finds expression in all world religions, but few can match the rich social teachings of Roman Catholicism. Highly developed and continuously refined, Catholic social teachings cover a broad range of subjects with a consistency that is a model of integrated thought. Of all its elements, the "focus on the other" is paramount. There is more to it than just a concern for the common good; "focus on the other" is the nucleus and driving force behind all of the Church's social teachings. This dictum is grounded in the belief that the human dignity of men and women must be respected, allowing no exceptions.

The principle of solidarity maintains that we are all obliged to be our brother's keepers. On the surface, this is highly unobjectionable, but in a world where "it's not my job" is the ruling mantra, the seemingly simple obligation to "focus on the other" belies the formidable challenge of putting it into practice. "It's not my job" is a disconcerting attitude in the workplace, but when it is applied to our duties toward our brothers and sisters, it is devastating to the social order. Indeed, the prevalence of this mind-set can kill the prospects of achieving the good society. This is the reason that Catholic social teachings need to be restated over and over again.

It is to the least among us that we are obliged to direct our attention. According to Catholic social teachings, the poor, the needy, the disabled, and the disenfranchised—all those who qualify as the dispossessed—are the obligation of individuals, social institutions, and the state. No one can legitimately pass the buck. At one level, this means that no man, woman, or child should be deprived of the basics. At another, it means that an equitable sharing of resources and responsibilities is required.

Catholic social teachings also have a global dimension; the concern for economic development, the rights of workers and equal opportunity know no geographical or class boundaries. Moreover, economic exploitation of any kind has long been criticized by popes, cardinals, and bishops, as well as by priests, nuns, brothers, and the laity. This has often won these Catholics the enmity of political authorities, but the Church has never sought to win a popularity contest—something even its detractors will admit. The Church has a moral duty, anchored in the pursuit of justice, to support equitable outcomes.

In 1986 the American bishops released a pastoral letter, *Economic Justice for All*, that urged Americans to "avoid a tragic separation between faith and everyday life"; this was an acknowledgment of the difficulties of turning beliefs into action. The bishops also released *A Catholic Framework for Economic Life*,[1] which listed ten prescriptions for economic justice. "The economy exists for the person, not the person for the economy," was listed first. The document also offered an index for judging success: "A fundamental moral measure of any economy is how the poor and vulnerable are faring." Of course, it said that everyone is entitled to the basic necessities of life, and the rights of workers must be respected, but it also said, "All people, to the extent they are able, have a corresponding duty to work, a responsibility to provide for the needs of their families, and an obligation to contribute to the broader society." Thus the bishops made clear that both sides of the ledger—responsibilities as well as rights—must be respected.

Catholic social teachings would carry little more than philosophical weight if they were not implemented by Catholic social institutions. They are, and the venues are many. In Catholic hospitals, hospices, social welfare agencies, orphanages, shelters for battered women, homes for the homeless, and elementary and secondary schools, orders of nuns and priests have built and serviced the dispossessed in all parts of the world. Collectively, these institutions represent the oldest and most visible demonstration of Catholic love the world has ever known. The Church does not get enough credit for the good that it has done, never mind the fact that its beneficiaries have never been confined to Catholics: Catholic social institutions have a long record of serving people of all races, ethnic groups, classes, and religions. They put into operation the universal meaning of the word *catholic.*

There are many Catholic national and international organizations that serve the common good, but most of the really impressive work is done at the local, or parish, level. There are approximately 18,000 parishes in the United States, and it is at the parish level that much of the tending to the aged and infirm is carried out. Although they are stretched today, priests and nuns still make house calls, bringing the necessities— and the Eucharist—to the needy. It is at the parish level, too, that most of the elementary schools are found. The parishes are also involved in services ranging from reaching out to unwed mothers to running soup kitchens.

Catholic activism is another way in which the dispossessed

are served. Dorothy Day, one of the great heroines in the annals of Catholic service, was born into an Episcopalian family in 1897. She said she viewed the Catholic Church as "the church of immigrants, the church of the poor." In her youth she was active in several radical causes, but always in a peaceful way. She fell in love at a young age and had an abortion when she was twenty-one; it was a decision she would deeply regret. Then she married an anarchist, a nonbeliever who did not want children. When she got pregnant and gave birth to a girl, her husband was not pleased, and he objected further when she said she wanted the baby baptized in a Catholic church (she had been moving toward Catholicism for some time). The day Tamar Teresa was baptized was the day he left. "I knew I was not going to have her floundering through many years as I had done," Day later wrote.[2] She then converted to Catholicism.

Her life changed again when she met Peter Maurin, a French immigrant, former Christian Brother, and social activist. Together they devoted their lives to the needy, building the Catholic Worker movement in 1933, during the depths of the depression. They launched the *Catholic Worker* newspaper, hoping to offer a religious perspective on contemporary social and economic issues. They then recruited volunteers to offer shelter to the homeless and food for the hungry. In 1936 there were thirty-three Catholic Worker houses across the nation. They stood out from other safe houses because they were populated by the so-called non-deserving poor—the prostitutes, drug addicts, and alcoholics. Not as well known was Day and Maurin's criticism of New Deal programs, which they believed enslaved the poor in a state of dependency; Day believed in serving the poor on a one-to-one basis. She died in 1980, and before he passed away, John Cardinal O'Connor proposed the cause of her canonization.

The good work of people like Dorothy Day is an example of Catholics putting into action Catholic social teachings. These teachings find their most cogent expression in papal encyclicals, which are the ultimate guides to economic justice.

Papal Encyclicals

Certainly the most authoritative of all the papal statements on economic justice, and one that has bearing on modern times, is *Rerum Novarum* (*On Capital and Labor*), an encyclical of Pope Leo XIII in 1891. It offers the strongest possible defense of private property. Not only does man have a right to private property, the encyclical states, but man possesses this right "by nature."[3] Leo makes it clear that although God has given the earth for our use and enjoyment, the right to private property "is in accordance with the law of nature," and must therefore be respected by government.

In addition to making a principled defense of private property, Leo underscores its utility: it is an important vehicle in helping the poor. He even goes so far as to say that the "first and most fundamental" way to "alleviate the condition of the masses" is to recognize "the inviolability of private property." In doing so he echoes Aquinas, who also took private ownership of property seriously. But what about the poor?

Both Aquinas and Leo XIII understood that all of us have a duty to take care of ourselves and our family first, but we are also summoned to give what we can to the less fortunate. It is not, however, out of a claim of justice that we do so: charity, not fairness, should direct our almsgiving. The distinction is important. The *Catholic Encyclopedia* explains that "the assistance to which a man in need has a claim does not belong to him in justice before it is handed over to him, when it becomes his. His claim to it rests on the fact that he is a brother in distress, and his brotherhood constitutes his title to our pity, sympathy, and help."

One of the more attractive aspects of Catholic social thought is that while it favors some economic principles and systems over others, it always draws a line at extremes. For example, while Leo is quick to endorse private property, the nucleus of a market economy, he is just as quick to denounce greed, the charging of excessive interest (what he calls "rapacious usury"), and monopolies. Yes, he respects the rights of employers, but he is not going to give anyone a blank check. Pulling no punches, Leo condemns "the hardheartedness of employers and the greed of unchecked competition."[4] It is no wonder that those on the left and the right of the political spectrum never seem to find unqualified support for their economic proposals in Catholic teachings.

That said, it is as clear as can be that Leo's sympathies are not with socialism. In theory, property is either owned by private persons, which is the capitalist or market ideal, or is it owned by government, which is the socialist model. In practice, there is often a complex blend, involving private ownership and government subsidies or tax incentives. What bothered Leo about socialism, at least in its purest form, was its tendency to deprive the wage earner "the liberty of disposing of his wages, and thereby of all hope and possibility of increasing his resources and of bettering his condition of life." In other words, Leo understood that self-interest is built into the human condition, and while it needs to be properly channeled, any economic system that stifles its expression works against the common good. As he saw it, the problem with socialism is its paternalism: it seeks to play father by "setting up State supervision."

Leo was insistent that both employer and employee should show mutual respect, recognizing their responsibilities to each other, as well as their rights. But he put most of his emphasis on the rights of workers. From Leo onward, every pope has endorsed the right of workers to unionize as one of their fundamental rights. Leo XIII was adamant about saving "unfortunate working people from the cruelty of men of greed, who use human beings as mere instruments for moneymaking."[5] The pope is hardly giving voice to unrestrained enthusiasm for capitalism, although as we have seen he had nothing good to say about socialism. A market economy, one that respects private property, works best, but in order for justice to prevail, government must have a role.

Forty years after Leo XIII's *On Capital and Labor* appeared, Pope Pius XI gave us *Quadragesimo Anno* (*On Reconstruction of the Social Order*). In many ways, Pius XI built on Leo's contribution, especially in denouncing socialism. But he was even more pointed in his criticism of those among the faithful who had one foot in the Christian camp and one foot in the socialist camp. Pius brooked no compromise. "If they truly wish to be heralds of the Gospel," he said, "let them above all strive to show to socialists that socialist claims, so far as they are just, are far more supported by the principles of Christian faith and much more effectively promoted through the power of Christian charity." This advice has subsequently been offered to many well-meaning but nonetheless highly politicized priests and nuns.

Just as Leo was no thoroughgoing capitalist, Pius referred to the individualism associated with market economies and the collectivism associated with socialism as "twin rocks of shipwreck" that must be "carefully avoided."[6] Another point of agreement lay in their views on the relationship between employer and employee: both need each other, thus it is important to avoid adversarial positions. This "focus on the other" directive also applied to the state. Government, Pius taught, had obligations to the community, "but in protecting private individuals in their rights, chief consideration ought to be given to the weak and poor."

Where Pius broke new ground was in his enunciation of the principle of subsidiarity. This principle posits that individuals and institutions closest to those in need are in a better position to serve them than are those individuals and institutions that are most distant from them. Pius XI said it was "an injustice and at the same time a grave evil and disturbance of right order to assign to a greater and higher association what lesser and subordinate organizations can do." He stated further that "in observance of the principle of 'subsidiary function,' the stronger social authority and effectiveness will be the happier and more prosperous the condition of the State."[7] This was a call for government to back away, not to absorb local institutions. Moreover Leo instinctively knew that one-on-one help is more efficient and more personal: "no human expedients will ever make up for the devotedness and self-sacrifice of Christian charity."[8] By contrast, large-scale organizations, often run by government, while they have a role, can never be a ready substitute for the face-to-face interactions of donor and recipient.

The Catholic Church is not against government serving the dispossessed—it even implores it to do so—but the Church is strongly opposed to the government pushing individuals and voluntary local organizations aside, in effect denying them their right to take care of their own needs and the needs of their brothers and sisters. That is why G. K. Chesterton and Hilaire Belloc were both proponents of subsidiarity; they incorporated this principle into their economic philosophy.[9]

In his 1961 encyclical *Mater et Magistra*, Pope John XXIII conjoins the principle of solidarity to the principle of subsidiarity. The subject of his concern was economic development. The message was that we owe it to our fellow man in the developing nations to express our solidarity with him by offering economic relief, but in doing so we must not compromise our commitment to subsidiarity. This can be done most efficiently by aiding and abetting the poor to help themselves. As the adage says, it is better to teach the poor how to fish than to give them fish.

At the time when John XXIII wrote, the disparities between rich and poor in the developed countries were gaining much attention. But so were the disparities between rich and poor nations, or between the developed countries and the less developed ones. "We contemplate the sorry spectacle of millions of workers in many lands and entire continents condemned through the inadequacy of their wages to live with their families in utterly sub-human conditions," he wrote.[10] He called for workers to be paid "a wage that allows them to live a truly human life and to fulfill their family obligations in a worthy manner." This was not a call for socialism; it was a call for social justice.

John XXIII invoked "justice and humanity" in calling on the rich nations to assist the poor ones. But he was quick to say that in doing so, the former must not yield to the temptation to control the latter. He admonished the advanced nations not to dominate the developing nations, and thereby introduce "a new form of colonialism—cleverly disguised, no doubt, but actually reflecting that older outdated type from which many nations have recently emerged." The goal, he said, was to offer financial and technical aid that would help the poor nations to "achieve their own economic and social growth." Six years later Pope Paul VI, in *Populorum Progressio* (*On the Development of Peoples*), said that while the poor nations cannot be isolated and neglected by the richer ones, "they have the prime responsibility to work for their own development."[11]

Pope John Paul II knew from his firsthand experiences that socialist governments delivered political and economic poverty—to say nothing of spiritual deprivation—and that is why he saw socialism as anthropologically flawed. In his 1991 encyclical *Centesimus Annus* he condemned socialism for its treatment of the individual "as an element, a molecule within the social organism." Because this economic system denies freedom of choice to the individual, stripping him of rights and responsibilities, "the concept of the person as the autonomous subject of moral decisions disappears, the very subject whose decisions build the social order."[12]

If socialism is not capable of being transformed, being poisoned at its very core, it does not follow that a market economy is without problems. In particular, John Paul II was critical of the nineteenth-century model of unrestrained capitalism, and he condemned conditions in which man "is treated as an instrument of production." When it came to the question of efficiency, he acknowledged that capitalism won hands-down. But an economic order should not be stripped of moral considerations, he advised, and it should not be exclusively driven by profit. The dignity of the human person and the "focus on the other" can never be subordinated to any economic index of progress.

Centesimus Annus was a tribute to the hundredth anniversary of Pope Leo XIII's *Rerum Novarum*. In his document John Paul picked up on Leo's embrace of "lesser" social units, and what Pius XI more explicitly referred to in his discussion of subsidiarity, by citing the role that "intermediary groups" have. These groups, or associations, are agents that intercede between the individual and the state. Such entities as the family, the church, and community and voluntary associations are the heart and soul of civil society. They not only allow the individual to establish an anchor in those social institutions that are closest to him, but they also act as a barrier to state penetration. As John Paul saw it, as did Burke and Tocqueville before him, these mediating institutions are a bedrock of political and economic liberty and a cornerstone of social and cultural well-being.

Subsidiarity, as carried out by mediating institutions, was central to John Paul's wariness of the welfare state. He said that "the principle of subsidiarity must be respected," and he maintained that "needs are best understood and satisfied by people who are closest to them and who act as neighbors to those in need." The Holy Father did not mince words when he said that the welfare state "leads to a loss of human energies and an inordinate increase of public agencies, which are dominated more by bureaucratic ways of thinking than by concern for serving their clients, and which are accompanied by an enormous increase in spending." Referring to emergency situations, he cautioned even then that such government interventions "must be as brief as possible, so as to avoid removing permanently from society and business systems the functions which are properly theirs, and to avoid enlarging excessively the sphere of state intervention to the detriment of both economic and civil freedom."[13] There is a mountain of sociological literature that provides empirical evidence that he was right.

Pope Benedict XVI punctuates what John Paul said in *Caritas in Veritate*. Benedict puts it plainly: "[S]ubsidiarity is the most effective antidote against any form of all-encompassing welfare state."[14] He expressly calls upon us to practice solidarity with the poor, but to do so in ways that do not promote state paternalism. Social scientist Charles Murray once warned against the development of a "custodial democracy,"[15] one in which the government essentially takes custodial responsibility for the welfare of the poor. It is precisely this kind of paternalism that Benedict rejects; instead of enabling the poor, it enfeebles them.

Benedict was the first pope to directly address globalization, the process by which international organizations, laws, and markets have come to dominate economic development. He has his criticisms, but overall he realizes this is a condition of economic life that has its benefits also. His biggest concern is about the impact of global institutions on the family, and whether globalization engenders increases in economic inequality. He is very concerned about the need of workers in some countries to migrate for the purpose of economic well-being, and what this does to the family. He also cautions against the concentration of wealth in the hands of an international elite. At bottom, his main interest is in seeing that moral considerations are not lost in the pursuit of economic gain.

Lessons Learned

The maturation of Catholic social thought has been the springboard for many social and economic ideas. Catholic theologian Michael Novak, for example, offered us one of the most influential concepts of Catholic thought by describing the workings of "democratic capitalism." With fidelity to papal pronouncements, Novak showed the natural affinity that exists between a democratic polity and a market economy. Both depend upon individuals being allowed to make choices unimpeded by government, and both assume that civil society—the home of mediating institutions—must be vibrant and participatory; subsidiarity is central to the equation. It is also true that the underlying supposition of both a democratic government and a market economy is the belief that self-interest is ingrained in human nature, and this proclivity is something those who craft social institutions need to respect.

Father John Ryan was the first to attempt to apply the lessons of *Rerum Novarum* by penning a book in 1906, *A Living Wage*, which would influence a generation of Catholic social thinkers. Father Ryan fought valiantly for workers' rights, whether in the form of a minimum wage or an eight-hour workday. In his writings he encouraged government support programs assisting the elderly, the unemployed, and the disabled. Considered at the time too much of a firebrand and a socialist-leaning priest by some, he is ironically remembered today as someone who pushed hard for a concept that was later condemned by feminists in the 1960s, namely, the "family wage."

Father Ryan was a fierce advocate of the idea that every breadwinner should earn a wage that was sufficient to support his family. In practice, this meant that employers would intentionally, and with the best of motives, pay breadwinners a higher salary than single persons for doing the same work. The paying of a family wage was not considered a slight to unmarried, divorced, or widowed workers; it was considered a just pay scale that put the family first. Ryan's beliefs found their way into the New Deal programs, and his service on the panel that created the Social Security Act of 1935 was pivotal. Today, of course, the individual takes precedence to the family in the setting of pay scales, and the results of this policy are a source of debate. In any event, Father Ryan's role in promoting the family wage was historic.

We've also learned that sympathy for the poor cannot be allowed to override our Christian moorings. In the 1980s Church leaders such as Joseph Cardinal Ratzinger excoriated some priests for promoting "liberation theology," the belief that the poor can be served by blending Christian and Marxist ideas. But Marxism is inherently inimical to Christian ideals and must never be allowed to blend with Catholic teachings. The fear was that concern for the poor would make serving them hostage to ideology, and the result would be a politicization of the Gospels and losing sight of transcendental matters. Ratzinger was right on target when he criticized liberation theologians for putting their faith in new social structures that would create a "new man," thus pushing aside the role reserved in Catholic thought for the Holy Spirit, the real source of renewal.

As Pope Benedict XVI, Joseph Ratzinger took aim at the other end of the spectrum when he met with eleven new ambassadors in December 2008; they were there to present their credentials. The Holy Father took the occasion to say that economic development and financial policies must be grounded on firm ethical grounds. With the Western nations in a deep recession, the result of a financial crisis without borders, the pope drew attention to the ultimate problem—the lack of a moral basis undergirding the economy. This was not really novel turf for him: he has been calling the Western world to turn back to its Christian roots for some time.

Greed is a sin. It is not just a problem. Although it has always been a staple of mankind, there are times when it has been culturally celebrated, and the early part of the third millennium has certainly been such a time. When well-educated men and women go to work every day with the single goal of borrowing more money to make more money—and are lavishly rewarded for doing so—there is something seriously wrong on Main Street, and not just on Wall Street.

Of all the lessons we can learn from Catholic social thought, this one rings true today: the extent to which the radical pursuit of wealth corrupts. In such an environment, why are we surprised when legions of financiers put their own interests above the interests of their clients? Why are we surprised that we were lied to by some of the "best and the brightest"? Why are we surprised when unscrupulous lenders extend irresponsible loans to equally culpable borrowers? Why are we surprised when unethical banks offer endless credit cards to equally unethical individuals, all of whom think they can roll over their debt until they die? But in a society where self-denial is looked upon as a source of sickness, such manifestations of greed can be expected. All of these things are traceable to tossing Christian values out the window.

Greed and materialism are surely stubborn problems today, but when it comes to economic justice, most of the Church's teachings and practices have been directed toward achieving economic equity. Some have mistakenly interpreted this objective as a call for equal outcomes, but the Church has never pursued an egalitarian agenda. For instance, the Church has never advocated the notion that everyone should be afforded the same standard of living. But economic equity is something altogether different: its primary objective is fairness, a condition that presumes equal opportunity, not equal results. Before considering the history of Catholic social thought put into action, we need a basis of comparison. We need to assess how secular institutions have fared in serving the dispossessed. Only then will the true significance of the Catholic response be appreciated.

The Secular Response to the Dispossessed

England was the first nation to launch a society-wide effort to address the problem of poverty. Up until the late sixteenth century, the Catholic Church catered to the needs of the poor. The Elizabethan Poor Laws changed all that, instituting a legal, compulsory system of relief on a national basis; the law lasted for three and a half centuries and was not replaced until after World War II. The system oscillated between punitive and compassionate measures, but its most noticeable effect was a change in the way the poor viewed themselves. Instead of taking moral responsibility for themselves, many—and this was true most conspicuously of the able-bodied—acted in a manner consistent with what happens when social responsibility eclipses individual accountability.

In the 1830s Tocqueville wrote what remains to this day the most cogent analysis of the deleterious consequences of the welfare state, *Memoir on Pauperism.* He explained the radical differences in the conditions of the poor in Europe. In Spain and Portugal he saw "an ignorant and coarse population," people who were "ill-fed, ill-clothed, living in the midst of a half-uncultivated countryside in miserable dwellings." In England he saw "the Eden of modern civilisation—magnificently maintained roads, clean new houses, well-fed cattle roaming rich meadows, strong and healthy farmers, more dazzling wealth than in any country of the world, the most refined and gracious standard of the basic amenities to be found anywhere."[16] Yet in Spain and Portugal there were few indigents, beggars, homeless persons, and their ilk, and in England such depraved persons were in abundance.

Marx used the term lumpenproletariat to describe roughly the "scum of the earth." As a direct consequence of the Poor Laws, England saw legions of these people. "Pauperism grew more rapidly in Great Britain than anywhere else,"

Tocqueville wrote. "Any measure which establishes legal charity on a permanent basis and gives it an administrative form thereby creates an idle and lazy class," he warned, "living at the expense of the industrial and working class." After observing the conditions of the poor in countries where private charity was the rule, and seeing what had happened to England, Tocqueville concluded that "any permanent, regular, administrative system whose aim will be to provide for the needs of the poor will breed more miseries than it can cure, will deprave the population that it wants to help and comfort," and will wind up soaking the rich and depleting savings.[17] It was for reasons like these that Tocqueville much preferred the response to the poor in the Catholic nations to that of the Protestant ones.

The War on Poverty in the United States followed the same logic of the Poor Laws, and reaped similar results. In the 1980s Charles Murray wrote a blistering account, *Losing Ground*, which sought to explain why the Great Society reforms under President Lyndon B. Johnson yielded such depressing results. "We tried to provide more for the poor and produced more poor instead," he said.[18] That's because the War on Poverty created a dependent class, stripped the poor of their dignity, and triggered an onslaught of social problems. No one suffered more than blacks, as welfare ate away at self-reliance and disabled the family. This happened largely because those who drove the welfare state, meaning the academicians, community organizers, and government specialists, replaced moral responsibility with social responsibility. This kind of policy created pauperism in England, and in America it generated an underclass and racial strife.

It didn't have to be this way. Thomas Sowell, a black economist who is perhaps the nation's clearest thinker on this subject, points out, "The most dramatic reduction in poverty among blacks occurred between 1940 and 1960, when the black poverty rate was cut almost in half, without any major government programs of the Great Society kind that began in the 1960s."[19] Moreover, the black family was intact during this period. It is instructive that the black family held relatively tight through Jim Crow segregation policies and the Great Depression but cracked under the weight of welfare dependency. In the 1950s, the number of out-of-wedlock births was low, one in six, but today they account for over 70 percent of all births to black mothers. That this should happen after African Americans have achieved political and legal rights makes this condition all the more disturbing.

This did not happen by accident, nor was it a function of racism. It occurred because the "focus on the other" was misplaced. Instead of enabling the poor, empowering them to climb the ladder of upward social mobility, government sought to take care of them. It is often said that the intentions were good, but in some instances they were not benign.

In 1966 two Columbia professors, Richard Cloward and Frances Fox Piven, wrote an influential article in the *Nation* magazine calling for several reforms. They wanted to convince every social worker in New York City to find every person who was even remotely eligible for welfare and get them on the dole immediately. The goal? To bankrupt New York. If this happened, then the federal government, Cloward and Piven reasoned, would be forced to come to the rescue and institute socialism.[20] Well, the welfare rolls expanded. For a few years, under Mayor John Lindsay, *anyone* who applied for welfare was automatically put on the rolls. Not surprisingly, New York essentially went bankrupt in the 1970s. Socialism, however, never materialized. But moral destitution spread like wildfire.

In the 1990s welfare was reformed, and officials at the federal, state, and local levels sought to weed out its most pernicious elements, foremost among them being the state of dependency it created. But the damage that has been done to human lives is not revocable by law. It lasts. Had there been more respect for the human dignity of the poor, the kinds of problems recorded by Tocqueville could have been avoided. Human nature is not a social construct that can be changed at will; there are certain constants that need to be respected. Most damaging of all, the prospects for economic justice are retarded whenever the "focus on the other" is translated into a bureaucratic response.

We should have learned from Gibbon even before Tocqueville. In the eighteenth century Sir Edward Gibbon detailed what happened in ancient Athens: when security is valued more highly than freedom, everything is lost. In *The History of the Decline and Fall of the Roman Empire*, he recorded the social effects that naturally occur once people look to society to do for them what they should do for themselves. The skirting of personal responsibility, Gibbon warned, is a direct consequence of state paternalism.

As we have learned from reading papal encyclicals, there is no substitute for personal responsibility. Not so evident, however, is how this ideal applies to those who want to help the poor, as well as to the poor themselves. The lesson is that those who champion the cause of the dispossessed should ideally be personally invested in the outcome. For reasons that make eminently good sense, the research shows that those who believe in God are much more likely to get involved in serving the poor than are nonbelievers. For example, two sociology professors from the University of North Carolina, Mark D. Regnerus and David Sikkink, drew on data gathered by the Religious Identity and Influence Survey, and found that the more religious a person is the more likely he is to give to the poor. Nonreligious persons gave the least.[21]

Arthur C. Brooks, president of the American Enterprise Institute, looked at mountains of social science data and came to the same conclusion. "Religious people are far more charitable than nonreligious people," he wrote in *Who Really Cares*. "In the years of research, I have never found a measurable way in which secularists are more charitable than religious people." This applies across the board. Religious people give more in terms of "secular donations, informal giving, and even acts of kindness and honesty" than do secularists. They give more blood and are 57 percent more likely to give to the homeless than are secularists. What is really astounding is that in the aftermath of 9/11, Brooks wrote, "People who never attended church were 11 percentage points less likely than regular churchgoers to give to a 9/11 cause (56 to 67 percent)."[22]

The same kinds of outcomes were more recently obtained by David Campbell of Notre Dame and Robert Putnam of Harvard. In the most authoritative study to date, *American Grace*, they concluded that religious people are more likely than nonreligious people to do good deeds—whether it is giv-

ing blood, helping someone find a job, volunteering, or donat-
ing their money, Americans who are religious are the most
generous. Religion, they concluded, was good for America.[23]

The differences in giving among believers versus nonbelievers cannot be explained by referencing income disparities. In fact, "an average secularist nongiver earns 16 percent
more money each year than a religious giver," Brooks emphasizes. Yet these secular liberals give 19 percent less each year
than do religious conservatives. How do we account for this
phenomenon? Much has to do with who we think should be
responsible for helping the poor. The secularists want government to do the job. To be sure, there is a role for government,
as the papal encyclicals confirm, but to look exclusively to
government is wrong morally and economically. As Brooks
says, with added emphasis, "*Government spending is not charity.*"[24] Thus does Brooks, a Catholic, nicely capture this very
Catholic truism: charity means personal giving; it does not
mean picking someone else's pocket to give to someone else.

By any fair measure, not only does the Catholic response to
the poor cost a fraction of the cost of the secular approach; it
gets the kinds of results that count: it helps the poor to improve
their condition. It succeeds where government programs usually fail because in the Catholic philosophy the human dignity
of the recipient is considered paramount. Moreover, the principle of subsidiarity may be a Catholic contribution, but one
does not have to be Catholic to embrace it. Americans who
respect representative government, and the three-tiered vertical federalist system of government—federal, state, and local
levels of authority—have already accepted a political model
of what subsidiarity entails for society. There is no question

that Catholic priests and nuns have given life to the principle of subsidiarity, showing why Catholicism really matters.

The Catholic Response to the Dispossessed

There is no monolithic Catholic response to the needy, the exploited, and the suffering. Rather there are many ways in which the dispossessed are served. Historically, it is true that those who have done the serving have drawn on the same Catholic teachings for inspiration and guidance, but the manner, timing, and means they used depended on who was doing the serving and the resources they had to work with. The charitable activities of monks are legion. Less well known is their welcoming of strangers in their monasteries—often providing emergency relief. This is a particularly noble chapter in the history of the Catholic Church. Moreover, their yeoman efforts serving the needs of the shipwrecked are equally commendable. Monks also built roads and bridges during the Middle Ages, accounting for much of the infrastructure.

For sheer courage alone, the missionaries have a special place in the heart of the Church. Imbued with the Holy Spirit, they initially took on burdens that most of their contemporaries found incomprehensible. Many of the better-known missionaries, such as the Society for the Propagation of the Faith, were established in the first half of the nineteenth century in France; they achieved great success despite the fact that most of the Church's property was confiscated. Their work today, which reaches parts of the world that most of us would never travel to, is still looked upon with awe; most important, it is a source of deep gratitude on the part of the recipients. Let us also not forget the great deeds of the religious orders in meeting the needs of the dispossessed, especially in faraway lands. Closer to home, the selfless giving of many nuns merits attention.

In the early eighteenth century, the Ursuline Sisters started Catholic health care in the United States. They quickly became nurses and teachers, caring for the indigent and orphans. With approximately six hundred hospitals in all fifty states today, the Catholic Church offers nonprofit services to everyone, independent of religion or any other social consideration. Not only do Catholic hospitals play a vital role in serving parts of the country where no other hospitals exist; they are superior in quality. A study in 2010 by Thomson Reuters found that "Catholic and other church-owned health systems demonstrated significantly better, more efficient care than for-profit health systems."[25] These facilities also scored higher than secular not-for-profit health systems. The difference? Governance. "Our data suggest that the leadership of health systems owned by churches may be the most active in aligning quality goals and monitoring achievement of mission across the system," said an official quoted in the study.

In addition, the Catholic Church provides approximately four hundred health care centers and fifteen hundred homes meeting a variety of needs, as well as hundreds of orphanages. Homes for the poor, as well as renovations to existing homes are paid for with Catholic contributions, and approximately 70 percent of the dioceses sponsor housing and related services. The Church provides relief services overseas with assistance going to those ravaged by war and environmental disasters; Catholic Relief Services reaches tens of millions of people annually in approximately one hundred nations.

Catholic Charities, founded as the National Conference of Catholic Charities in 1910, is one of the nation's largest nonprofits, and one of the most efficient: 90 percent of the money is spent on programs and services. Although it is heavily dependent on government funding, its 1,600 agencies reach millions of persons annually, providing food, clothing, medicinal services, financial assistance, housing, disaster relief, immigration services, and refugee assistance. "The mission of Catholic Charities and all Catholic social ministries is not humanitarian but religious—to proclaim by our words and deeds the love that God has shown to the world in Jesus Christ." Those are the words of Philadelphia Archbishop Charles J. Chaput, one of the most influential bishops in the nation. He sees Catholic Charities doing something only a Church-sponsored organization can do. "Government cannot love," he instructs, and that is because "[i]t has no soul and no heart."[26] It is through Catholic men and women working for Catholic Charities that love can be delivered.

What Archbishop Chaput says about government programs is so true. Important as they may be, they can never be a substitute for the work accomplished on the ground, and they most especially can never substitute for the love that is generated by the faithful. There are so many Catholic heroes, men and women who have selflessly given of themselves without fanfare or adulation, that if their accomplishments were bound in cloth their contribution would fill any college library. One such hero was Father Damien.

Father Damien's "focus on the other" took the form of a

lifetime of service to lepers. Born in Belgium, he was ordained a priest in Honolulu Harbor in 1864, and he immediately set out to build chapels to bring the word of Jesus to the natives. Less than ten years later, Damien made his way to the Hawaiian island of Molokai, where he accepted the invitation of the vicar apostolic, Msgr. Louis Maigret, to work with lepers. Maigret had mixed feelings, knowing that Damien's service could mean his eventual death. "You know my disposition," Damien told him. "I want to sacrifice myself for the poor lepers."

Father Damien cared for the lepers by washing their bodies and bandaging their wounds. But tending to their physical needs was not his top concern. What he wanted to do more than anything was to give the lepers something they seriously lacked—a sense of self-worth. He sought to restore their dignity as human persons, and he succeeded in ways that subsequently won him the praise of people like Mahatma Gandhi, the famous leader of India. Indeed, Gandhi credited Damien with inspiring him to work among the "untouchables," persons who were pariahs in their own land.

That Damien succeeded there is no doubt. Five years before he arrived in Molokai, an American writer, Charles Warren Stoddard, had traveled to the island and found horrible conditions. When he returned in 1884, he saw firsthand what Damien had accomplished. In place of rotting huts there were two villages of white houses. There were gardens and cultivated fields, a hospital and two orphanages. And the people were not sitting and waiting to die; they were up and about. Damien didn't build these institutions all by himself. Because of his commitment to the human dignity of the person, he motivated the lepers to take pride in themselves and take command of their lives. It was the lepers who built these small monuments to God. Pity is not what Father Damien offered them; he offered them hope. Because of his commitment to working with people suffering from such a terrible disease, he is considered the patron saint of those with HIV and AIDS. Leprosy claimed him in the end, and in 1995 he was beatified by Pope John Paul II.

The Role of Nuns

The greatest Catholic contribution to the dispossessed has been that of the nuns. More than any other segment of the Catholic community, sisters have made supreme contributions. At the top of everyone's list is Agnes Gonxha Bojaxhiu, Mother Teresa of Albania.

Of all the values Jesus gave us, love ranks the highest. It was so fitting, then, that when Mother Teresa was asked what galvanized her and the religious order she founded, the Missionaries of Charity, to give their lives to the poor, she answered: "We are not social workers, we are not nurses, we are not doctors, we are religious. . . . All we do is for Jesus."[27] And what she accomplished was prodigious. She operated hundreds of missions all over the world (which are now run by her order) serving the dispossessed in hospitals, hospices, and orphanages. She worked with lepers, those dying of AIDS, the blind, the homeless, the mentally and physically disabled, and children afflicted with deadly diseases; she even searched the slums looking for the indigent. She made her mark in Calcutta, and it is hardly surprising that she is regarded by the people in India as the most revered person in their history next to Gandhi.

In 1952 Mother Teresa opened the first Home for the Dying in Calcutta. Like Father Damien, she knew she could not possibly save everyone suffering from disease, but she could comfort them in their last days. She did this because, like Damien, she knew that human dignity is something that is rightfully ours, and it is something that no government or authority of any kind has a legitimate right to take away from us. Once this belief becomes a hardened conviction, it cannot be shaken. It was for her a hardened conviction; she successfully lived the tenets outlined in the papal encyclicals.

Mother Teresa did not stay put. She traveled to various parts of the world afflicted by environmental and man-made afflictions. Most important, she never sought the limelight. Had it not been for an English scholar, Malcolm Muggeridge, who made a documentary film about her, she might never have been awarded the Nobel Peace Prize, the Presidential Medal of Freedom and the Congressional Gold Medal, UN recognitions, and well over one hundred other awards from all over the world. Muggeridge was so moved by her work that he was converted. Father Brian Kolodiejchuk, who knew Mother Teresa for twenty years and is the postulator for her cause for sainthood, said, "She never took credit for her accomplishments and always tried to divert the attention she received to God and 'His work' among the poorest of the poor. Yet it was not in God's providential plan for her to remain unknown."[28]

No government program could do what Mother Teresa did. "The miracle is not that we do the work," she once said, "but that we are happy to do it." There was no money in it for her. Obviously, she took money from the rich, and she was occasionally criticized for doing so (should she have taken it from the middle class, or the poor?), but she spent it on others. "I try to give to poor people for love what the rich could get for money," she said. "No, I wouldn't touch a leper for a thousand pounds; yet I willingly cure him for the love of God." To those who say "I am only one person, I can't save the world," she replied, "If you can't feed a hundred people, then feed just one." Always the realist, she offered, "Jesus said love one another. He didn't say love the whole world." She also knew there was something worse than material deprivation: "Being unwanted, unloved, uncared for, forgotten by everybody, I think that is a much greater hunger, a much greater poverty than the person who has nothing to eat."[29] It is impossible to understand her work without understanding what she meant by this statement.

The truth of the matter is there are many, many other Mother Teresas in Catholic history, although in most instances their contributions are without a global effect. In the United States, nuns taught the immigrants and their children and served them in hospitals run by their orders. There have been more than four hundred religious orders in the United States, and each carved out a turf and made good on their pledge. Unfortunately, for many reasons, after Vatican II there has been a substantial exodus of sisters from their orders, the result of which has been widely felt by the laity at the parish level.

Many of the nuns who came to America from Europe had suffered greatly in their home country. In Ireland there was English oppression and later the famine; in the late eigh-teenth century in France there was the deadly fallout of the French Revolution; the conditions in Germany were harsh under Bismarck. When they got to the United States a lot of the sisters were met with nativistic fears of a Catholic take-over, and there was a growing literature of hate speech aimed at the Catholic clergy and laypersons, although nothing was worse than the vicious lies told about the sexual habits of priest-seducing nuns. Anti-Catholicism was written into state constitutions and was taught in the schools under the guise of social studies.

Even before the mid-nineteenth century, American bish-ops worried there weren't enough nuns to do the job, so they began recruiting them from abroad. No nation proved to be more obliging than Ireland. Pittsburgh bishop Michael O'Connor got the ball rolling when he arranged with an Irish bishop to have nuns board a ship and set sail to America. He was there to greet them when they disembarked and struck up a good relationship with Frances Warde. In time, she would become a great leader of the Sisters of Mercy, and would be known as Mother Frances Xavier Warde.

The conditions in Pittsburgh at the time were brutal: with coal and iron being the mainstays of the economy, infamous smokestacks polluted the air. Three out of four Pittsburghers were Protestant and many of them looked askance at the nuns dressed in their habits. In time, however, the residents came to know the sisters for what they did: they went about the city tending to the needs of the sick. Mother Warde proved to be entrepreneurial, building schools and orphanages.

Another Irishman, New York bishop John "Dagger" Hughes,

followed the lead of his Pittsburgh colleague and started recruiting nuns from his home country; he got his nickname
because of his pugnacious style. He traveled to Ireland in 1845,
during the famine, to recruit Sisters of Mercy. When they
reached New York, many of the sisters were ill from the famine themselves, yet they set about visiting hundreds of the
sick and dying, providing medicinal and pastoral care. They
offered shelter and helped the unemployed find work, and
they visited Irish prisoners in the wretched jails known as the
"Tombs." With no public funds, they relied wholly on private
philanthropy, working with Bishop Hughes for support and
contacts with the laity.

By the middle part of the nineteenth century, there were
over 130 Catholic schools in the United States, all the work
of the nuns. Hospitals and orphanages were being built at a
record pace. Ten years later, on the brink of the Civil War,
the Irish-Catholic presence was profound: of the 2.2 million
Catholics in the United States, 1.6 million were Irish. The
Irish foothold was especially visible among the nuns: the Sisters
of Charity, the Sisters of Mercy, and the Sisters of the Good
Shepherd (a French order) were a major force, especially in
New York City. There were other orders of nuns, such as the
French Sisters of the Holy Cross and the Sisters of Notre
Dame from Germany, and there were some that settled in the
mid-Western states. One such order was the Sisters of St.
Joseph of Carondelet, CSJ, from France.

Like so many other orders, the Sisters of St. Joseph were
service-oriented, working in education, nursing, and social
agencies. The order drew from a wide array of women, recruiting from cities and the countryside, and from rich and

poor families. They founded communities in places like St. Paul, Minnesota, and Kansas City, Missouri, and made their way westward to Arizona and California, ending up in the Rocky Mountain states.

It is hard to imagine what Catholic life would have been like without the efforts of these nuns. They ran everything: schools, hospitals, orphanages, shelters, social services of every kind. And in the best of the Catholic tradition, they never turned away the dispossessed because of their religion or any other social consideration. Their service to Native Americans was proof of their commitment; they built schools, hospitals, and orphanages for Native Americans in both St. Paul and Minneapolis. Carol K. Coburn and Martha Smith, authors of the definitive book on the Sisters of St. Joseph of Carondelet, *Spirited Lives: How Nuns Shaped Catholic Culture and American Life, 1836–1920*, detail the sisters' heroism: "The CSJ contribution to American Catholic culture and service in St. Paul/Minneapolis encompassed thousands of schoolchildren and hospital patients and hundreds of art/music students, orphans, and young women in secondary and post-secondary education."[30] The Sisters of St. Joseph opened the first private hospital in Kansas City, St. Joseph's. They made their way to the Denver area in the 1860s and 1870s, building hospitals and schools; the mining community was most appreciative of the health care centers the sisters established, and this certainly included the Protestants among them. The sisters' outreach even extended to reducing friction between different ethnic groups in the Catholic community. They tried, with less success, to ameliorate the social conditions of those who lived in Mexico. Interestingly, at the close of the

nineteenth century the Sisters of St. Joseph were making pil-
grimages to Ireland in search of more nuns.

Nuns in the United States have done so much good, in so
many areas, that it would be difficult to single out any one endeavor as being the most important. But surely their work in
providing health care, and in meeting the needs of children,
in the establishment of both orphanages and schools, ranks
at the top. These efforts deserve a closer look.

Florence Nightingale, the founder of modern nursing, studied under the Sisters of Charity. Impressed with their dedication and commitment to the needy, the Italian-born British
nurse enlisted them in 1854 to work with her in tending to soldiers during the Crimean War. It was during the war in Turkey that she became known as "The Lady with the Lamp," a
reference to her nighttime visits to wounded patients. Her top
priority was sanitation; the living quarters used to house the
soldiers were infested with rats; drinking water was in short
supply; and fleas were everywhere. When the war was over,
Nightingale returned to London, making quality hygiene
in the hospitals her most important goal.

Before Nightingale was born, the Sisters of Charity, under
the inspiration of Saint Vincent de Paul, were working with
the sick and dying in hospitals. Their efforts in the poorhouses,
places where the indigent and homeless wandered, were yeoman, as was their service to inmates in the asylums. In 1809
the nuns, who later changed their name to the Daughters of
Charity, made their way to America, where they cared for
hospital patients. The Sisters of St. Joseph were active during
the first part of the nineteenth century as well, working with
cholera victims in Philadelphia in the 1840s; they established

their first American hospital there. They also opened a hospital in Wheeling, West Virginia. In fact, nuns founded more hospitals in the United States than did any other organization between 1850 and 1960.

When the Civil War broke out, no group in the nation had a better history of service to patients than did the nuns. Almost 20 percent of all the female nurses were sisters from twelve different religious orders; most of them were Daughters of Charity. They served on land and at sea, working aboard hospital ships that set anchor in the middle of the Mississippi River, allowing them to proceed by small boats to shore. In typical Catholic fashion, it made no difference to them who they rescued and brought back to the ship: Confederate and Union soldiers were treated as equals. Selfless work like this helped to convince many Protestants that their anti-Catholic misgivings were without foundation.

By the turn of the century, the nuns were running just about every Catholic institution, from the hospitals to the schools. When the *Titanic* went down in 1912, sisters gathered rescue boats for 174 injured adults and children and ferried them to New York Harbor; most of the passengers were treated at St. Vincent's Hospital in Greenwich Village, run by the Sisters of Charity. During the Depression the sisters offered food, clothing, and shelter to the needy and continued their service in urban hospitals. And when World War II broke out, they volunteered their professional services again.

No one in Catholic history is more well known for tending to the needs of orphans than Saint Vincent de Paul. In the early seventeenth century he drew women of all classes to work with him offering services to children regardless of their

situation. Whether they were abandoned, orphaned, or indi-
gent, they were given the care they deserved. The Sisters of
Charity did most of the work, and by the time of the French
Revolution they had established hundreds of orphanages.

The Ursuline Sisters founded the first American orphan-
age in New Orleans in 1727. Other orders of religious women
followed suit, among them the Sisters of Charity. Many of the
children were considered too unruly for other social agencies,
but none were turned aside by the nuns. By the thousands
the children arrived at Catholic orphanages because they had
no recourse to government programs. They were delivered by
parents, relatives, police officers, and priests; other children
were simply abandoned. There were occasional private grants,
but without the voluntary services of the nuns, many of these
children would have died on the streets. The sisters did not
neglect the women who gave their children up for adoption,
the widowed and the working women.

There was considerable controversy in the nineteenth century over the policy of "placing out," a term used to describe
the practice of placing children with families, instead of at
orphanages. The theory behind this initiative was unexcep-
tional: children reared in families would be better off than
those housed in institutions. But "placing out" also referred
to taking children away from the allegedly uneducated, un-
couth, and highly sexual poor Catholic women who were
their mothers: the main idea was to give the boys and girls a
better life by introducing them to the manners and customs
of more refined and affluent white Anglo-Saxon women. The
class and religious implications were provocative, leading

many of the Catholic clergy and laity to fight back by expanding their outreach and improving services for children.

The "child savers," as the Protestant women were called, were particularly bent on "rescuing" Catholic children from their Irish moms. "From the early 1850s through the mid-1870s," writes Professor Maureen Fitzgerald, "Protestant elite reformers removed tens of thousands of poor immigrant children from New York City streets and homes and sent them to Protestant homes in the Midwest."[31] The idea that there was a great benefit in taking urban kids and placing them on farms, far away from vice, was an unshakable conviction in the Protestant well-to-do community, but it was also a practice that provoked nuns to lobby for "parental rights." By this the sisters meant the right of nuns to house these children in their care, keeping them away from the "child savers." By 1885 the sisters were rearing more than 80 percent of New York City's dependent children.

Not all children in need were dependent; some were merely abandoned all together. For them, the sisters established what was known as the Foundling Asylum, or "Foundling Hospital." Besides providing care for these children, the nuns also attended to the needs of "fallen women," the young women who found themselves unable to cope with their children. There weren't too many professionals who wanted anything to do with these women, but the nuns didn't care what others thought; they had a duty, and their "focus on the other" included serving abandoned women, as well as abandoned children. The sisters sought to give these women work, enabling them to earn enough money, in time, to care for their own children. This was another way of avoiding the "placing out" services of Protestant women. The goal of the nuns was to reunite the children with their mothers.

Education

The Catholic contribution to education, especially at the elementary and secondary levels, would not have been possible without the decades of service that so many orders of sisters have provided. Today, lay Catholic women are at the forefront in this area; what they learned from the nuns best explains their continued success. When it comes to Catholic education in the United States, no one is better known than Elizabeth Ann Bayley Seton, the first native-born canonized saint in America.

Born in New York in 1774 to a wealthy Episcopalian family, Seton lost her mother when she was three years old. Married at nineteen, she had five children, and after her last child was born her husband died of tuberculosis. To make matters worse, the business he had run had just gone bankrupt. Distraught, she sought comfort with her friends, some of whom introduced her to the Catholic Church. She converted on Ash Wednesday, 1805. After becoming a teacher, she agreed to a request by the president of the College of St. Mary in Baltimore and opened a school, St. Joseph's Academy the first free Catholic school in the nation. Seton made sure it was open to African American children. She soon moved her school to Emmitsburg, and it was there that she founded the Sisters of Charity.

In the 1830s, as a result of the efforts of Horace Mann,

the "common schools" were developed across the nation. The chief purpose was to provide a common culture and education to immigrant children, so they could be assimilated into American society. This was fine for the majority of people, but not for Catholics. The public schools carried the heavy imprint of Protestantism: the King James Bible was read in the classroom, Protestant hymns were sung, and patently anti-Catholic texts were assigned. Mann himself was anti-Catholic, and he accused Catholics of an inability to think for themselves. But Catholics pushed back, and no one led the charge more effectively than did New York Bishop John "Dagger" Hughes. He lobbied Catholics to give up the pipe dream of reforming the public schools; the time had come, he argued, to establish a separate parochial system of education.

The goal of Catholic schools was more cultural than educational: the nuns sought to instill in children a sense of pride in being Catholic, and to introduce them to the faith. Literacy was never neglected, of course, but the dominant culture was so hostile to all things Catholic that a strong identity had to be instilled in the children before academic achievement could be tackled. Typically the schools were segregated by sex, and each school reflected the ethnic composition of its neighborhood.

Today Catholic schools comprise the largest segment of private schools in the nation. Their graduation rates continue to outperform both the public and the private nonsectarian schools. In 2010 the graduation rate of Catholic schools was 99.1 percent; 85 percent go to a four-year college, compared to only 44 percent of public school students. In terms of academic achievement, Catholic students continue to outperform their counterparts in other schools in most instances. That they are able to do this with so little money, as compared to what is spent on public education, is seen as another one of the strengths of Catholic schools. On the other hand, having so little to spend on anything but the basics has had an alembic effect: it forces administrators, who are tiny in number compared to their public school cohorts, to concentrate on what is important.

What accounts for the success of Catholic schools? According to researcher Helen Marks and Professor Mark Berends, there are two factors: the influence of Catholic values and the fostering of Catholic faith and morals.[32] This finding dovetails with the earlier work of Rev. Andrew Greeley and others.[33] As important as test scores are, it would be myopic to measure success on the basis of academic achievement alone; schools are also incubators of citizenship. In this regard, Catholic schools excel as well. "As both history has shown and researchers have documented," writes New York Archbishop Timothy Dolan, "there are plenty of reasons for all American Catholics to take proud ownership of Catholic schools."[34]

But the true success story is what Catholic education has achieved in the inner city. In New York City, two-thirds of the students served by Catholic schools come from families at or below the poverty line, and more than one-third are non-Catholics. To say they that these schools have not been given enough credit is a wild understatement. Today much of the tribute belongs to the laity.

When I spent four years teaching in a Catholic elementary school in Spanish Harlem, I saw firsthand what a success story

Catholic education is. The public school that was across the street was so bad—violence and rape were commonplace—that New York City had to shut it down. But at St. Lucy's these kinds of problems were unheard of. There were occasional fights, and the neighborhood was dangerous, but the kinds of things that went on in the public school were never tolerated at the Catholic school. The parents, which is to say the mothers (the fathers were rarely around), wanted it that way. The number one reason mothers sacrificed to send their Puerto Rican and black children to St. Lucy's was not for an education (that was second); it was because of safety concerns. They knew when they dropped their children off in the morning that they would be unharmed when they picked them up at the end of the day.

It is often said, especially by public school union officials, that the reason that Catholic schools outperform public schools is because the Catholic schools can afford to be selective; they don't have to take the incorrigible students. Nonsense. Where do they think unruly public school students often wind up? Catholic schools cannot afford to turn students away; they need all the tuition money they can collect. While there is certainly an adjustment period for these miscreant students, eventually they learn the ropes and settle down.

Discipline is not an option; it comes with the territory. Uniforms help a lot, cutting down on silly and sometimes violence-producing competition over clothing and footwear. Moreover, there is a price to be paid for misconduct. Daily homework, and lots of it, yield impressive results, and that is one reason that students at Catholic schools excel. Class size is supposed to matter, and no doubt it does, but this was just one more luxury the children I taught were not afforded; there were between forty and fifty students per class (compared with roughly half that in public schools). Another luxury was heat. When the boiler went out during the winter at the Catholic school in Spanish Harlem, classes were combined, leaving some teachers to handle one hundred students at a time; there were no rows because the desks were aligned next to each other.

The law in the United States is that parochial students are entitled to taxpayer-funded textbooks but not maps. This once led former New York Senator Daniel Patrick Moynihan to wonder whether an atlas, a book of maps, could be provided with public funds. The textbooks the Catholic schools received were used, and many were badly damaged. At that time, U.S. law also mandated that remedial teaching for Catholic students, offered by public school teachers during the day, could not take place in a room containing religious symbols. For example, crucifixes needed to be removed when public school teachers taught. Some schools rented trailers to house the remedial instruction, parking them across the street from the parochial school, and these trailers were occasionally run into by reckless drivers.

It cannot be seriously maintained, then, that quality education depends on money. It does not. It is made possible by cooperation and a steely commitment on the part of parents, administrators, and teachers. The record of Catholic education, especially among minority students, is one of the greatest, and least appreciated, success stories in American history. If this contribution were appreciated more, then school vouchers would be a reality, but they are not. What do we have instead? In Washington, D.C., there is public money available to pay for a poor woman's abortion, but there is none available to pay for her choice of school if she decides to carry her baby to term; she is forced to send her child to a school that no president, congressman, or senator would choose for their own children.

Father Rick

The "focus on the other" that is a staple of Catholic social thought rises to a new level when "the other" is a stranger. In one sense, everyone outside our kin and close associates may be considered a stranger, but there is something altogether different when we're talking about encountering people from foreign lands who speak and act in a manner that we are not accustomed to dealing with in everyday life. Often these people present a challenge and test the limits of our ability to "love thy neighbor." Catholic social teachings have not neglected this phenomenon, but the true test is how Catholic sons and daughters have dealt with this situation.

Mother Teresa is not the only Catholic champion of the dispossessed not to seek recognition or applause; the same is true of Father Richard Frechette. His mission, which is still ongoing, is to serve the dead and dying in Haiti in the double role of priest and doctor. In this instance, Father Rick is the stranger.

Father Rick belongs to the Passionists, an order of priests known for their "focus on the other." He has recorded his experiences in a powerful little book, *Haiti: The God of Tough*

Places, the Lord of Burnt Men, a riveting volume that requires a strong stomach. It should make Catholic readers proud to claim him as one of their own.

Father Rick has lived in Haiti for two decades (he hails from Connecticut) and is the founder and director of Nuestros Pequenos Hermanos (Our Little Brothers and Sisters). He also runs Haiti's only free pediatric hospital, appropriately named St. Damien's. On Thursdays Father Rick likes to avail himself of Marlboros and rum. This habit is not driven by weakness; it is occasioned by the need to cope with the stench of burnt bodies. To be specific, on Thursdays Father Rick makes his weekly morgue run and blesses the bodies of the dead and comforts the family and friends of the deceased. Without the smokes, and a little libation, the smell of the corpses would simply overwhelm him. But just as he never misses saying daily Mass at 7:00 a.m., he never misses his Thursday obligation.

Haiti is a nation long riddled with massive exploitation, abject poverty, natural disasters, kidnapping, gangs, and unrelenting violence. So what's in it for Father Rick? The same prize that attracted Mother Teresa. Just as she said she would not touch a leper for money but only for the love of God, he gives of himself to these poor people all the love that cannot be bought.

What energizes him is the Haitian people: they never give up. Surrounded by horror stories, many of which are their own, they possess a will to live that would astound most of us in the developed nations. "The idea of assisted suicide, or of determining who should be helped to live and who should be left to die, are hot and controversial topics in our world today," Father Rick writes.[35] Then he lowers the boom. "It is just that

I have not yet come across someone who said to me, 'Thanks for offering the help, but I really would just rather die.'" He concludes, "I am waiting for such a moment, and its accompanying wisdom."

It is fascinating to ponder. Why are so many self-identified champions of compassion in North America and Europe obsessed with promoting doctor-assisted suicide, while the indigents in Haiti just want to live one more day? The idea that life is valued more highly by the wretched than by the wealthy, and by the ignorant more than by the intellectuals, seems counterintuitive by most standards. But then again the "deep thinkers" have often seen the poor as nothing more than the miserable masses, not realizing how the least among us still find room for joy and a reason for living.

Surely the assisted-suicide enthusiasts could not make heads or tails of why so many people in Port-au-Prince rallied around a young man named Joseph. Father Rick never met him, but he risked his life trying to find the young man's dead body. Joseph was an American college graduate who worked at a mission hospital trying to eradicate a terrible mosquito-borne disease. He was murdered in the worst section of Port-au-Prince, his body left to rot in a car. No one from the police or the United Nations would grant his wife's wishes to go into the neighborhood to find him. Father Rick tried but failed.

Why would Cathy, married to Joseph for only a year, want to risk so much for his rat-eaten body? Because she wanted to give her husband a Christian burial. The people who joined the search for his body were men and women plagued with tuberculosis and AIDS. That none of them knew Joseph made their heroism all the more remarkable.

Father Rick reflected on what happened: "In the face of the arrogant and horrible display of hell, there appears a powerful force of good capable of defying it, and often this goodness is in a seemingly very feeble form. That force of goodness has made its home in you and I."[36] Spoken like a true priest.

Father Rick does what he does for the sake of Christ. There is no other reason. He is, at heart, an optimist, but there is nothing Pollyannaish about him. He knows what suffering is, having experienced it himself and having served those whose sufferings make our own seem trivial. But he never gives up. He says, "We are encouraged to offer our works, our trials, our sufferings to God in union with those of Christ so that they might be redemptive."[37]

Father Rick's efforts have touched many. How else can we account for the blessed determination of those who risked their lives, tragic as they were, for others? Surely self-interest would not propel desperate people to go into gang-infested villages looking for the body of a loved one. This is evidence of the goodness that he mentioned, the goodness that we all possess and are capable of demonstrating.

As the apostles showed, it is not just us plain folk who are weak without Christ. Father Rick hits home when he says that the apostles were stronger after Christ died. "These timid, ordinary men," he writes, "who were afraid of their own skins, suddenly were guided by a force that carried them valiantly into the future and into the world. They became fully servants of the gospel of life: articulate, fearless, leading by example, traveling far and wide to spread the Word, even at great danger to themselves."

Beyond question, Father Rick's apostolate gives further

evidence of the Spirit of Christ, which makes it possible for him—the stranger—to "focus on the other" in a way almost unimaginable to most of us. "The vast slums of Port-au-Prince are pretty rough places," he observes. "Yet they are home to hundreds of thousands of people. Most of these are children. If people are there, God is fully there too." It strains credulity that any atheist could look at what Father Rick has given of himself and what he has learned about the human spirit from these destitute people and not appreciate his insights. They are to be pitied for having elected to trim their own horizons.

But if God is good, how do believers make sense of evil? God, Father Rick tells us, is all about setting boundaries. "Boundaries between light and darkness, between good and evil. Unbelievable horrors, like tsunami and Shoah, show us what is at stake when boundaries disappear. Hell is in the business of trying to destroy all boundaries. And resisting hell is about fighting to restore them."[38]

At bottom, there is hope for the human condition. "Most sin is the perversion of something good," the Haitian hero says. For example, "Hatred is a perversion of love." Here's his optimism: "That is why there is hope for us sinners. The basic stuff for something very right is still there and can be reworked with God's grace."[39]

Father Rick does not brag about himself, but he does not hold back in giving due praise to the nuns who serve the Haitian poor. He quotes the advice of a Canadian Sister of St. Joseph: "If it's old and ugly, paint it a bright color. If it's barren, plant a flower." Most important, "If they are sick, sit with them on the bed. If they are hungry, make soup."[40]

Mother Teresa opened the first Missionaries of Charity

mission in Haiti some three decades ago. Father Rick tells the tale of Sister Abha, one of the sisters who opened the first mission with Mother Teresa, and how she endured. One night she was shot. Worse, the man who ordered the hit was one of the men whom she had taken off the streets and raised from the time he was a child. How she responded to what happened is Catholicism at its best. "We will all die one day anyway," she said. "It does not matter how or when or where we die. It only matters how we have lived."

Father Rick exemplifies the best in the Catholic tradition, and he is able to do what he does because he sincerely believes that all of us are destined for greatness. "We have a triple dignity," he says. "God made us, redeemed us and prepares us for life eternally." We will suffer, he writes, but "we are made in the Divine image, held by God's hand, considered the apple of God's eye, with every hair on our head counted, and our names engraved in God's heart."[41] Father Rick is a gift to Haiti and to the Catholic Church.

Immigrants

The ministry of "welcoming the stranger" is more typically performed by those who greet the immigrant. Mother Frances Xavier Cabrini, an immigrant herself, is known as the "saint of immigrants." She was born in Italy and arrived in New York in 1889 with six of her sisters from the Missionary Sisters of the Sacred Heart. Their work was not confined to New York; they made their way to every region of the country, founding schools, hospitals, and orphanages. But money was tight, so Mother Cabrini wrote to Leone Reynaudi, the commissioner general of emigration for the Italian government, asking for funding from the Italian government.

"In the orphanages are gathered Italian girls who have lost their parents in work-related accidents or misfortunes," Mother Cabrini wrote. Numbering approximately five thousand, the youngsters were taught Italian and the domestic arts. She noted with pride that Columbus Hospital was exclusively Italian, although she hastened to say that non-Italians were taken care of there as well. "The dispensary connected with the hospital has given proof of great vitality," she said. "During the past year about 5,000 Italians received free medical treatment; 22,000 were medically examined; 22,400 prescriptions were filled out for them, and 10,500 received surgical care," she wrote. She also mentioned the schools and the churches that served the immigrants. With a nice touch, she added, "Only a person who has lived far from the country, separated from the most precious domestic joys . . . can value the sweetness that lies in the Sunday gathering of our workers who hurry to us in their best attire."[42]

Mother Cabrini died on December 22, 1917, in Chicago's Columbus Hospital, which she founded. Her work has been carried on by over a thousand Missionaries of the Sacred Heart of Jesus working in dozens of venues on two continents.

Today the work of Mother Cabrini is institutionalized in Church organizations such as Migration and Refugee Services. Its main goal is to work with immigrants, refugees, and migrants, helping them find housing and work, and directing them to government and community services. Over one million refugees have been resettled by this organization in the last three decades, and this doesn't count the work done by parishes; there is another program, Parishes Organized to Welcome Refugees, that is staffed by volunteers. For those who need legal help, there is the Catholic Legal Immigration Network, which provides services to indigent and low-income immigrants. This group's "focus on the other" includes welcoming government detainees, refugees, asylum seekers, families in need of reunification, and victims of human trafficking and domestic violence (most of whom are women and children).

When the American Revolution began in 1776, there were approximately 25,000 Catholics out of a population of 2.5 million in the thirteen colonies. Today Catholics number approximately 70 million in a nation of 313 million. Many of the early immigrants were the beneficiaries of Catholic outreach programs that put into action the Gospel imperative of welcoming the stranger. By 1920, 75 percent of American Catholics were immigrants, and most of the recent arrivals were from southern and eastern Europe. Fortunately, at the parish level there were mutual-aid societies, fraternal and sororal groups, schools, charities, and an array of educational and medical services.

In 1850 Bishop Hughes boasted that the Catholic Church would "conquer America." While this was pure hype, it was no exaggeration to say that the Catholic imprint would be significant and lasting. The Catholic presence would also be felt along ethnic lines, at least initially. In the 1860s there were already more Irish in New York City than in Dublin, and by 1880 nine in ten of New York's foreign-born were English, Irish, or German. While the Irish congregated almost exclusively in cities in the Northeast, the Germans made their way to the Midwest, since most of them were farmers from southern Germany. Not as deeply rooted in their Catholicism as the Irish were the Italians, but unlike the famine-ridden Irish, the Italians were more self-supporting. Although the Catholic Church was heavily Irish at the time, when the Poles and other eastern European ethnics began to arrive, there was nothing to stop them from establishing Polish communities and parishes that reflected their own heritage. All of these ethnic groups were settled in large part with the help of the Catholic Church.

Every Catholic ethnic group had its own fraternal and sororal groups to help integrate them into American society. America's oldest Irish Catholic fraternal group, and the oldest Catholic ethnic organization, is the Ancient Order of Hibernians (AOH). Founded in 1836, it was born of necessity—to protect the clergy and churches from violent nativists. The AOH resembled the groups, many of which were secret societies, that had developed in the 1500s in Ireland to safeguard the welfare of the priests and their churches. At that time in Ireland, the English dominated, and after the Penal Laws of 1691, these societies were needed more than ever to provide assistance to the clergy and laity alike, many of whom were driven underground. So when the Irish landed in New York, they had a ready model to emulate in the United States. The AOH took its cues from the secret societies of the old country and introduced the Irish to America. So, too, did the Irish Emigrant Society, a group that with the leadership of Bishop Hughes, set up the Emigrant Savings Bank; it was instrumental in settling the immigrants and catering to their financial needs.

Another Irishman, Father Michael McGivney, founded

the Knights of Columbus in New Haven in 1882. The organization provided fellowship and low-cost insurance to Catholic immigrants, independent of ethnic origin. Its emphasis on service and faith was especially in need in a time when anti-Catholicism was prevalent, and when the Freemasons were attempting to lure immigrants. Central to the Knights of Columbus was a death-benefit program that catered to wives and children, who needed such assistance given the high mortality rate of men working in harsh conditions. Today the Knights give generously to the episcopal conferences of the United States, Canada, and Mexico; the Catholic University of America, the John Paul II Institute for Studies of Marriage and the Family, the Missionaries of Charity, the Eternal Word Television Network, and many other worthy organizations.

African Americans

The only immigrant group to come to America involuntarily, Africans, were not initially welcomed in the Catholic community, a function of their status as both slaves and non-Catholics. But in time they would be welcomed. Mother Mary Elizabeth Lange and Saint Katharine Drexel created orders to assist African Americans. Lange was Haitian and Drexel was from a wealthy Philadelphia family, yet both saw that in serving black Americans, Catholics had an opportunity to break racial barriers.

There were other Catholics, not well known, who lost their lives because they stood up to white racists. On August

11, 1921, Father James Coyle, an outspoken critic of racism, was shot to death in Birmingham, Alabama, by a Methodist minister who was also a member of the Ku Klux Klan. His crime? About an hour before he was murdered by Rev. Edwin R. Stephenson, Father Coyle had officiated at the wedding of the minister's daughter to a Catholic migrant from Puerto Rico; Stephenson regarded the groom as a "Negro." Although the minister was clearly guilty, because of the anti-Catholicism that permeated the South at that time, coupled with the antics of Stephenson's defense lawyer, Hugo Black, Stephenson got off. Attorney Black, who hated Catholics and was also a member of the Ku Klux Klan, was later appointed to the U.S. Supreme Court; he used his role on the high court to marginalize the Catholic Church with spurious First Amendment rulings on the establishment of religion (for example, the denial of school vouchers to parents who want to send their children to parochial schools). Worse, his revisionist interpretation of the First Amendment inspired future judges to take a narrow view of religious liberty.

Perhaps the best known Catholic to reach out to blacks was a Jesuit priest, Father John LaFarge, who was active in the first half of the twentieth century. At a young age LaFarge was disturbed to learn of the racism and injustice that blacks endured. He was also not too happy with some in the Catholic clergy whom he saw as failing to combat racial discrimination. What inspired him to work for racial equality was an experience he had in a rural area of southern Maryland in 1911. Although he was proud to see that the Jesuits had established mission churches there in 1663, he was distraught over the

Catholic passivity on racial injustice at the time. Blacks were exploited and few whites reached out to them. This experience left more than an impression on him; it convinced him that he had to personally involve himself in the cause for racial equality.

In 1926 LaFarge took a position working for *America*, the influential Jesuit magazine in New York. He immediately immersed himself in reading and writing about race relations, and in 1934 he founded the Catholic Interracial Council of New York; it proved to be a model of other such groups. By bringing whites and blacks together for the purpose of dialogue and coalition efforts designed to end racial injustice, LaFarge was a pivotal force in ending discrimination. Following Aquinas, he maintained that everyone possessed natural rights equally, and that government had no option but to recognize them.

In 1937, his seminal work, *Interracial Justice: A Study of the Catholic Doctrine of Race Relations*, was published by America Press. LaFarge cited the encyclicals of Pope Leo XIII and Pope Pius XI as having had a great effect on him; Pius XI honored him by asking him to help write an encyclical on racism. Pius XI also used LaFarge's natural law writings to undercut the racist policies of the Nazis. When A. Philip Randolph, a powerful figure in the African American community, organized a rally in 1942 at Madison Square Garden to protest racial discrimination, LaFarge was the only white person invited to sit on the dais with him. Efforts like those of La Farge paved the way for Catholic outreach to black Americans, thus inspiring many priests, nuns, and lay Catholics to march with Rev. Martin Luther King in the 1960s.

Latinos

Today it is the Latino community that is the focus of conversation among students of immigration. As well it should be; in the past twenty years, the number of Latinos under the age of eighteen in the United States has doubled to 16 million. It is estimated that by 2035 a third of all Americans will be of Hispanic descent. Because Latinos are largely Catholic, they have drawn the attention of the Catholic bishops.

In 1984 bishops issued a pastoral letter, "The Hispanic Presence: Challenge and Commitment," in which they addressed an array of issues, ranging from poverty to political participation. Hispanics in the United States were characterized as a "blessing from God,"[43] as people who are entitled to the same respect as any other ethnic group. Calling attention to their fragile social and economic status, the bishops urged Catholics to develop a "more welcoming attitude" toward America's newest strangers. Importantly, the bishops pledged financial assistance, invoking the Church's "preferential option for the poor" as a guidepost. They also lauded Latinos for their apostolates, mentioning the contributions of Cursillos and Encuentros.

In 1995 Pope John Paul II delivered a message for World Migration Day wherein he dealt forthrightly with the issue of illegal immigrants. "The illegal migrant comes before us like that 'stranger' in whom Jesus asks to be recognized," he said, and he asked Catholics to receive these people "whatever their illegal status with regard to state law." His words were timely. Today one of the hot-button issues is the problem of illegal immigrants, and Mexicans are at the center of the controversy.

Impoverished in their home country, and unattended to by their government, many Mexicans find the lure of a better standard of living in the United States irresistible. Largely Catholic, Mexicans are caught in the crosshairs of religious, ethnic, and national politics. In 2003 the bishops of Mexico and the United States issued a joint pastoral letter, "Strangers No Longer: Together on the Journey of Hope," in which they make it clear that "Christ is present in migrants,"[44] and remind Catholics that we will be judged by the way we treat the dispossessed. Stressing the fact that both Mexico and the United States are immigrant nations, the bishops said that states have a right to secure their borders, although they insisted that it is not an absolute right; it must be measured against the needs and conditions of migrants. Economic opportunities must be made available in one's own country, they said, and refugees from persecution and war should be received without recrimination. Respect for human dignity and human rights demand no less.

These kinds of statements are not to be interpreted as dogma, so that means that they are subject to revision. In 2007 the American bishops issued a document, *Forming Consciences for Faithful Citizenship*, that called for comprehensive immigration reform. It emphasized that reform "should include a temporary work program with worker protections and a path to permanent residency; family reunification; a broad and fair legalization program; access to legal protections, including due process and essential public programs; refuge for those fleeing persecution and exploitation; and policies to address the root causes of migration."[45]

Regarding the right to control the border, an issue that is pressing in states like Arizona, they said that they do not support "open borders"; they argued that the United States has every right to secure its borders. Nonetheless, as Bishop John Wester put it, it is important to have "generous, but reasonable, immigration policies that serve the common good."[46]

The issue of borders has generated much discussion, some of which has been vitriolic. It is worthy to note that Pope Pius XII long ago affirmed the right of nations to secure their borders, although he hastened to say that all related issues must be addressed with care, and that fundamental human rights should be respected. The Catechism asserts, "Political authorities, for the sake of the common good for which they are responsible, may make the exercise of the right to immigrate subject to various juridical conditions, especially with regard to the immigrants' duties toward their country of adoption." But the Catechism also places a responsibility on "the more prosperous nations" to welcome foreigners to the extent they can.

Msgr. George Higgins, who died in 2002, repeatedly called on Americans never to forget their immigrant roots, reminding them that the newest immigrants are confronted with many of the same issues that confronted the immigrants who came before them.[47] His advice was quintessentially Catholic. There are legitimate national interests that must be attended to, but in the process, the duty to "welcome the stranger" is never out of date. Indeed, this compassion toward immigrants is one more reason why Catholicism matters, not only to Catholics, but to everyone else.

FORTITUDE

N o world religion condones oppression, but few have
actually had the fortitude to do something tangible
to fight it—except the Catholic Church, which
has delievered a lot more than sentiment. The Church's fight
against fascism, especially under Hitler, and its efforts to undermine communism, especially in the Soviet Union, are deserving of much commendation. Unfortunately, many people
remain wholly unaware of the Church's efforts, so thoroughly
politicized has scholarship become; that is why a fresh look
at the historical record is merited. Understanding the roots
of totalitarianism is also important, lest we fail to check its
reemergence. But before we examine how the Church courageously fought the twin evils of fascism and communism, it is
important to debunk some myths about the Church itself.

Martyrs

The best of intentions do not alone make for the development
of the good society. Sometimes it takes fortitude to do what is
right. Although acting prudently is critical, and the pursuit of
justice is noble, there are times when all the goodwill in the
world matters little unless we are willing to take a hit for the
cause. At the most profound level, this means carrying our

cross for Christ. Jesus warned us that when we work to do what is right we will be met with resistance and rejection, and that is why the exercise of fortitude figures so significantly in His game plan.

The ultimate expression of fortitude, in the Catholic tradition, is martyrdom. Pope John Paul II defined martyrdom as "an affirmation of the inviolability of the moral order." He saw martyrdom as "an *outstanding sign of the holiness of the Church*" (his emphasis), a heroic deed that allows everyone to see with clarity the difference between good and evil. "By their eloquent and attractive example of a life completely transfigured by the splendor of moral truth," John Paul says, "the martyrs and, in general, all the Church's Saints, light up every period of history by reawakening its moral sense."[1] During his papacy John Paul canonized 482 saints, 402 of whom were martyrs. From Korea alone he canonized 103, all of whom had been martyred during the mid-nineteenth century. Today North Korea is the most violent place on earth for Christians to live.

In their own special way, then, martyrs make good on the Catholic imperative of "focusing on the other." Almost all the apostles died as martyrs, and many of the most popular saints did as well. The number of faithful who were persecuted and killed, beginning in the Roman Empire, are too numerous to appreciate, and the barbarous means that have been used to kill Christians are worse than we could ever imagine. Perhaps most surprising is that more Christians were martyred in the twentieth century than in any previous century.

Robert Royal has nicely chronicled the story of Christian martyrs in the last millennium. The genocide of the Armenians in Turkey in the early twentieth century, he notes, is typically taught in the schools without mentioning that "many Christians, Armenian Catholics and Orthodox, died during the same massacre precisely because they were Christians."[2] Nor do most students learn of more recent examples of martyrdom such as that of Archbishop Oscar Romero, an outspoken champion of the poor in El Salvador, who was murdered in 1980 while saying Mass. Nuns and priests were also murdered there, for no other reason than that they sided with the oppressed.

In today's world, radical Muslims pose the biggest threat to Catholics and Jews, although there is reluctance on the part of the media to highlight martyrs who have died at the hands of Muslims. In the 1990s, nuns were murdered in Yemen by Muslims for tending to the poor; their killers were suspicious of their proselytizing efforts. The terrorist attacks of September 11, 2001, of course, killed Muslims as well as people of other faiths, but all of the killing was done in the name of Islam. In Nigeria in 2010 Christians were massacred in retaliation because a Christian woman had tried to cross a road while a group of Muslims were praying, and the killing received little attention. Similarly, the media largely downplayed what happened to Bishop Luigi Padovese, president of the Turkish Catholic Bishops Conference in 2010. A twenty-six-year-old Muslim man showed up at the bishop's door and stabbed him at least twenty times, delivering eight wounds to his heart. After he decapitated the bishop, the assailant shouted, "I killed the great Satan!" These are not isolated instances: according to Open Doors, which monitors Christian persecution, 100 million Christians around the world live in fear, and eight of the top ten most violent places for them to live are ruled by Muslims.

Regensburg Address

Pope Benedict XVI has not shied away from addressing the subject of Islamic extremism. The fortitude he has shown in directly confronting this issue makes him exceptional among world leaders. Unfortunately, some have mischaracterized his remarks, especially the ones he made at the University of Regensburg in 2006. In that speech the pope quoted a fourteenth-century Byzantine emperor who said, "Show me just what Mohammed brought that was new, and there you will find things only evil and inhuman, such as his command to spread by the sword the faith he preached."[3] This was quickly interpreted as an attack on Islam, yet any fair-minded person who actually read the Regensburg address in its entirety would say just how unfair this criticism is.

At its core, what Pope Benedict XVI was trying to get at was a statement on how fanaticism is the child of both faith without reason and reason without faith. The quote about Mohammed was selected to highlight the former; in other words, when faith abandons reason, trouble follows, often in the form of violence. The opposite is also true: reason without faith has a disastrous track record, although few spoke out on this part of the pope's address. In 2010 Benedict warned us again about the evils of religious fundamentalism *and* radical secularism: "A society that would violently impose or, on the contrary, reject religion is unjust not only to individuals and to God, but also to itself."[4] The problem with both extremes is that they "absolutize a reductive and partial vision of the human person," thus cutting us off from our God-given nature.

There have been plenty of examples, drawn from every religion, where religious fanatics have embarked on an irrational quest for purity. So convinced were they of their own righteousness, they proceeded as if reason is a dispensable faculty, if not a liability. But when reason is uncoupled from faith, as Benedict teaches, the result is bad fruit, poisoning the prospects for the good society. Getting this idea through the heads of religious zealots is not easy; they resist because they see all genuflections towards reason as a betrayal of faith. What they don't understand is that faith and reason go hand in hand, complementing each other in a most efficacious way. Although it may be unpopular to say so, it is undeniably true that at the outset of the third millennium, Islam poses the greatest threat to world peace, precisely because so many of its adherents cling to faith without reason.

Pope Benedict XVI is not only a masterful theologian but also a first-rate academician. He drew on his academic background when in the Regensburg address he pointed to the problems that have manifested when professors, particularly in the humanities and social sciences, have proceeded as if faith is an impediment to the creation of the good society. Yet as the totalitarian regimes of the twentieth century proved, when faith is abandoned, the body count is high. Fascism and communism have more commonalities than differences, and it is their utopian bent—creating heaven on earth—that accounts for their plunder. Just as the religious fanatic treats reason as the enemy, thoroughgoing secularists treat religion as the enemy. The consequences, in both instances, are dripping with blood.

As if to underscore the veracity of the pope's criticism of faith without reason, a cleric in Somalia urged Muslims who objected to the pope's remarks to "hunt down" the pope and kill him. Similarly, the Mujahideen Shura Council referred to the pope as "the worshipper of the cross," and pledged to "break the cross and spill the wine" in the "house of the dog from Rome." This was not idle talk. Seven churches were firebombed in the West Bank and Gaza by gun-wielding Palestinians, who used lighter fluid to set the churches on fire. And in the Pakistani-controlled section of Kashmir, Muslims took to the streets chanting, "Death to the pope," burning him in effigy.

In fairness, there were Muslims who applauded what the pope said. Irshad Manji, a Muslim feminist writer, commented that what the pope said was hardly inflammatory. "Actually," she opined, "he called for dialogue with the Muslim world." She emphasized that the pope's critics were not focusing on the "larger context" of his address; she compared their exclusive concentration on "a mere few words of the speech" to those who reduce the Koran "to its most blood-thirsty passages."[5] Reuel Marc Gerecht, a Jewish writer, praised the pope for his frankness, saying it was "a welcome change from the pabulum that passes for 'interfaith' dialogue."[6] Catholic scholar George Weigel caught the essence of what the pope said. "His lecture in Germany was, first of all," he wrote, "a celebration of human reason—the human capacity to know the truth of things." Weigel pointed out that "[t]rue faith is reasonable faith, faith that makes sense," and that reason and faith "cannot be in conflict."[7]

The Crusades

It would be unfair to single out Islam as the only religion in which one can find examples of what happens when people of faith discard reason. The Crusades and the Spanish Inquisition are blots on Christianity, although here I must object that the most common condemnations of Catholicism are patently absurd and historically inaccurate.

After the events of September 11, 2001, St. Louis University professor Thomas F. Madden was asked by many reporters what the connection is between the Crusades and the attack on America. Madden, who specializes in this period of history, said the Crusades were a medieval phenomenon with no connection to 9/11. To drive home his point, he made it clear that "medieval Muslims had no understanding or interest in the crusades." Indeed, he said, it was not the Crusades that brought about 9/11; it was "the artificial memory of the crusades constructed by modern colonial powers passed down by Arab nationalists and Islamists." Reporters were stunned.

"The simple fact is that the crusades were virtually unknown in the Muslim world even a century ago," Madden writes. "The term for the crusades, *harb al-salib*, was only introduced into the Arabic language in the mid-nineteenth century."[8] How can this be? Because in the course of their history, Muslims have long been at war with so-called infidels, and the skirmishes that mark the Crusades never stood out as distinct. Indeed, as Madden says, "A western traveler in the eighteenth century would have been hard-pressed to find a Muslim in the Middle East who had heard of the crusades. Even in the nineteenth century they were known only to a handful of intellectuals. In the grand sweep of Islamic history the crusades simply did not matter."[9] Madden concedes, of course, that Muslims today cite the Crusades all the time, but "[t]he 'long memory' of the crusades in the Muslim world is, in fact, a constructed memory—one in which the memory is much younger than the event itself."[10]

The idea that the Crusades were a bloodthirsty war declared by Christians against Muslims without provocation may be the conventional view, but it is totally wrong. Historians of the Crusades such as Jonathan Riley-Smith have just about given up trying to set the historical record straight, so unshakable is the myth of Christian conquest.[11] The fact is the Crusades were a defensive action. Princeton's Bernard Lewis, one of the world's most noted historians, has written, "At the present time, the Crusades are often depicted as an early experiment in expansionist imperialism—a prefigurement of the modern European countries. To the people of the time, both Muslim and Christian, they were no such thing."[12] So what were they? "The Crusade was a delayed response to the jihad, the holy war for Islam, and its purpose was to recover by war what had been lost by war—to free the holy places of Christendom and open them once again, without impediment, to Christian pilgrimage."

The crusaders were volunteers, not papal conscripts. Small

in number, they enjoyed widespread support. They saw themselves as making a collective act of penance, as being involved in a just cause. They were not a band of roving barbarians wildly attacking everyone in sight; they had limited and defined goals. Madden points out, "All the Crusades met the criteria of just wars."[13] They were a reaction to Muslim aggression. The First Crusade, for example, was called in 1095 in response to the Turkish conquest of Christian Asia Minor, as well as the earlier conquest of the Christian-held Holy Land. The crusaders saw their sacrifice as a holy mission. One thing the Crusades were not; they were not campaigns motivated by the desire to reap material gain. If anything, the holy wars were expensive. They were also deadly: an estimated 35 percent died in these efforts that largely failed.

The Inquisition

The Inquisition is similarly misunderstood, to put it mildly. As Madden says with authority, "The Catholic Church as an institution had almost nothing to do with it."[14] Most of what is related in the grossly exaggerated tales of horrors never happened, and in any event the secular authorities, not the Catholic Church, were at the center of events. The source of the many anti-Catholic myths is not in doubt; they stem from the "Black Legend" writings that were disseminated in the aftermath of the Protestant Reformation. The propaganda against Catholicism continues today, although these days the source is academia.

Whatever the Inquisition was, it was not some pervasive

operation orchestrated by an elite at a command center. The preeminent scholar of the period, Henry Kamen, lays to rest all the conspiratorial theories.[15] There were many Inquisitions, spread out over hundreds of years, with different targets and different objectives. What began in the 1480s because of the fear that converted Jews were returning to their faith ended in the eighteenth century with little else to inquire into. Kamen makes it clear, too, that contrary to many myths, the Inquisition did not stifle culture or have any effect on the distribution of literary works.

"One of the most enduring myths of the Inquisition," writes Madden, "is that it was a tool of oppression imposed on unwilling Europeans by a power-hungry Church. Nothing could be more wrong. In truth, the Inquisition brought order, justice, and compassion to combat rampant secular and popular persecutions of heretics."[16] Heresy was defined differently by the Church than by secular authorities. The Church saw heretics as lost sheep who needed to be brought back into the fold. Those suspected of heresy were subjected to an inquiry, hence the term *inquisition!* But the secular authorities saw heresy as treason; anyone who questioned royal authority, or who in any way challenged the idea that kingship was God-given, was guilty of a capital offense. And because they defined heresy in this way, the secular authorities—not the Catholic Church—burned heretics. Although it may strike the modern reader as bizarre, Madden says, "The simple fact is that the medieval Inquisition *saved* uncounted thousands of innocent (and even not-so-innocent) people who would otherwise have been roasted by secular lords or mob rule."[17]

The secular authorities were highly critical of the Catholic Church's limited role in the Inquisition, branding the pope's efforts as weak and ineffectual. As the Inquisition grew, so did opposition from the Catholic Church. Many in the Church's hierarchy protested the practice of burning heretics at the stake, and popes leant their support. Innocent VIII wrote twice to the king of Spain pleading for greater leniency for the *conversos*. Successive kings characterized the Church's response as weak, and muscled their way into the Inquisition; this relegated the Church to an ancillary role.

At the heart of the Inquisition were the *conversos*, Jews who had recently converted to Catholicism. Most converted initially in response to anti-Semitism, but even after the King of Aragon decreed that any Jews who accepted baptism to avoid death could return to their religion with impunity, most decided to stay Catholic. They were not secret Jews; they were recognized by rabbis as true Christians. "The vast majority of *conversos*," Madden says, "were good Catholics who simply took pride in their Jewish heritage"; they were not dishonest persons seeking to retain their old faith.[18] Moreover, they were investigated with an eye toward making sure they were in good standing with the Church. Jews, per se, were never the subject of the Inquisition. Madden says, "Spain's Jews had nothing to fear from the Spanish Inquisition."

As for all the talk about violence and the Inquisition, it is mostly bunk. "No major court in Europe executed fewer people than the Spanish Inquisition," says Madden.[19] The actual number of executions, according to most students, is 2,000, but Kamen, who has done more independent research on this issue than any other scholar, says the figure is too high: he puts the number at 1,394.[20] The relatively small number is explained by sociologist Daniel Bell as proof that the Inquisition "was primarily interested in conversion, not execution."[21]

As Kamen points out, the French under Henry II executed twice as many heretics; under England's Queen Mary, three times that number were executed; and in the Netherlands, ten times that number were executed. In fact, Kamen notes that some seven thousand clergy were killed in Spain in the 1830s, yet this number is rarely cited.[22] Solzhenitsyn compared the number of people executed by the Inquisition to the number of people who died under the Bolsheviks: "In a period of sixteen months (from June 1918 to October 1919) more than sixteen thousand persons were shot, which is to say *more than one thousand a month*" (his italics).[23] The famous Russian freedom fighter says that in order to appreciate on a historical scale what happened, it is important to realize that at the height of the Inquisition, an average of ten heretics were executed per month.

Resisting Evil

It is one thing to counsel against evil, quite another to combat it. This is especially true when government is the principal source of the evil. Historically, the means that have been available to the Catholic Church to resist evil have been few, although their use has paid many dividends. Diplomacy is an option, manifested in either a public or a private way; rescue efforts are another; aiding and abetting resistance movements is yet another; and there is always the possibility of a just war. There is no all-purpose solution, but the prudent application of any one of these tactics, or a combination of them, is a worthy alternative to the wanton destruction of innocent human life. It takes fortitude, and plenty of it, to follow through with these methods in the face of formidable odds.

Sometimes diplomacy must be public to have an effect, such as Pope John Paul II's open defiance of communism. But there are other times when prudence dictates that efforts to undermine evil not be too confrontational, lest conditions deteriorate further. Pope Pius XII was wise to follow this course in resisting the Nazis. Rescue efforts have saved innocents and stymied evil, especially under Hitler's rule. John Paul's efforts to support the workers in Poland, especially the Solidarity movement, are a textbook case of how to defeat evil by facilitating a resistance movement. As we will shortly see, Popes Pius XII and John Paul II acted nobly and wisely, playing an integral role in undermining fascism and communism in the twentieth century.

The Catholic Church also believes there are times when war may be necessary to protect the loss of innocent human life. The concept of a just war has quite specific criteria; it is not something that can be promiscuously invoked. Indeed, there are specifics tenets, such as the need for a proportionate response to aggression. Essentially, the concept of a just war is an extension of the right to self-defense. In *Evangelium Vitae*, Pope John Paul II wrote that "the intrinsic value of life and the duty to love oneself no less than others are the basis of *a true right to self-defense*" (his italics). The Catechism, John Paul reminded us, is quite clear about this, asserting that "legitimate defense can be not only a right but a grave duty for someone responsible for another's life, the common good of the family or of the state."

All of these measures are available and have been used by various popes throughout the ages. Stalin dismissively quipped, "How many divisions does the pope have?" The answer is he doesn't have any, but that hardly means he is without other means. Indeed, in his noteworthy address in 1968, Eugene V. Rostow, the Under Secretary of State for Political Affairs under President Johnson, discussed the many ways in which the Catholic Church has played the role of peacemaker in history.

"As the oldest continuing international organization in the world today," Rostow told a Boston College audience, "the Vatican has a well-deserved reputation for diplomatic expertise." He was referring to the Vatican's many contacts with foreign nations, its "benevolent neutrality," as well as its "unrivaled sources of information through church universities, schools, monasteries, convents, and other institutions." He was quick to point out that this expertise was nothing new: "It goes back to the civilizing mission of the Church in the Middle Ages."[24]

Rostow emphasized that the greatest influence the Church has had as a peacemaker has been through the dissemination of its "great ideas." He listed as examples "equality or the principle of self-determination," as well as "love." Rostow concluded his remarks by pointing to the Church's "remarkably balanced" vision of reality—appreciating heaven and hell and rendering unto Caesar the things of Caesar, all of which "prepare men for fortitude in the face of adversity and courage in the face of evil."

Megamurders

R. J. Rummel, a professor emeritus at the University of Hawaii at Manoa, has spent his professional career tracking what he calls democide, or what may also be dubbed as megamurder, that is, genocide, politicide, and mass murder. Genocide is the term used to describe the mass slaughter of a national, racial, political, or cultural group; Rummel more specifically uses the term to refer to the mass slaughter of Armenians and Jews. The killing of clergy, as well as "enemies of the people," counts as politicide; and mass murder is employed to describe the fate of religious and ethnic groups.

One of the conclusions Rummel came to in his exhaustive study of these related phenomena is that democracies almost never go to war against each other; they settle their disputes peacefully. This is not true of authoritarian regimes, or what are essentially political dictatorships, and it is even less true of totalitarian governments, regimes that are at once political, economic, social, and cultural dictatorships. Franco's Spain was authoritarian; he ruled absolutely but did not care what anyone believed about him, or anything else. Hitler's Germany, Stalin's Russia, and Mao's China were totalitarian in every sense of the word: the functionaries of these states were masters of thought control, leaving no aspect of life off-limits to the omnipresent state. In such regimes, the public sphere constitutes everything; there is no such thing as the private sphere, including even one's conscience.

It would be hard to think of any institution in history that is more diametrically opposed to totalitarianism than the Roman Catholic Church. The Catholic Church believes in faith and reason; the pursuit of truth; the human dignity of every man, woman, and child; a culture of life; natural rights and natural law. But under fascism and communism, these beliefs are not only disagreeable; they are dangerous. That explains why under these regimes anyone who entertains such ideas must die. History shows that there has never been a situation where a totalitarian regime has had anything but contempt for the Catholic Church, trying by every means possible, including murder, to shut it down. Horrendous though these deeds are, they offer, in a backhanded way, positive proof of the extreme incompatibility between Catholicism and totalitarianism.

If power corrupts and absolute power corrupts absolutely, as Lord Acton said, it is also true, as Rummel maintains, that "Power kills and absolute Power kills absolutely." He arrived at this conclusion by studying what has happened in history when governments have assumed too much power: the natural outcomes are deadly. Moreover, it matters not a whit what the ideology of the regime is: fascism and communism, as totalitarian expressions, have much in common. They are totalistic ideologies that reject human nature and nature's God, seeking to create a utopia on earth as part of their quest to create the "new man." They always fail because human nature is fixed, and human beings are not pieces of putty that can be refashioned at whim. Moreover, God the Almighty is a reality, something which atheists bent on total domination can never acknowledge. Interestingly, the word *utopia* means "nowhere"—an apt description of their futile attempts to create one.

Under Hitler an estimated 21 million people met their deaths, including most astoundingly 6 million Jews, who were murdered only because they were Jews. Under the Soviet Union, Rummel says 61 million people were killed; Stalin was responsible for killing 43 million of them. Under Mao, Rummel puts the number killed at 77 million. Proportionately, Pol Pot beat everyone: between April 1975 and December 1978, he killed 2 million Cambodians out of a population of 7 million.[25] It could have been worse. For instance, Mao told the Russians in 1957, "We are prepared to sacrifice 300 million Chinese for the victory of world revolution." He told his closest comrades, "Working like this, with all these projects, half of China may well have to die."[26] By contrast, he lived well: he had at least fifty villas and was immensely wealthy.

A common misunderstanding is that if the people of these countries had been properly educated, these regimes of megamurder wouldn't have been possible. Yet no nation in the world had better educated people than did Germany in the first half of the twentieth century, and they succumbed to Nazism. As Solzhenitsyn said, Stalin did not pervert Marxism—he perfected it. No matter, he was loved by legions of Western intellectuals. Unbelievable though it may sound, Mao is still revered; indeed, Christmas ornaments with his picture on them were displayed in the White House of the Obama administration in 2009 (no display of Hitler would ever be allowed). And Pol Pot and his most trusted advisors were all educated at the Sorbonne. What Hitler, Stalin, Mao, and Pol Pot had in common, besides having the blood of well over 150 million innocent men, women, and children on their hands, was atheism. As Pope Benedict XVI suggested at Regensburg, when reason is uncoupled from faith, disaster follows.

If education truly made people moral, lawyers would be moral exemplars. In the end, what matters is not education, per se, but deeply inculcated moral values. Moral education can be instructive, but as many in the clergy of all religions show, passing an academic test is no guarantee of moral behavior. A strong moral code, one that is internalized, is a necessary condition of acting morally, but unless a person acknowledges God as the author of universal norms, such a moral code is not likely to be of much utility. The Ten Commandments are a good starting point—indeed, they are a must—but unless they form a constitutive presence in defining who we are, they will not constructively direct our actions.

Benedict also spoke at Regensburg about those who kill innocents in the name of God, in other words, those who uncouple faith from reason. Waller R. Newell, a political scientist at Carleton University in Ottawa, Canada, has looked at today's Islamic terrorist organizations and finds commonalities with fascist and communist regimes. According to him they all seek to create the "new man," thereby rejecting the belief that only God can redeem the world. "Looking through the charters and pronouncements of groups like the PLO, the Taliban, and Hezbollah," Newell writes, "one discovers, never far beneath the pseudo-religious surface, the language of socialism (both national and international), the levelling of classes, and the eradication of individual liberty under a monolithic dictatorship."[27] Importantly, Newell adds, "[T]he jihadists, like their fascist and Bolshevik predecessors, cannot be considered true men of faith, because all three Abrahamic faiths deny that man can save the world through secular political action, much less through mass violence."[28]

The Roots of Totalitarianism

We will see shortly exactly what the Catholic Church has done to combat fascism and communism. But first we need to consider what made these megamurders possible. The bottom line is that fascism and communism triumphed precisely because these ideological schools of thought entertained a vision of man and society that was the polar opposite of what the Catholic Church teaches. In other words, what made Hitler, Stalin, Mao, and Pol Pot possible was the total rejection of Catholic thought and the total acceptance of a radical secular worldview.

In two of his encyclicals Pope John Paul II wrote that "if there is no ultimate truth to guide and direct political activity, then ideas and convictions can easily be manipulated for reasons of power."[29] Standing against this verity are many strands of thought that deny the existence of truth. For example, Darwin maintained that there was no such thing as a universal morality that was understood by men in every culture. He held that morality was a process and an accident of natural selection. Marx also believed that morality had no independent meaning, moral codes being nothing more than "phantoms formed in the human brain." No wonder he believed that truth was whatever serves the cause.

Unfortunately, those who believed his views and put them into operation aided and abetted mass murder.

Materialists such as Darwin and Marx are not inclined to look kindly on religion. Indeed, those who deny that truth exists are naturally prone to have a hostile view of religion, and they reserve a special hatred for Roman Catholicism. Nietzsche certainly did. He spent his adult life trashing the teachings of the Catholic Church, contending, "There are no truths, only interpretations." This kind of thinking was exactly what made it possible for megamurders to happen. Who is to say that purges are always wrong? Who is to say that sacrifices in the short term—including the sacrifice of innocent human lives—are not morally justifiable? Martin Heidegger also embraced Nietzschean relativism, a vision of man and society that was completely at odds with the Judeo-Christian ethos. Not surprisingly, he was a fan of Hitler. More recently, Jacques Derrida, the French philosopher, picked up where Heidegger left off, challenging the belief that there is a final external authority. Yet the rejection of moral absolutes inevitably leads to a state of cultural nihilism, the breeding ground for evil on a massive scale.

Derrida is the intellectual father of deconstruction, a school of thought that originated in France in the 1960s. He questioned the idea that there are inherent meanings, even to the point of challenging the belief that words mean what an author seeks to explain. In other words, there are no truths, the world being a fiction. His views achieved wide currency in the United States through the work of Paul de Man. Many intellectuals were shocked, although they should not have been, when it was revealed that de Man had been a Nazi collaborator in Belgium. If they understood the logical consequences of denying moral truths they wouldn't have been shocked. Just as another French secular radical, Jean-Jacques Rousseau, did, de Man abandoned his family. Why not? If nothing matters, what earthly difference does it make? De Man also borrowed money from his father to start a business, ran it into the ground, and then left his father destitute. That's what happens when people treat the idea of a moral compass as a fiction.

Those who reject religion, especially the tenets of Catholicism, still have a need to nourish themselves spiritually, even if they won't admit it. Typically they embark on a quest for wholeness. Believing that there is no such thing as human nature, they seek to construct a "new man." This may sound appealing on the face of things, but in reality it leads to extremism; it's a way of greasing the slide toward totalitarianism.

Paul Johnson, an English historian, has explained better than anyone what happens historically when moral relativism triumphs. Trotsky, he shows, paved the way for communism in Russia when he scoffed at the idea that moral criteria exist. "Moral relativism in monstrous incarnation"[30] is how Johnson describes Stalin's regime. Johnson points to another example of relativism, the "Marxist habit of thinking in terms of classes instead of individuals"[31]—it's like putting on blinders so you can't see personal human suffering. Hitler, Johnson says, "defined the virtues of the SS, the embodiment of Nazi 'morality,' as loyalty, honesty, obedience, hardness, decency, poverty, and bravery."[32] Mao, the greatest mass murderer of them all, succeeded, Johnson says, precisely because of the triumph of moral relativism. The essential problem with moral relativism, Johnson says, is that it eliminates "any fixed anchorage," allowing no check on evil. Every idea that springs from this atheistic philosophy is totally incompatible with everything the Catholic Church teaches.

To get an idea of how these pernicious ideas work, consider Albert Speer, Hitler's closest confidant. "If I had to draw one single lesson from the horror of World War Two," Speer said in 1971, "it would be not to depersonalize your enemy. Once this happens—whether it is a case of Nazi or Jew, Communist and capitalist, or black and white—the greatest crimes are not only feasible but inevitable." When asked specifically how he could carry out orders to kill millions of Jews, Speer confessed, "I did not hate them. I was indifferent to them." Yes, he said, "by depersonalizing them"[33] he was able to murder Jews with the same lack of conscience as a sociopath. Think of it this way: when we get angry at someone, we acknowledge his humanness, but if we think of humans the way we do ants on the street, we can walk on them—even stomp them to death—without remorse.

According to Herbert C. Kelman, who has studied how ordinary Germans were able to become mass murderers, there are three conditions that allow for this transformation: the violence is authorized; the actions are routinized; and the victims of violence are dehumanized. All three conditions represent a wholesale rejection of natural law, natural rights, and the inherent dignity that each of us possesses. In other words, only by rejecting Catholicism is totalitarianism possible.

Fascism

"It should never be said that Christians were responsible for the Holocaust—Nazis were. Blaming Christians would be as unjustified as holding Jews accountable for the death of Jesus. Individuals were responsible in both situations."[34] So true. Those are the words of Ed Koch, former mayor of New York City. Marc Saperstein, who is also Jewish, came to the same conclusion: "The fundamental responsibility for the Holocaust lies with the Nazi perpetrators. Not with Pope Pius XII. Not with the church. Not with the teachings of the Christian faith."[35] Regarding this last point, Professor Saperstein says, "Nazi texts provide no evidence that the antisemitism of Hitler or Himmler was informed by the Christian characterization of the Jews as Christ-killers, condemned by God because they refused to recognize the messiah." Nazi rhetoric, he makes plain, was drawn from "exacerbated nationalism" and "pseudo-scientific" racist theories.[36]

What Koch and Saperstein say is convincing. That it has to be said at all is disturbing, but there are those who continue to blame the Catholic Church for the Holocaust. Some have called Pope Pius XII "Hitler's Pope," and others have said that the Church "paved the way" for Hitler. But even the man who labeled Pius "Hitler's Pope" subsequently retracted his accusation, and those who want to blame the Church fail to distinguish between anti-Judaism, which is a theological animus, and anti-Semitism, which is hate based on ethnicity. Only the latter found a role in the Holocaust.

For almost two decades after World War II, the consensus

of scholars and statesmen was that no one did a better job of resisting the advances of Hitler than Pope Pius XII. Indeed, as we shall see, the pope was singled out for his heroics by almost everyone in the Jewish community, as well as those in other quarters. But everything changed after 1963. Astonishingly, there was no new evidence to cast doubt on the pope's courageous role, but there was a new play on Broadway.

The Deputy opened in Berlin and London in 1963 before opening on Broadway in 1964. The work of a Protestant left-wing German radical, Rolf Hochhuth, the play portrays the pope as a Nazi collaborator who did nothing to combat Hitler. Thus began the myth about the pope's "silence" on the Holocaust. Hochhuth was not well known, but he was part of an artistic trend called "Documentary Theatre" or "Theatre of Fact," a theatrical genre that was considered quite persuasive at the time. Although the play was fictional, Hochhuth said his depiction of Pope Pius XII as a coward was based on "provable facts." That not a single historian has ever remarked on the factual accuracy of this play tells us all we need to know about Hochhuth's "facts." No matter, although attitudes toward the pope did not change overnight, in time they would as people with their own agenda got on board.

Recent scholarship suggests that although Hochhuth probably acted on his own, he was used by people who had a vested interest in smearing the pope. Indeed, it now appears, as Professor Ronald Rychlak has discovered, that Hochhuth was an "unknowing dupe" of the KGB.[37]

In 2007 Ion Mihai Pacepa stated that in 1960 Soviet Premier Nikita Khrushchev approved a plan to discredit Pope Pius XII. Pacepa was in a position to know; he was a former

Romanian intelligence chief and the highest-ranking official ever to defect from the Soviet Bloc. The idea was for Pacepa's operatives to penetrate the Vatican Archives and to coordinate a disinformation campaign. To put it bluntly, the goal was to intentionally distort the truth about the pope. Three officials got access to documents, which they stole, but it was to no real effect—there was no dirt showing the pope had been some kind of weakling in Hitler's pocket. But the operation did give the spies an idea how the Vatican works, and in the end they accumulated ideological fodder that found its way into the script of *The Deputy*.

Hochhuth, of course, denies any KGB role. But former CIA director James Woolsey has testified to Pacepa's character, so it is likely, according to Rychlak, that Hochhuth was manipulated. Rychlak notes, "Hochhuth may not have knowingly cooperated with the Soviets, but he was the perfect candidate to be an unknowing dupe."[38] His was certainly not a first-class mind, and he was deeply involved in radical causes, having a special hatred of the Catholic Church. We also know that using the arts as a propaganda tool was vintage KGB. As far back as 1944 the Soviet organ *Izvestia* attacked the Vatican for being "pro-Fascist"—a charge that caused the *New York Times* to go ballistic *in defense of the pope*; four years later a fabricated report by M. M. Sheinmann for the Historical Institute of the Soviet Academy of Sciences in Moscow was released alleging a link between the Nazis and the Vatican. In other words, there are historical reasons to believe Pacepa's account.

Hochhuth's play, now long forgotten, nonetheless became the catalyst behind a wave of anti-Pius books. Three of the most vicious were written by an ex-priest and two ex-seminarians; one was written by a highly controversial historian. James Carroll and Garry Wills in the United States, along with England's John Cornwell, have all been exposed by Rabbi David Dalin as harboring an agenda: their real interest was not to smear Pius, but to discredit the Church's past so as to weaken its credibility in the present.[39] Similarly, Daniel Jonah Goldhagen's contribution has been skewered by Dalin, as well as by many others, because of Goldhagen's lack of accuracy.

The fact that all of these men call for radical changes in the Catholic Church regarding matters having nothing to do with the Holocaust shows their real agenda. But if the goal is to tarnish the Church's past so as to weaken the resolve of the hierarchy today, then perhaps in their minds it makes sense to smear Pope Pius XII as a tactic to demand Vatican III. Regarding Carroll, Wills, and Cornwell, Dalin writes that these "lapsed or angry liberal Catholics exploit the tragedy of the Jewish people during the Holocaust to foster their own political agenda of forcing changes on the Catholic Church."[40] As for Goldhagen, Dalin chastised him for "factual errors, historical misrepresentations, and suppression of overwhelming counterevidence to his argument."[41]

Some of Pius's critics fault him for not excommunicating Hitler. There are several misunderstandings here. Excommunication does not mean expulsion from the Church; it means the offender cannot receive the sacraments until he reconciles himself with the Church. But why should we believe that excommunication would have meant something to Hitler when he did not identify himself as a Catholic? If anything, he hated the Church. And as Rychlak points out, if James Carroll, an embittered ex-priest, admits that his own excommunication meant nothing to him, it is silly to think Hitler would have lost sleep over being excommunicated.[42] No matter, Hitler had long since excommunicated himself ipso facto. Moreover, it needs to be said that many of those who have been excommunicated did not receive notice in the overnight mail; they did it to themselves, as defined in the Church law *latae sententiae*, which is a penalty that automatically follows acts of a very serious moral nature.

Some have also criticized the pope for not excommunicating Catholics who were Nazis. "Theoretically," writes professor William D. Rubinstein, "and in hindsight, the Pope might have excommunicated all Catholic members of the SS (or of the Nazi Party) although the only likely effect of such a pronouncement would have been that the Nazis denounced the Pope as an agent of 'Judeo-Bolshevism' and an imposter."[43]

If Pope Pius XII was supposedly an accomplice of Hitler's, then why did the Nazi leader try to kidnap the pope? As soon as Italian dictator Benito Mussolini was forced out of power on July 25, 1943, Hitler began his plan to kidnap the "Jew-loving" pope; the minutes from a meeting that occurred the next day show this to be true. Moreover, Hitler discussed his plan of invading the Vatican with Ernst von Weizsäcker, the German ambassador to the Holy See. According to notes taken by the SS commander in Italy, Hitler said in September of 1943, "I want you and your troops to occupy Vatican City as soon as possible, secure its files and treasures, and take the pope and the curia to the north" (probably Liechtenstein).[44] One of the letters that made its way among SS leaders was titled "Massacre of Pius XII with the Entire Vatican." Dan

Kurzman, who authored a book on the plot to kidnap the pope, reveals the contents of an SS letter that settles the issue: the plot to kidnap the pope was hatched to avenge "the papal protest in favor of the Jews."[45]

The plot was known to the pope. In fact, Pius XII called a meeting of cardinals to choose a possible successor in the event that the scheme succeeded. Von Weizsacker, who befriended the pope, warned him that if he didn't keep quiet, Hitler would target the entire Vatican and go after the hundreds of thousands of Jews who were hidden in churches, convents, and with other Catholic institutions. But Hitler was also worried; if the pope did speak out, he might unleash an uprising. In the end, neither the kidnapping nor the revolt took place.

The Risks of Confrontation

Should Pope Pius XII have thrown down the gauntlet? Should he have directly confronted Hitler in public? Would that have shown what real fortitude is made of? Or would it have violated the test of prudence? The answer can be gleaned, in part, by considering how those in the Jewish community reacted at the time.

When Hitler took over Germany in 1933, he wasted no time showing his hatred for Jews. American Jewish leaders quickly got together to discuss public demonstrations against Hitler. Plans were made for an anti-Hitler parade in New York City on May 10, 1933. But then the American Jewish Committee and B'nai B'rith put out a joint statement condemning "public agitation in the form of mass demonstrations." They feared such actions would only "inflame" matters.[46]

In 1935 the Nuremberg race laws were enacted, effectively stripping Jews of all civil rights. American Jews, led by Rabbi Stephen Wise of the American Jewish Congress, worked against legislation that would have made it easier for Jews to emigrate to the United States from Germany. Similarly, on November 9–10, 1938, during what is known as Kristallnacht, the "Night of Broken Glass," American Jewish leaders counseled restraint, even though Hitler's storm troopers in Berlin had gone on a rampage killing Jews, entering their homes, destroying their businesses, and burning synagogues. Were the Jewish people in America wrong to reject a more "forceful" approach? No, not given the realities that existed at the time. All moral decisions must be judged in context.

Following Kristallnacht, the General Jewish Council met to discuss what to do. The American Jewish Congress, the American Jewish Committee, B'nai B'rith, and the Jewish Labor Committee debated how to reform immigration rules in order to alleviate the plight of German Jews. In the end, they said, "at least for the time being, nothing should be done with regard to this matter." In addition, all of these Jewish organizations went on record saying that "there should be no parades, demonstrations, or protests by Jews."[47] Even in 1942, after Gerhard Riegner of the World Jewish Congress notified his colleagues in London and New York of an "alarming report" about plans to exterminate Jews, Jewish organizations failed to lobby on behalf of a bill sponsored by Rep. Emanuel Celler that would have eased restrictions on Jews emigrating from France to the United States.

The *New York Times*, which is quick today to indict Pope Pius XII for not having done enough to condemn the Holocaust, chose a restrained approach during the Holocaust. For example, when in 1942 it reported that two million Jews had been killed in the Nazi extermination campaign, the newspaper placed the story on page ten surrounded by ads for Thanksgiving Day turkeys. The newspaper not only buried stories about what was happening; it ran only nine editorials criticizing the Nazis in the years 1941, 1942, and 1943 (three each year). Moreover, when the Nazis arrested a cousin of Arthur Sulzberger, the *Times* chief instructed his Berlin bureau chief to do "nothing." Sulzberger said he didn't want to antagonize the Nazis. The cousin, Louis Zinn, was so despondent that after he left prison he hanged himself.[48]

In hindsight, perhaps a more confrontational approach might have been a better choice. On the other hand, it might have made matters worse. We will never know. One thing is for sure: the Jewish leaders who implored the pope not to be confrontational—and there were many of them—cannot be faulted morally. They knew, as the pope knew, that the Nazis were monitoring his every word. Pope Pius XII said in June 1943: "Every word from Us in this regard to the competent authorities, every public allusion, should be seriously considered and weighed in the very interest of those who suffer so as not to make their position even more difficult and more intolerable than previously, even though inadvertently and unwillingly."[49]

Pope Pius XI

In order to appreciate the fortitude exercised by Eugenio Pacelli, Pope Pius XII, it is instructive to consider his predecessor, Pope Pius XI (r. 1922–39), and the role Pacelli played in serving him; as cardinal, Pacelli was Vatican secretary of state under Pius XI, starting in 1930. During his pontificate, Pius XI condemned racism as sinful and later condemned Charles Maurras's anti-Semitic political movement, Action Française. Pius XI's 1931 encyclical, *Non Abbiamo Bisogno* (We Need Not), was a statement against fascism. In September 1933, after Hitler came to power, the *Jewish Chronicle of London* praised the pope for his unyielding rejection of the Nazis' racial policies. Long before other religious and secular leaders had spoken up against Hitler, in 1933 the pope summoned Jewish leaders and intellectuals to the Vatican to express his outrage at what was already happening. In the same year, the pope signed a concordat, an agreement, between Germany and the Vatican. Critics of the agreement say that the pope essentially sold out to Hitler, but this interpretation cannot stand scrutiny.

Pius XI signed the concordat to protect German Catholics from persecution. Rabbi Dalin says that it was a protective measure; it was not an endorsement of Nazism.[50] The agreement, which essentially enabled the Church to continue to exist in Germany as long as it did not interfere with Hitler's regime, was violated by Hitler almost immediately. According to Zsolt Aradi, a Jewish writer who covered Pius XI, "the little freedom that the Concordat left for the clergy and hierarchy was widely used to save as many persecuted Jews as

could be saved."[51] In any event, the pope didn't have a whole
lot of options to choose from at the time. It is also important
to note that the pope never gave even tacit support to Hitler's
agenda.

Catholic writer Ralph McInerny counts at least thirty-four
letters of protest to the Nazis between 1933 and 1937.[52] They
culminated in the 1937 encyclical, *Mit Brennender Sorge* (*With
Burning Anxiety*), which not only condemned the Nazis' vio-
lations of the concordat; it took aim at their racial ideology.
The encyclical was written in the vernacular (rather than in
Latin), smuggled out of Italy, and distributed on Palm Sunday
to the faithful in Germany, all to the intense displeasure of
the Nazis; they charged that the pope was half-Jewish. Sister
Margherita Marchione, one of the most prolific chroniclers
of the Catholic Church's role during the Holocaust, explains
what happened: "No one who heard the pontifical document
read in the church had any illusion about the gravity of these
statements or their significance. Certainly the Nazis understood their importance. An internal German memorandum
dated March 23, 1937, called *Mit Brennender Sorge* 'almost a
call to do battle against the Reich government.' "[53]

Fortitude is the only word that accurately describes how
Pius XI responded to the Nazis' persecution of the Jews. Invoking natural law and inalienable rights, he condemned the
invidious racial policies and anti-Semitism of the Nazis. The
encyclical, which had been written by Pacelli, was roundly
attacked in the German newspapers, which wrote that it
was the product of the "Jew God and His deputy in Rome."
Some media outlets said that the encyclical "calls on Catholics to rebel against the authority of the Reich," a conclusion

that was entirely warranted. Priests in Germany quickly denounced Nazism, saying it was no better than Stalinism. The Nazis banned publication of the encyclical, but in defiance, German bishops had it reprinted and it was read from pulpits all over the nation.

Pius XI did not hold back his criticism of Mussolini either. In 1938 the pope announced, "The entire human race is but a single and universal race of men. There is no room for special races. We may therefore ask ourselves why Italy should have felt a disgraceful need to imitate Germany." Shortly thereafter he proclaimed that "Abraham is our Patriarch and forefather. Anti-Semitism is incompatible with the lofty thought which that fact expresses. It is a movement with which we Christians can have nothing to do. No, I say to you, it is impossible for a Christian to take part in anti-Semitism. It is inadmissible! Through Christ and in Christ we are the spiritual progeny of Abraham. Spiritually, we are all Semites."[54] Thus he made crystal clear the position of the Catholic Church.

Pope Pius XII

Long before Eugenio Pacelli became Pope Pius XII in 1939, he had a strong record of opposing anti-Semitism. In 1916, while working for Pope Benedict XV, he played a role in preparing a Vatican document that the *New York Times* reported on with the headline "Papal Bull Urges Equality for Jews." In 1923 Pacelli wrote to the Vatican Secretary of State denouncing Hitler's failed attempt to unseat the Munich government. When Pacelli became secretary of state in 1930, the first thing he did was to send a statement of protest to Germany against Nazi anti-Semitism. His abhorrence of anti-Semitism was so strong that while visiting the United States, he snubbed Father Charles Coughlin; the radio priest was widely seen as anti-Semitic. Rabbi Dalin writes that it was shortly thereafter that Coughlin was banished from the airwaves; he blamed Pacelli.[55]

While he was secretary of state, Pacelli issued fifty-five protests against the Nazis, and in 1938 he repeated the idea of Pius XI: "Anti-Semitism is inadmissible; spiritually we are all Semites." When Pacelli was installed as Pius XII, Jewish groups were elated, citing his role in writing *Mit Brennender Sorge*. But the Nazis were not cheering; they knew what they were in for. In fact, the day after his election, March 3, 1939, the Nazi newspaper *Berliner Morganpost* reported, "the election of Cardinal Pacelli is not accepted with favor in Germany because he was always opposed to Nazism."

In response to the first encyclical of Pope Pius XII, the *New York Times* summed up the substance of the document with the headline "Pope Condemns Dictators, Treaty Violators, Racism; Urges Restoring of Poland."[56] In *Summi Pontificatus* the pope condemns racism and totalitarianism, stressing the necessity of natural law principles. Heinrich Mueller, the head of the Gestapo, accurately understood that the encyclical was "directed exclusively against Germany,"[57] because even though the pope did not mention the Nazis by name— for fear of inflaming conditions for the Jews—everyone knew whom he was talking about. The pope was more explicit on Vatican Radio, where he denounced the Nazis.

In 1939 German bishops, following the pope's lead, published a pastoral letter that was so strong that the *New York Times* branded it "one of the sharpest attacks ever made by Catholics against Nazis."[58] Not surprisingly, the Nazis then seized Catholic presses and closed down their printing facilities. On March 14, 1940, under the headline "Jews' Rights Defended,"[59] the *Times* described what it dubbed the pope's "burning words" delivered to the German foreign minister, Joachim von Ribbentrop. Two months later the pope publicly condemned the Nazi invasions of Belgium, Holland, and Luxembourg. In its Christmas Day, 1941, editorial the *Times* wrote, "The voice of Pius XII is a lonely voice in the silence and darkness enveloping Europe this Christmas." Setting the record straight on Pius XII is important if for no other reason than that it shows how utterly baseless are the contemporary criticisms of Pius XII—including those published in the *New York Times*—accusing him of being silent about the treatment of Jews in Germany. He was the very one singled out for *not* being silent at the time!

In January 1942 Gestapo officials formalized plans for the "Final Solution." Two days later Vatican Radio lashed out at Nazi persecution of the Polish people. The Nazis responded by arresting and executing priests and teachers. It was this kind of scenario that weighed heavily on Pius XII: the bolder the Vatican's actions, the sharper the Nazi response. The situation was much the same elsewhere in Europe. Pius XII blasted the mass deportation of Jews from Nazi-occupied France, and the German bishops followed through by issuing a pastoral letter that was read from every Catholic pulpit warning of Hitler's plans to obliterate "every vestige of Christianity."[60]

The supreme test case of the consequences of publicly

condemning the Nazis came in June 1942, when the Vatican and the bishops in Holland picked up the tempo. Nowhere else in Europe was the Catholic Church more resistant to the Nazis, and nowhere were Hitler's henchmen more vicious in their retaliation. In fact, Holland was the only place where the Nazis began revoking the waiver they had given to Jews who had been baptized Catholics. Because of this new policy the Discalced Carmelite nun Edith Stein, a brave Jewish intellectual who had converted to Catholicism, was gassed at Auschwitz, along with her sister, who had recently converted to Catholicism.

Eighty percent of Holland's Jews were deported—the highest percentage of any nation in Europe—precisely because of the forceful Vatican response. Jewish writer Pinchas Lapide attributes the pope's reticent approach later on to what happened in Holland. Indeed, the Dutch experience convinced Pius XII to burn the draft of his own public condemnation. "If the protest of the Dutch Bishops has cost the lives of 40,000 people," he said, "my intervention would take at least 200,000 people to their deaths."[61] After the war many prominent rabbis testified that the pope's worst fears would likely have been realized.

On December 25, 1942, for the second consecutive year, the *Times* ran a Christmas Day editorial citing the magnificent work of Pope Pius XII. "No Christmas sermon reaches a larger congregation than the message Pope Pius XII addresses to a war-torn world at this season," the *Times* said. Not only that, but once again, the newspaper singled out the pope for *not* being silent: "This Christmas more than ever he is a lonely voice crying out of the silence of a continent." The *Times* even went so far as to say, "The Pulpit when he speaks is more than ever like the Rock on which the Church was founded, a tiny island lashed and surrounded by a sea of war." No other world leader, not even religious leaders, was praised this effusively by the *New York Times* for having the fortitude to stand up to Hitler.[62]

Yet the pope's bravery was not without a cost. By 1943 the Nazis had had it with him, and with the bishops. So when in July 1943 all the bishops signed a protest against the Nazis for their plan to extend the mandated wearing of the Star of David to the offspring of mixed marriages, the Nazis responded by seizing convents, hospitals, and other Catholic property throughout Germany. Catholic labor organizations were banned in Germany, and religious symbols were removed from the schools. In August 1943 the *New York Times* commented on the 1,200 German priests interned at Dachau: "The arrests are linked with strong anti-Nazi and anti-war movements in the predominantly Roman Catholic section of Germany."[63] At the end of the year the Vatican protested Mussolini's internment of Jews, which included Catholics of Jewish descent.

If Holland was the test case showing what happened when the Catholic Church stepped up its condemnation of Hitler, the rescuing of Jews in Italy shows what happened when the Church directly interceded. Nowhere did the Church have more leverage, and nowhere were the Church's efforts more spectacular. Had the Church failed to rescue Jews in Italy, critics of Pius XII would have something tangible to point to, but the fact is that his intercession proved heroic, and were it more widely known it would silence the charges of his critics.

When the Nazis occupied Rome, the pope made his way into the streets. Sister Margherita Marchione describes in vivid detail what happened next: "He stood in the midst of the terrorized people as buildings collapsed in piles of smoldering rubble, and bombs exploded on all sides. The Romans ran toward him for guidance and strength. With his hands and cassock smeared with the blood of the dead and the wounded, he blessed and consoled them, and took care of their immediate needs."[64] This was a compassionate thing to do, but the policies he carried out in the wake of the occupation mattered more. The pope immediately ordered all Vatican buildings, churches, convents, and monasteries opened as places of refuge for Jews. The result was historic: throughout Europe 65 percent of Jews were exterminated, but in Italy 85 percent of Jews were saved.

Sir Martin Gilbert, perhaps the foremost historian of the Holocaust, notes that Catholics were among the very first victims of the Nazis and that the Church responded by taking a tough stance against Hitler. About Pius XII's role, he says that "the test for Pacelli was when the Gestapo came to Rome in 1943 to round up Jews. And the Catholic Church, on his direct authority, immediately dispersed as many Jews as they could."[65] Historian William Rubinstein takes a wider view in evaluating the role of Pope Pius XII; he compares the Catholic Church's efforts overall to the Protestant response. "The dramatically higher survival rate for Jews in Central Europe brings us to the central question in evaluating Pius

XII and his response to the Holocaust," he writes. "Can it be that, with all its frustrations, inadequacies, and apparent failures, the policy of 'silence' pursued by Pacelli was actually the most effective possible, given Hitler's obsessive and overriding intention to kill every Jew in Europe?"[66]

In the spring of 1944 the Nazis moved to crush Hungary, and by the fall of that year they had taken control of Budapest. The Vatican chose to work diplomatically to save Jews, and the approach paid off. A Jewish scholar and an authority on Hungary, Jeno Levai, describes what happened: "Over 20,000 passports had been issued by the papal Nuncio—on the average of 500 a day." He added that "there was practically no Catholic Church institution in Budapest where persecuted Jews did not find refuge," the effect of which was that more than 100,000 Jews were rescued in Budapest and some 200,000 throughout Hungary.[67] No other religious denomination came even close in its efforts to save Jews.

Nazi Persecution of Catholics

When Hitler said he was going to "crush [the Catholic Church] like a toad,"[68] he meant it. Father Edward Krause says, "[I]t is not uncommon to ignore the fact that at least 8,000 priests or more than $1/3$ of the German Catholic clergy had come into open conflict with the Nazi regime. Over 500 were killed in the concentration camps or deported." The situation in Austria was also dire. Moreover, the Nazis infiltrated the Catholic Church,[69] seeking to monitor diocesan offices and the organizations run by religious orders and the laity. Heinrich

Himmler and Martin Borman were in charge of the espionage ring, and the operation, Krause says, "was clearly ordered to the eventual destruction of the Church." The Nazis feared priests like Jakob Gapp, a Marianist who refused to buckle under Nazi pressure. He was warned not to continue with his anti-Nazi sermons, but he refused and was murdered as a result. He was beatified in 1996.

Whole books could be written just on the meritorious actions taken by priests like Father Gapp, but the names of most would not mean much to historians today. But there is one priest whose name will forever be etched in the conscience of all those who study the Holocaust: the Franciscan father Maximilian Kolbe.

Father Kolbe was sent to Auschwitz because he had been sheltering refugees and Jews at his friary. No matter how severe the conditions at the camp, he led his fellow prisoners in prayer, reciting the Rosary, to the astonishment of the Nazis. Although he was suffering from tuberculosis and was very weak, he allowed others waiting in line for medical treatment to go ahead of him. His faith kept him going, an unshakable faith that made guards wonder what kind of man he was. Father Kolbe really stunned them when he made an incredibly potent Christian sacrifice: he offered his life in exchange for that of a man with a family. In German, he told the Nazi officer, "I would like to die in place of one of these men." When asked why he wanted to do this, he explained how he was old and sick and wanted to spare a man who had a wife and a family. His request was granted.

No Catholic nation suffered more under the Nazis than did Poland. Three million Catholics and three million Jews were killed in Poland under Hitler, and it is a source of some dismay, if not anger, on the part of Catholic survivors of the Holocaust that the deaths of so many Catholics are often ignored. No one doubts the Holocaust is of special significance to Jews—they were killed *because* they were Jews—but to deny a place to Catholics who died in the Holocaust is intellectually dishonest and a slap in the face to those Catholics who survived. Some, like Catholic survivor Bozenna Urbanowicz Gilbride, have written about their ordeal, but for many more there is no written legacy of their experiences.

Nazis hated priests almost as much as they hated Jews. Auschwitz was the most infamous death camp, but it was not alone. At Dachau, nearly three thousand clergymen were imprisoned, making it the largest "monastery" in the world; more than one thousand of them were murdered. Many nuns met their fate there as well. Not only do all these Catholics need to be remembered at Holocaust commemorations, their story needs to be taught in schools as well. This is not a matter of competing with the Jews—they were clearly punished with a single-minded determination by the Nazis—but it is a matter of truthfully acknowledging that millions of Catholics suffered and died under Hitler.

Pius XII Testimonials

Who knows history better than those who lived it? If the answer is obvious, it still needs to be said, if only because the critical comments made about Pope Pius XII—almost all of which have been made in recent times—conflict sharply with the testimony of the people who witnessed his efforts at the close of the war and shortly thereafter. And since there has been no new evidence that would cast doubt on his great efforts (the evidence, in fact, only buttresses his heroics), we can only conclude that ideology, not fact, is motivating the criticism. In any event, no amount of criticism can discount what was said about the pope's outreach during the Holocaust.

The contributions of Pope Pius XII were so substantial that as early as 1940 they were being heralded by people like Albert Einstein. "Only the Church stood squarely across the path of Hitler's campaign for suppressing the truth," he told *Time* magazine.[70] Three years later, *Time* did a cover story on the pope's efforts. "No matter what critics might say, it is scarcely deniable that the Church Apostolic through the encyclicals and other papal pronouncements, has been fighting against totalitarianism more knowingly, devoutly, and authoritatively, and for a longer time, than any other organized power," the story said. "Moreover," it continued, the Church "insists on the dignity of the individual whom God created, in his own image, and for a decade has vigorously protested against the cruel persecution of the Jews as a violation of God's Tabernacle."[71]

There is no question that the fortitude of Pope Pius XII was recognized at the time. In 1943 Hitler's biographer John Toland said, "The Church, under the Pope's guidance, had already saved the lives of more Jews than all other churches, religious institutions, and rescue organizations combined, and was presently hiding thousands of Jews in monasteries, convents, and Vatican City itself."[72] There is no question that the survival rates of Jews in Catholic countries were considerably higher than elsewhere in Europe. Sir Martin Gilbert writes, "In Italy, churchmen across the whole spectrum of Roman Catholicism, including leading Jesuits, saved Jews from deportation. Many hundreds of Polish priests and nuns are among the 5,000 Catholic Poles who have been recognized by the state of Israel for their courage in saving Jews."[73]

Those who were on the ground came to the same conclusion. Jan Hermann and Dr. Max Pereles, who spent time in a concentration camp during the horror, delivered a letter to the Vatican in 1944 praising what the pope had done: "While our brothers were hunted, imprisoned, and threatened to death in almost every country in Europe, because they belonged to the Jewish people, Your Holiness . . . fearlessly raised his universally respected voice, in the face of our powerful enemies, in order to defend openly our rights to the dignity of man."[74]

In 1943 the World Jewish Congress pleaded with the pope to persuade the Italian authorities to remove 20,000 Jewish refugees from internment camps in Northern Italy. The members of this distinguished world organization turned to the pope because, they said, "Our terror-stricken brethren look to Your Holiness as the only hope for saving them from persecution and death."[75] The officials were not disappointed, and thanked the pope profusely. Nor were officials from the National Jewish Welfare Board, who in 1944 wrote to the pope expressing their appreciation for protecting Jews during the German occupation of Italy.[76] Also appreciative was Chaim Weizmann, the future first president of Israel, who in 1943 wrote that "the Holy See is lending its powerful help wherever it can, to mitigate the fate of my persecuted co-religionists."[77]

As the war was winding down, the praises for the pope's

words and deeds were mounting. Perhaps the most moving statement came from Einstein. "Being a lover of freedom, when the Nazi revolution came in Germany, I looked to the universities to defend it, but the universities were immediately silenced. Then I looked to the great editors of the newspapers, but they, like the universities, were silenced in a few short weeks. . . . Only the Church stood squarely across the path of Hitler's campaign for suppressing the truth," he said. With breathtaking honesty, Einstein admitted that he had changed his mind about the Catholic Church. He said, "[N]ow I feel great affection and admiration." Indeed, he said that he was "forced to confess that what I once despised, I now praise unreservedly."[78]

Many leading Jews agreed with Einstein. Moshe Sharett, who would become Israel's second prime minister, thanked Pius XII in person, extending his gratitude to the entire Catholic Church. Paying tribute to what had been done "in the various countries to rescue Jews," Sharett concluded by saying, "We are deeply grateful to the Catholic Church."[79] In November 1943, Rabbi Isaac Herzog, the Chief Rabbi of Israel, sent a note to Msgr. Angelo Roncalli (the future Pope John XXIII), thanking him for "the invaluable help given by the Catholic Church to the Jewish people in its affliction."[80]

Similarly, Dr. Joseph Nathan, representing the Hebrew Commission, stated, "Above all, we acknowledge the Supreme Pontiff and the religious men and women who, executing the directives of the Holy Father, recognized the persecuted as their brothers and, with great abnegation, hastened to help them, disregarding the terrible dangers to which they were exposed."[81] At the end of the war, the World Jewish Congress was so appreciative of the pope's efforts to save Jews that it gave 20 million lire to the Vatican.

After Rome was liberated, the Chief Rabbi of Rome, Israele Anton Zolli, formally expressed the gratitude of Roman Jews "for all the moral and material aid the Vatican gave them during the Nazi occupation."[82] That was a nice gesture, but a more profound acknowledgment came one year later, in 1945, when Rabbi Zolli was received into the Catholic Church. He asked Pius XII to be his godfather and chose the name Eugenio as his baptismal name; it was the pope's given name. In his book, *Why I Became a Catholic*, Zolli said, "No hero in history has commanded such an army; none is more militant, more fought against, none more heroic than that conducted by Pius XII in the name of Christian Charity."[83] Zolli's wife also converted to Catholicism.

The tributes to Pope Pius XII did not end there. In 1955, when Italy celebrated the tenth anniversary of its liberation, the Union of Italian Jewish Communities made a major statement thanking the pope for what he had done; gold medals were given to priests and nuns for their heroics deeds. This was followed by an even more significant demonstration of appreciation: the Israeli Philharmonic Orchestra flew to Rome to perform Beethoven's Seventh Symphony at the Vatican's Consistory Hall. But when Pius XII died, in 1958, the Jewish community throughout the world pulled out all the stops.

Golda Meir, then Israel's foreign minister (she would later become prime minister), telegraphed the Vatican saying, "When fearful martyrdom came to our people in the decade of Nazi terror, the voice of the Pope was raised for the victims. The life of our times was enriched by a voice speaking out on the great moral truths above the tumult of daily conflict. We mourn a great servant of peace."[84] New York Philharmonic director Leonard Bernstein was so moved by news of the death of the pope that he tapped his baton for a moment of silence. Among the Jewish organizations that praised the pope were the following: the Anti-Defamation League, the Synagogue Council of America, the Rabbinical Council of America, the New York Board of Rabbis, the American Jewish Committee, the World Jewish Congress, the Central Conference of American Rabbis, and the National Council of Jewish Women.

The effusive response by the Jewish community was entirely warranted. Former Israeli diplomat Pinchas Lapide estimated that approximately 860,000 Jewish lives were saved by Pope Pius XII. No historian has ever claimed that any world leader, secular or religious, ever came even close to saving as many Jews as Pius XII did. Lapide makes an astounding comparison: "The Catholic Church saved more Jewish lives during the war than all the other churches, religious institutions, and rescue organizations put together. Its record stands in contrast to the achievements of the International Red Cross and the Western democracies."[85] In fact, it was proposed in the 1940s that 860,000 trees be planted in the hills of Judea, a just tribute to the pope.

Today Rabbi David Dalin, an expert on the Catholic Church's response to the Holocaust, says the time has come to proclaim Pope Pius XII a "righteous gentile." He writes that "it needs to be more widely recognized and appreciated that Pius XII was indeed a very 'righteous gentile,' a true friend of the Jewish people, who saved more Jewish lives than any other person, including Raoul Wallenberg and Oskar Schindler."[86] That day may yet come, and when all of the Vatican Archives are finally made available to the public, the chances of it happening will surely be enhanced.

Communism

Communism and Catholicism are diametrically opposed to each other; indeed they are so wholly irreconcilable that there is no room for the two of them on earth. Communism rejects natural law, natural rights, nature, and nature's God; Catholicism proudly embraces them all. Given the disposition of many intellectuals, it is not surprising that in the last century many of the most learned men and women in Europe and North America lined up on the side of communism. Intoxicated with Marxism, they defended Lenin and even justified the genocidal policies of Joseph Stalin. As history has shown, there has never been a shortage of people with PhDs ready to defend the most monstrous acts of oppression; the blood on their hands is incalculable.

There are still communist nations today; North Korea is home to the most enslaved people in the world. And although conditions have improved in China, human rights are still a very serious problem there. Catholic activist Harry Wu, who is on China's most wanted list, is trying hard to get the word out about a little known phenomenon, the Laogai, the

"Bamboo Gulag," a collection of labor camps in China where political prisoners continue to suffer. He was tortured and starved in one of these camps for nineteen years. The similarities to the Soviet Gulag are striking. "All churches and temples are government property," says Wu. "There is a religion of the state, which is communism. I was Catholic, and for this reason I was persecuted."[87]

Fortunately, communism does not play the role it once did in the world, and this happy circumstance is owing in no small way to the role played by the Catholic Church. To be specific, the story of Pope John Paul II's efforts to help bring down Soviet communism shows why Catholicism matters.

The first freedom, Solzhenitsyn once said, is freedom of conscience. This freedom is ineluctably tied to freedom of religion, and it has proven to be the greatest bulwark against totalitarianism the world has ever known. Lenin understood this, and that explains why he moved quickly to short-circuit the independence of the Catholic Church in the Soviet Union. By nationalizing the schools and seminaries, prohibiting churches from owning property, and registering religious leaders as "enemies of the people," Lenin effectively neutralized the rights of Catholics. The arrest of Archbishop John Cieplak of the Latin Catholic Mogilev archdiocese, and his assistant, Msgr. Constantine Budkiewicz, showed that Lenin meant to enforce penalties against those who engaged in anti-Soviet activities. The two churchmen were put on trial, along with other priests, and in 1923 they were sentenced to death. Although officials spared the archbishop, bowing to international pressure led by the Vatican, Budkiewicz was shot on Easter morning, thereby becoming the first Catholic martyr in Soviet history.

In the 1930s Stalin went on a rampage, ordering the killing of any suspected Catholic rebels. In large numbers Catholics and Jews were rounded up and sent to concentration camps. Robert Royal describes what Father Léopold Braun, an American priest stationed in Moscow, observed. By 1934, Royal writes, "the 3,300 Catholic churches and 2,000 chapels on Russian soil had been reduced to two active churches, primarily meant to serve foreigners and serve as a public demonstration that Catholicism existed in Soviet Russia despite claims of persecution."[88] Conditions quickly deteriorated in the late 1930s, when Stalin instituted the Great Terror. The genocide of the Ukrainians was the most grotesque expression of communism to date.

Religious oppression continued under Nikita Khrushchev, although the mass murders ceased. It wasn't until Mikhail Gorbachev came to power that the persecution of religious leaders ended. To be sure, Soviet communism was still a formidable force for evil, but there were signs that its influence was waning. The threat to Soviet dominance was not taking place at home; it was in Poland, a Soviet satellite, where the cracks in the Soviet empire became most visible.

Pope John Paul II

Two weeks before Christmas in 1970, workers at the Gdańsk Lenin Shipyards went on strike. The strikes quickly spread to other Polish cities. As Catholic scholar George Weigel said, the central problem was not inept communist leadership; "the problem was that the system was economically insane."[89] But the Polish people were enduring more than economic havoc. John O'Sullivan describes the conditions of Polish Catholics at the time:

> Priests were taxed excessively, and often followed and beaten up; students were denied admission to universities if their parents were churchgoers; permits for the building of churches were withheld when new towns were developed; the state abolished old religious holidays and invented ersatz national ones; and there was a constant ideological campaign of lies in the media designed to weaken religion and reduce it to an expression of patriotic nostalgia.[90]

Against this backdrop of oppression some resistance developed. With dogged determination, Karol Cardinal Wojtyla, archbishop of Kraków, dug in his heels and challenged the communist regime head-on. He was not only a Polish leader; he also led his fellow bishops around the world to understand what communism was doing to society. At that time, some bishops were enthralled with hope of "liberation theology" and did not appreciate how Marxist ideology corrupts. Wojtyla saw clearly what was happening and unleashed what Weigel calls "cultural resistance" to communism. He avoided a direct political response and instead mobilized those who worked in the universities, church groups, and the theater, as well as those who wrote for magazines, to enter the debate on the good society. Although the appeal was made at the level of culture, its political implications were evident.

"During the 1970s," writes Weigel, "as the credibility of the Polish communist regime waned, the stature of the Church continued to wax."[91] More than 90 percent of the population of Poland was Catholic, and there were thousands of seminarians and 21,000 catechetical centers. Stoking the fires of the cultural resistance was a Catholic newspaper based in Kraków, *Tygodnik Powszechny* (Universal Weekly), which reported on what was really happening. Although attempts were made to censor the news, *Tygodnik Powszechny* succeeded in linking Catholic and non-Catholic intellectuals in a way that ultimately proved fateful for the communist regime. So when workers went on strike again in the late 1970s and priests disappeared from public life, important social networks were already in place.

The scene was set for a showdown when Karol Wojtyla was elected Bishop of Rome in 1978. Pope John Paul II's ascension to the Chair of Peter was not overlooked by the KGB. Yuri Andropov warned the Soviet Politburo that the Holy Father was nothing but trouble, citing his role in fomenting dissension in Poland. Andrei Gromyko, the Soviet foreign minister, wasn't overjoyed either, and paid a personal visit to the pope at the Vatican in January 1979. When the two met, the pope did what he always did: he broached the subject of religious liberty. It was precisely the pope's statements on religious liberty that had prompted Gromyko to meet with the pope in the first place, so when the Soviet foreign minister heard John Paul II mention the lack of such rights in the Soviet Union, he was not surprised, but he was not exactly happy. One person who was happy with the election of the new pope was

Solzhenitsyn: "It's a miracle! It's going to change the face of the world!" he said.[92] In time, events would validate the prediction of the famous Russian civil rights activist.

If unhappiness is an accurate description of how Gromyko felt after meeting with John Paul II, trembling better describes what all the Soviet officials would soon experience. When in June 1979 Pope John Paul II visited his homeland, he set in motion a series of events that eventually led to the collapse of Soviet communism and the liberation of the Soviet Union's satellite states. Even before he arrived, Soviet ruler Leonid Brezhnev warned Polish leaders that the pope would "only cause trouble."

The pope did not shy away from confronting the communist menace on his visit to Poland; he was fortitude personified. He stood up to the communist leaders by speaking openly and forcefully about the need for human rights. In particular, he spoke of the need not to exclude Christ, an idea that resonated with the exuberant crowd. He also took a direct shot at Marxism, comparing it unfavorably to Christianity. The human being, John Paul II said, does not derive his worth by measuring his role in the means of production; rather men and women are valued because they are made in the image of Christ and possess a dignity that cannot be violated. Over the course of the nine days he spent in his native homeland, his words proved to be music to the ears of the 13 million Poles who heard him speak in person—fully one-third of the nation—not counting the millions more who watched him on TV. No wonder one Polish political scientist labeled the pope's trip a "psychological earthquake."[93]

What caused the "psychological earthquake" was neatly

understood by Bronisław Geremek, a former Solidarity activist and a former foreign minister of Poland. "When the pope came in 1979, he brought a very simple message," Geremek said. "He said, 'Don't be afraid.' "[94] That message was not lost on either the Polish people or the KGB, accounting for the former's resilience and the latter's fears. The pope's every word, we have since learned, was under scrutiny by Soviet intelligence agents. But nothing could stop the Holy Father. In October 1979 he repeated his demand for religious liberty and human rights before the United Nations. He even excoriated those who stood in the way of educating children freely, a reference to Soviet policies. Daniel Patrick Moynihan, the U.S. ambassador to the UN, said that the Soviet delegates "knew exactly what [the pope] was talking about and, for once in that chamber, looked fearful rather than bored."[95]

The pope's 1979 trip to Poland bore its most productive fruit fourteen months later, in the summer of 1980. That was when the Gdańsk shipyard strike took place, the unraveling of which led to the ultimate collapse of the Soviet regime in Poland. A quarter century later, Soviet expert and diplomat Zbigniew Brzezinski recalled that "the strikers, fearing that they would be crushed in the first few days by police, hung out by their fence the Polish flag and a picture of the pope. He was, in a sense, a spiritual umbrella for what they were doing. And, probably, in a mysterious way, a source of their reassurance."[96] Solidarity, the movement that was formed at this time, proved to be the most powerful force combating communism. The great irony of having a workers' strike take place in an alleged workers' paradise, as lionized by Marxism, was not lost on Lech Wałęsa, a union leader who had a special affection for Pope John Paul II.

The workers had many grievances, among them the inflated prices for meat. But they also pressed for political rights. What disturbed the communists more than anything was the obvious role that Catholicism was playing in the protests. It was one thing to witness the strike in August 1980, quite another to witness the first public Mass that month; thousands of workers and their families attended. The pope stoked the fires of freedom even more when he spoke on Vatican Radio in defense of the strikers. The government knew it was up against a force larger than life, and on the last day of the month it yielded to the workers' demands and allowed the formation of independent unions. As Weigel notes, "The Solidarity movement had been born."[97]

By the end of the year, the Soviets had had enough and were planning an invasion of Poland. The troops were assembled and a two-day occupation had been mapped out, but in the end there was no invasion. The pope had written to Brezhnev warning against what he labeled "the preoccupation of Europe," stating that such a move would violate détente. Although the pope's missive carried weight, what mattered most to the Soviets was the growing power of Solidarity; because it was a force to be reckoned with, Brezhnev counseled restraint. A month later, Solidarity leaders met with the pope at the Vatican. The Holy Father not only pledged his support, he went further; at Mass, during his homily, he spoke of the "great cause" of freedom that Solidarity represented.

The Soviets wanted the pope dead. They almost succeeded. On May 13, 1981, Mehmet Ali Agca, a Turk, shot and almost killed John Paul II. Although there was speculation at the time that the Soviets were behind this attempted assassination, not all the evidence was collected until 2006. Then an Italian parliamentary commission concluded "beyond any reasonable doubt" that Soviet officials "took the initiative to eliminate the pope Karol Wojtyla."[98] It was the Soviet military intelligence, not the KGB, that was behind the plot.

Solidarity's role in challenging communism, and the central role played by John Paul II, prompted the Soviets to seek to kill the Holy Father. Not only did Agca fail to do the job, but the attempted assassination only emboldened the Polish people. *Newsweek* correspondent Andrew Nagorski described what he saw in Poland during the summer of 1981: "The free trade union had been operating openly for a full year, and the country was flooded with the dissident labor unions' banners, pins, stickers, and other mementos, including those that celebrated the pride of Poland, Pope John Paul II."[99] By the end of the year, the pope was saying it was lights out for communism. "In Rome," writes John O'Sullivan, "the pope told a delegation of Polish intellectuals associated with Solidarity that Communism was ultimately finished."[100]

In 1982 John Paul II met with President Ronald Reagan; it was the beginning of a historic friendship. As O'Sullivan points out, many of Reagan's top advisors were Catholic: William Casey, Richard Allen, Alexander Haig, Zbigniew Brzezinski, Vernon Walters, and Judge William Clark. Not surprisingly, they all saw eye-to-eye on the ambitions of the Soviets. It helped the president to have such a distinguished group of Catholics to draw on, and it made communication with the Holy See easier: Walters, Casey, Allen, and Clark had cultivated their contacts with Philadelphia archbishop Cardinal John Krol and Pio Laghi, the pope's representative in Washington. The pope, President Reagan, and England's prime minister, Margaret Thatcher, would all come together to defeat the Soviet Union.

The Soviets may have given up trying to kill John Paul II, just as Hitler had given up in his plans to assassinate Pius XII, but they did not give up their intention to rid the empire of what they considered Catholic troublemakers. In October 1984 a thirty-seven-year-old priest, Father Jerzy Popiełuszko, the former chaplain of Solidarity, was bound, beaten, and tortured to death and then thrown into the Vistula River. He had been arrested and harassed by the police for years. His crime? Speaking out for human rights. The former chaplain to Solidarity had long stood up to the communist regime, helping families of persecuted and imprisoned workers. Some 400,000 attended his funeral, sending more shockwaves through the corridors of the Kremlin. In December 2009 Pope Benedict XVI declared Popieluszko a martyr, opening the road to his beatification (the procedures had begun in 1997). On June 6, 2010, more than 100,000 Poles gathered in Warsaw for his beatification. Like other martyrs, the rebel priest was imbued with the virtue of fortitude. He once said, "[I]f we must die suddenly, it is surely better to meet death defending a worthwhile cause than sitting back and letting injustice win."[101]

By the end of the 1980s, the Soviet Union was unraveling at a blistering pace, thanks to Mikhail Gorbachev, the ruler who took over in 1985. When John Paul II met with Gorbachev in December 1989, the pope was impressed with Gorbachev's evident honesty. The pope was less impressed with the KGB.

Eric Margolis, a Canadian, was the first Western journalist inside the KGB headquarters in 1990. "The generals told me that the Vatican and the Pope above all was regarded as their number one, most dangerous enemy in the world," he said.[102]

Gorbachev was half realist, half idealist. He knew that the communist system was flawed, but he still thought he could fix it. In the end it proved to be an impossible task; the ideology the system was built on was corrupt from top to bottom. In 1991 Gorbachev presided over the death of the USSR: the Soviet empire finally collapsed of its own weight, with not just a little push from Pope John Paul II. Years later Gorbachev admitted that the Iron Curtain fell because of the Holy Father. "It would have been impossible without the pope,"[103] he said. And it had all begun in June 1979. Polish general Wojciech Jaruzelski called the pope's first trip to Poland "the detonator." George Weigel commented, "The Nine Days of John Paul II were the trigger for all the rest. And, of course: no John Paul II, no Nine Days."[104]

It is shameful that the textbooks assigned to most American students do not give credit to the role that Pope Pius XII played in saving Jews during the Holocaust, and to the pivotal role that Pope John Paul II played in the collapse of communism in Europe. But given the secular bent of the people who write and select these books, it is difficult to get an unbiased account. The evidence, however, is there for everyone to see, and no amount of ideological myopia can ultimately stop the truth from being told. Catholicism matters for many reasons, among them because of the exercise of fortitude that its martyrs and leaders have shown. The world is freer as a result, and that is no small matter in the annals of history.

TEMPERANCE

T HE exercise of the virtues of prudence, justice, and fortitude take for granted certain characterological traits, many of which are found in the virtue of temperance. One way to appreciate this is to consider the social impact of abandoning constraint altogether, as in the legalization of drugs, prostitution, and pornography. Social constraint, as well as chastity, merit reconsideration; that is why we need to take a fresh look at the reasoning behind the Catholic Church's teachings on sexuality. Its teachings matter not simply for Catholics, but for all of those who want to live in the good society. How we govern ourselves matters greatly.

The sexual revolution did not spring from a social vacuum, and its consequences went way beyond its most obvious victims; this is a topic that deserves an honest discussion. Discarding old truths may be popular these days, but doing so exacts a hefty price. To be sure, individual rights are important, but so are social institutions. When marriage and the family are treated in a cavalier fashion, no one wins, including those who see society as nothing more than an arena for the distribution of rights. In short, there are many social and cultural challenges ahead, but without the strong public voice of the Catholic Church—its wisdom in this area is unparalleled—society will be all the poorer.

Temperance and the Good Society

The fourth cardinal virtue, temperance, is as important to the makings of the good society as are the other three. Prudence, the chief cardinal virtue, affects every moral decision, playing a central role in decisions affecting liberty. The good society cannot exist without the sincere pursuit of justice, especially as applied to the poor and dispossessed. Without fortitude, the fight for freedom and justice cannot be won, and at the very least this means a commitment to fighting totalitarianism. Temperance is important because without it individuals self-destruct, and so may society.

It is fashionable in some circles to sneer at anyone who makes a plea for temperance. But temperance, properly understood, is not a call for repression; it is a call for moderation, the absence of which is excess. And excess is no friend to the individual, or society. For instance, food is a necessity, and eating is one of life's more pleasurable experiences. Eating in excess, however, may result in obesity. The contrary is also true: excessive weight watching may abet anorexia. Both obesity and anorexia are serious disorders because they violate the norm of moderation. The moderate use of alcohol brings pleasure, but in excess it is disordered. The sexual act, the function of which is the propagation of the species, was meant to be enjoyed as well, but not randomly: context and purpose matter (e.g., marital relations for the begetting of children). Moreover, sexual excess, promiscuity, is also problematic. It is not for nothing, then, that abstinence, chastity, and modesty are known as the three subordinate virtues of temperance.

It is hard to think of any healthy human act, from exercising to sleeping, that cannot be corrupted when carried to extremes. The same is true about the quest for material gain. There is nothing wrong with wanting to enjoy a comfortable lifestyle, but there is something seriously wrong when that end becomes consuming. Money is not the source of all evil, but its exclusive pursuit is positively unhealthy. That's why greed is a sin and charity is a virtue. Similarly, self-restraint is a check on lust; temperance is a brake on gluttony; diligence conquers sloth; patience contravenes anger; kindness is the antidote to envy; and humility disables pride. Human nature may incline us to give in to the temptations of the cardinal sins, but the seven virtues that counter the attraction to sin are also accessible to us. Catholicism matters because without its influence, it is easier for sin to trump virtue.

If temperance were only an endearing individual attribute, it might not loom large. But it is much more than that; it is a vital ingredient in the building of the good society. As we have seen, when society makes good on the Catholic value of "focusing on the other," everyone wins. Those who give of themselves typically feel rewarded, and those who are served typically feel grateful. But giving does not come easy; taking does. For many reasons, these days many more individuals find it harder to give of themselves than before. The prevailing weltanschauung prizes self-indulgence, and that is not a quality linked to giving. But self-denial is; indeed, it is critical to charity. Those who are willing and able to deny themselves are best prepared to "focus on the other," giving freely of themselves so that others may benefit. Fortunately, Catholicism has always had a special predilection for self-denial (and not just during Lent). Unfortunately, society has chosen not to adopt it.

Temperance and Liberty

The link between temperance and helping others, as well as between temperance and healthy living, makes a strong argument for nurturing more of it. But temperance fulfills another function, one that is perhaps less obvious, and that is the promotion of liberty. Temperance matters because without it self-government is not possible, and if self-government cannot be accomplished, then the prospects of living in a free and democratic society are doomed.

Here's how it works. A free society is one that keeps government in check; the more intrusive government becomes, the more despotic it is likely to be. A free society, like all societies, must have some degree of order, without which anarchy reigns. Anarchy, however, is never permanent; its subjects quickly demand order, and a lot of it. Which brings us back to despotism. So the only way to ensure order and to allow for liberty is for people to police themselves. Otherwise the police will do the job for them.

Temperance, then, enables self-government because it nurtures self-governing individuals. Not only is temperance not inimical to liberty, it is freedom's best friend. This is a tough sell, admittedly, and that is because we have been taught to see temperance as an intrusion on our liberty. It is this skewed view of freedom—one that interprets liberty as license—that is responsible for so many of our psychological and social disorders. It is about as far from the Catholic perspective as possible. Catholicism teaches the primacy of virtue, the necessity of restraint, the importance of boundaries, and the need for limits. In short, it values temperance.

It is not a good sign that the Western nations where freedom developed are resistant to the idea that temperance facilitates liberty. Intoxicated with secularism, and with grandiose notions of the advantages of the unencumbered self, these nations are experiencing unprecedented social problems, ranging from out-of-wedlock births to venereal diseases. That most of these problems can be checked by harnessing the passions, that temperance could be promoted with the kind of social support currently afforded to self-indulgence, cannot be logically rebutted. But it requires more than fortitude to say so publicly; it requires an admission that the near wholesale rejection of Western civilization's Christian heritage has resulted not in freedom but in moral destitution. That's a tall order given that so many members of the cultural elite have an ideological investment in the status quo.

Imagine the elites being asked to respond to Jesus's call: "Come, follow me." Imagine further their being asked to explain why they think Pope John Paul II called this plea "the greatest exaltation of freedom." They wouldn't know what to say. Nor would they know how to respond to what the Catholic Catechism says on the subject of freedom. In a section labeled "Threats to Freedom," we learn that "[t]he exercise of freedom does not imply a right to say or do everything. It is false to maintain that man, 'the subject of this freedom,' is 'an individual who is fully self-sufficient and whose finality is the satisfaction of his own interests in the enjoyment of earthly goods.'"

It doesn't get more countercultural than this. But think about it. How does one man's liberty to say and do anything he wants add to the fund of freedom? If this were true, then it would mean that the cause of freedom benefits by tolerating the right of any individual to advocate, and practice, such things as slavery and genocide. Now if it seems plain that this is going too far, then it must be admitted that a line must be drawn—limitations on speech and behavior must be acknowledged—if liberty is to reign. This is a good start, but it is hardly sufficient. Other laws are also required, but the heavy reliance on legal prohibitions is itself a problem. Would it not be preferable for individuals to police themselves? And if this is true, doesn't this path commit us to valuing temperance? So why do we trash it?

Pope John Paul II did not refrain from making moral statements that challenged conventional wisdom. In his magnificent encyclical *Veritatas Splendor,* the most important exposition on the connection between morality and liberty in modern times, he boldly proclaimed that the Ten Commandments were the foundation of freedom. But how could a series of "Thou Shalt Nots" have anything to do with liberty? Aren't these prescriptions for repression?

To see the logic in John Paul's reasoning, consider the subtext of the Ten Commandments: to command against doing something suggests that the acts being proscribed are morally wrong yet tempting. For example, there are occasions when we may be tempted to dishonor our parents, although it is morally wrong to do so. Similarly, murder cannot be justified, nor can adultery, stealing, defamation, and envy. We are commanded not to do these things precisely because, left to our own passions, unguided by reason, we may choose to do so. And that would be tragic not only for us, but for others. Put differently, no society that hopes to achieve a modicum of liberty can survive if what the Ten Commandments enjoins becomes commonplace. The link between temperance and freedom, then, should be clear: temperance facilitates the ability to internalize the Ten Commandments, thus paving the way for freedom and the establishment of the good society.

The Founders valued the virtue of temperance and counseled against the vice of intemperance. In Federalist No. 63, we learn from Madison that "liberty may be endangered by the abuses of liberty as well as by the abuses of power."[1] Almost everyone understands that power can abuse liberty, but it is not well understood how an excess of liberty weakens the cause of freedom. It does so by eviscerating temperance. President Washington understood this, which is why he took the occasion of his Farewell Address to speak to the indissoluble link between religion and freedom.[2] Similarly, John Adams warned that the Constitution was made "only for a moral and religious people."[3] The Founders got it. They knew that besides such important criteria as representative government, a separation of powers, a federalist system, and a Bill of Rights, the citizenry must be willing to practice self-control and self-reliance. In other words, a rule of law is a necessary condition of liberty, but it is not sufficient.

"Despotism may be able to do without faith," wrote Tocqueville, "but freedom cannot."[4] Tocqueville, a French Catholic who recorded his observations about America in the first half of the nineteenth century, wrote eloquently about the need of a free people to respect the mores, or unwritten laws of society, a process facilitated by religious faith. Even someone touted as a pure libertarian, John Stuart Mill, while always defending the rights of the individual, counseled the need to nurture virtue; he might not have considered virtue as being as important as Aristotle did, but he was not neglectful of its role. The Founders, relying on the wisdom of Christianity, embraced the practice of virtue as being central to citizenship.

But the nurturance of virtue is difficult these days, to say the least. Unfortunately, one of the negative side effects of affluence is radical individualism, and in such circumstances it is difficult to sow the seeds of virtue. Self-indulgence, not self-control, has become the norm.

In 1978, when Solzhenitsyn gave the commencement address at Harvard University, the faculty and students expected to hear him speak critically about Soviet communism based on his experiences. Instead he spoke critically about his experiences in America. "I have spent all my life under a Communist regime and I will tell you that a society without any objective legal scale is a terrible one indeed," he said. "But a society with no other scale but the legal one is also less than worthy of man."[5]

What bothered Solzhenitsyn was the way freedom was being interpreted in America; the reckless abandonment of temperance, he warned, was ubiquitous. Indeed, he said, "Voluntary self-restraint is almost unheard of." We are so wrapped up in the exercise of our rights, he counseled, that "[i]t is time, in the West, to uphold not so much human rights as human obligations." What this great freedom fighter decried the most was the "total emancipation" of our Christian heritage, and its replacement with a monistic fixation on radical autonomy; he called this condition *anthropocentricity*, a situation wherein man is seen "as the center of all."[6]

The condition that Solzhenitsyn described has only worsened; radical autonomy is the defining element of contemporary Western societies. It is not only deeply embedded in the culture; it is deeply infused in law as well. The communitarian vision of law and society that was a staple of Western nations has largely been upended by a highly individualistic, indeed atomistic, conception of reality. In this view, social solidarity typically loses in a confrontation with the rights of the individual. Worse, even pleas to balance the rights of the individual with the need for civility and community are seen as repressive. This could not be more diametrically opposed to the Catholic perspective, which is grounded in individual responsibilities, self-restraint, and a "focus on the other."

The anthropocentricity that Solzhenitsyn saw as characteristic of Western societies was nowhere defined in law more distinctly than in the U.S. Supreme Court's ruling in *Planned Parenthood v. Casey*. In 1992 the high court ruled, "At the heart of liberty is the right to define one's own concept of existence, of meaning, of the universe, and of the mystery of life."[7] This is the most asocial interpretation of freedom ever promulgated. There is no role for God, the Creator of the universe, nor for natural law. Indeed, what this concept promotes cannot honestly speaking be regarded as a society: this is a vision of a world where unhinged individuals go about their business creating and re-creating their world, without any collective end. Radical autonomy has never been more radically defined.

Standing against the anthropocentric view is the Catholic tradition of counseling the virtue of temperance. Although these days, sadly, temperance has taken on a negative connotation, it is the only virtue that can stem the corrosion of the social bond. More than that, its prudential application yields liberty, not oppression. Take, for example, what happens to the individual and society when temperance is considered irrelevant to the discussion of law and order.

Victimless Crimes

According to the tenets of *Planned Parenthood v. Casey*, people should be free to define existence any way they see fit. If they engage in behavior that others find immoral, so be it, just as long as the rights of others are not directly impacted. So-called victimless crimes figure prominently here because they involve behaviors that arguably affect no one but the actors themselves, yet these behaviors are criminalized under law. They include such crimes as gambling, drug use, prostitution, and pornography; homosexuality was once included, but the sodomy statutes have either been repealed or have gone unenforced throughout the Western world.

The case for the legalization of victimless crimes runs against the grain of Catholic thought. For example, the Church teaches that society has a legitimate interest in curbing self-destructive behavior. From this perspective, any behavior that erodes the practice of temperance necessarily undermines the requisites for freedom, thus undercutting as well the building of the good society. Tolerating such behaviors, as would happen if legislation for legalization were passed, is seen in Catholic thought as fundamentally mistaken.

Pope Benedict XVI, in particular, has spoken out against drugs, alcohol, pornography, and what he calls the "deceptive illusions of happiness." Sure, getting high allows us to jump outside our world, but what goes up must come down, and for many the ride down ends in a crash. The pope is interested in seeing liberty, reason, and the pursuit of truth inextricably linked; when the link is broken, serious problems *ensue*.

Some teachers who came before Benedict took a harder line in addressing the moral challenges of modern society. Archbishop Fulton J. Sheen, for one, offered an uncompromising essay in 1931, "A Plea for Intolerance." He pulled no punches: "America, it is said, is suffering from intolerance. It is not. It is suffering from tolerance: tolerance of right and wrong, truth and error, virtue and evil, Christ and chaos. Our country is not nearly so overrun with the bigoted as it is overrun with the broad-minded."[8] Sheen wrote this essay before the postmodern assault on truth became fashionable, yet even at that time his opinions were considered controversial. Today they would be branded as heresy in many secular quarters.

Narcotics

Let's apply these unconventional views to narcotics. Those who fancy themselves broad-minded instruct us to be nonjudgmental about those who partake in drug use. Never mind that those who hail the virtue of nonjudgmentalism are themselves making a judgment, what matters is whether drug use enhances or impairs the making of the good society. If the good society is defined as one in which the rights of the individual are paramount, making all other competing interests subordinate, then, yes, the case for legalization should proceed. But if the good society is defined as one in which rights and responsibilities must coexist, then it is difficult to understand how legalizing narcotics could expand our capacity to act responsibly. Quite the contrary: drug use undermines individual responsibility by celebrating intemperance.

Should the state have an interest in protecting people from themselves? If it has too much interest, the result is intrusive government that destroys individual choice. This seems easy to understand. Less easy to grasp, perhaps, is what happens if the state has no interest in whether its citizens self-destruct. At some point it must be asked whether there is any social condition in which it might be appropriate for the state to act. For example, if self-destructive behavior becomes widespread, should the state still sit on the sidelines? To be exact, those who make the case for the legalization of drugs need to explain why the good society is best served by having the government adopt a laissez-faire policy. Their reply—the government should not intrude on private decision making when what people choose to do has no effect on the rights of others—assumes too much about both the drug user and those with whom he or she interacts.

It is indisputable that drugs disorient the faculties of the people who use them. Depending on the quantity and quality of the substance, the disorientation may be extensive, and the consequences may be severe. Prolonged drug use can disable the drug user to such an extent that he can no longer contribute to his own well-being, never mind the well-being of others. Should the government be in the business of legalizing substances that promote self-destructive behavior? The refrain that alcohol is legal is of little utility; the decision to decriminalize booze after Prohibition did not commit society to legalizing every mind-altering substance. For prudential reasons, society may tolerate limited outlets for alcohol and gambling. It is equally prudent not to take a passive view of intemperate behaviors.

No society that prizes liberty will survive if too many of its members treat temperance as a nuisance. In other words, if enough members of society become drug addicts, their intemperate behavior will necessarily affect the well-being of everyone else. There can be a legitimate debate about when the tipping point is reached, that is, the point where individual self-destruction becomes a social liability, but there can be no serious debate about whether it can occur. The tipping point may be when 15 percent of society uses drugs regularly; or it may be at 20 percent. Whatever the point is, at some level it will be generally recognized that societal destruction follows self-destruction. The problem is that the awareness may come too late for it to matter.

There are other problems, as well. No government is ever going to allow unlimited quantities of drugs to be sold. Furthermore, no government is ever going to legalize every conceivable drug. Thus there is no way to stop an underground economy from developing to provide the contraband. Not only will legalizing narcotics lead to a new segment of users, some of whom will surely become addicted; it will not rid society of the black market and its attendant crimes.

Prostitution and Pornography

Prostitution and pornography are no more victimless crimes than is drug use. Although it is impossible to eliminate these vices altogether, it behooves the good society to keep them from flourishing. The Catholic Church sees prostitution and pornography as an attack on marriage and the family, and with good reason: they draw men away from their marital vows. In the case of prostitution, Catholic social thought has long condemned human trafficking of women and children and has repeatedly denounced the sins of the flesh as undermining marriage. Similarly, pornography appeals to our most debased appetites, objectifying women, thus making their exploitation easier. In the case of child pornography, the results are devastating to children.

Dr. Melissa Farley has studied what happens to prostitutes, and it is not pretty. "In prostitution, she is depersonalized; her name and identity disappear. She shuts down her feelings to protect herself. She becomes 'something for him to empty himself into, acting as a kind of human toilet.'"[9] How can the good society be realized if the dehumanization of women is legally supported by government? One does not have to embrace the Catholic value of "focus on the other" to realize that prostitution moves the individual further away from recognizing his social obligations, and toward a preoccupation with his own gratification. Instead of legitimizing intemperance, the good society needs to keep it in check.

The same is true of pornography. Catholicism opposes pornography because it contravenes God's will by inviting the individual to see sexuality as a solitary exercise. Sexuality is a gift, something to be enjoyed by men and women as an expression of their marital love; it was not meant to sever men from women. But that is what pornography does: it destroys the communion of men and women by focusing on the self, not the other. In doing so it corrupts the individual and coarsens human relationships.

Consider this: in 2010 an important statement on pornography was published that confirmed the Church's teachings on the subject without ever intending to do so. What makes the document so impressive is that it was signed by a wide array of scholars. *The Social Costs of Pornography: A Statement of Findings and Recommendations* found the support of agnostics and atheists, along with Catholics, Protestants, Jews, and Muslims. Those on the right and the left were represented, as were people who specialize in economics, medicine, psychiatry, psychology, sociology, journalism, and law.[10]

Its first finding was that the Internet has made possible a historic level of access to pornography. Second, it found that today's pornography is qualitatively different from what has been available in the past, and that addiction is now at record levels. The third finding describes how women have been harmed by this vice: "Several researchers report that women typically feel betrayal, loss, mistrust, devastation, and anger as a result of the discovery of a partner's pornography use and/or online sexual activity."[11] The harm done to children is the fourth finding; for example, children and adolescents use pornography to coerce each other into sexual behavior. The fifth finding outlines the demographics of Internet pornography. "Women of all ages comprise 80% of those trafficked, children comprise 50%, and of those women and children 70% are used for sexual exploitation." The effects on the users is the sixth finding: it undermines marital and other intimate relationships.

The seventh finding is particularly important: "Pornography consumption is philosophically and morally problematic." In other words, it is not just a private matter. Quoting one of the signatories, Hadley Arkes, a recent convert to Catholicism, the report says that pornography, like prostitution, is intrinsically wrong, and that "there is something of inescapable moral significance about sex in creatures who have moral reasons for extending or withdrawing their love."[12] Owing to its overriding social implications, then, pornography cannot be understood as a purely individual matter. The eighth finding therefore makes great sense: it calls for the regulation of pornography. The signatories do not see pornography (or prostitution) as a victimless crime; they see it as undermining the building of the good society. In sum, these scholars, most of whom are not Catholic, have successfully made the Catholic case for treating pornography as a vice that warrants criminalization.

Chastity

Chastity is an annexed virtue of temperance, one that is often misunderstood. The chaste person is not some uptight neurotic afraid of normal sexual desires; he or she is someone who values sexuality as an expression of love, finding complete reward in the marital state. Promiscuity, the opposite of chastity, is unquestionably a social liability because it does great harm to marriage and the family, the two building blocks of society. The Catholic emphasis on temperance and chastity, then, serves the best interests of society by nurturing those virtues that allow for marital fidelity. This healthy understanding of the meaning of sexuality originated not with Catholicism but with Judaism.

We learn in Genesis that sexuality is a gift from God; it is a tribute to the sexually complementary roles of males and females. Human beings are expected to control their sexuality and express themselves responsibly within marriage. The Old Testament is not ambiguous about the appropriateness of sexual relations being confined to marriage. Leviticus, for example, condemns incest, adultery, homosexuality, and bestiality. This teaching was truly revolutionary as it broke with the customary acceptance of nonmarital sex.

For Dennis Prager, an Orthodox Jewish author, Judaism, quite unlike the religious and secular traditions before it, "placed controls on sexual activity." By that he means that sexuality "was to be sanctified—which in Hebrew means 'separated'—from the world and placed in the home, in the bed of husband and wife." Prager says, "Judaism's restricting of sexual behavior was one of the essential elements that enabled society to progress." How so? "Societies that did not place boundaries around sexuality were stymied in their development. The subsequent dominance of the Western world can, to a significant extent, be attributed to the sexual revolution, initiated by Judaism and later carried forward by Christianity."[13]

When Prager argues that "Judaism has a sexual ideal— marital sex," he is also giving voice to the Catholic perspective. The New Testament accepts the Old Testament teachings on sexuality, fortifying them by referencing Jesus's role in deepening our understanding. In the New Testament we learn that chastity is a virtue, and that marital relations are sacrosanct. It is not without significance that the early Christian writers wrote against the backdrop of societies where sexual licentiousness was commonplace. Prostitution, divorce, abortion, and infanticide were not treated as social liabilities; those societies suffered as a result. It is important to keep in mind that three of the Ten Commandments address marriage and the family: the fourth demands parental respect; the sixth condemns adultery; and the ninth forbids lust. All show the role that chastity plays in society.

Chastity is valued by Catholicism because it is the key to self-mastery. Self-mastery, in turn, is the key to individual and social well-being. The great sociologist Émile Durkheim touted the virtue of self-mastery as the key to freedom. For Durkheim, self-mastery meant the ability of the individual to practice self-restraint. Without it, he maintained, it would not be possible for us to develop our resources or to realize our potential. Catholic thought is quite at home with this formulation—the Church has long defined freedom as self-mastery—only in the eyes of the Church, there is a defined link between chastity and self-mastery. That link finds expression in the marital union, where men and women can give of themselves without restrictions. True sexual liberation, the Church counsels, is contingent on self-control; that is, this freedom is achieved when our passions are mastered.

Priestly Sexual Abuse

If Catholicism values chastity and its priests take a vow of celibacy, how is it that a sexual abuse scandal has taken root in the Catholic Church? Similarly, on what moral grounds does the Church condemn sins of the flesh when some of its own priests succumb to it? These questions, and questions like them, are totally legitimate and deserve an honest response.

The sexual revolution that hit Western nations like a hurricane in the 1960s and 1970s left no institution untouched, including the Catholic Church. It was a time when sexual liberation was being touted in the schools and the media, as well as in the workplace and many of the divinity schools and churches. Elementary standards of moral behavior collapsed under the weight of radical autonomy; from the boardroom to the bedroom, celebrations of individualism were the new norm. Tragically, many of the seminaries were hit as well; some of them not only tolerated the sexual revolution, they trumpeted it.

Some priests, as well as bishops, were caught up in this whirlwind and dropped their guard. Moreover, they misread the reforms of Vatican II, thinking they had a green light to "get in step" with the changing culture. "The programme of renewal proposed by the Second Vatican Council was sometimes misinterpreted,"[14] Pope Benedict XVI said in his 2010 pastoral letter to Catholics in Ireland. Referring explicitly to the sexual abuse scandal, he said, "In particular, there was a well-intentioned but misguided tendency to avoid penal approaches to canonically irregular situations." It might also be said that standing up to the prevailing libertinism, which waged war on traditionalism, took courage. Regrettably, too many in the Church opted to go along and not challenge the zeitgeist. Worse, protecting minors from predatory priests was not the priority it should have been.

The evidence on the timeline of the scandal is not in dispute: most of the damage was done between the mid-1960s and the mid-1980s, the very period when the sexual revolution was running its course. It started in the Age of Aquarius and ended with AIDS, the dreaded disease that was uncovered in 1981, putting the brakes on the sexual revolution. Bad as the scandal was, it is important not to overstate its scope. "Out of 100,000 priests in the U.S. in this half-century," Philip Jenkins noted in 2010, "a cadre of just 149 individuals—one priest out of every 750—accounted for over a quarter of all allegations of clergy abuse."[15]

The reason the scandal seems more recent has to do with what happened in 2002; that's when stories of priestly sexual abuse started hitting the major media outlets. But they were stories of mostly old cases. Similarly, while the media continue to run stories today of sexual abuse, almost all of these stories refer to alleged cases that took place decades ago. Quite frankly, there is no institution today, religious or secular, that has less of a problem with the sexual abuse of minors than the Catholic Church; it has implemented programs to deal with this issue that cover every employee and volunteer.

The Catholic Church is very much a part of the larger culture. It is not an isolated ghetto. Indeed, it can no more resist being affected by the prevailing cultural winds than can any other institution. To be sure, the fact that it is not insulated from these forces is no excuse for adopting some of the culture's more pernicious elements. Had everyone in the Church stood fast, rejecting the dominant cultural norms and values of the day, there would have been no scandal.

Matters worsened when some bishops, following the advice of psychologists and psychiatrists, thought they could "fix" wayward priests by sending them to therapy. The fact is that many of those who molest minors are not capable of being "cured" through therapy. But therapy was the chosen route for handling these problems at the time, not simply in the Catholic Church, but in *all* institutions. Although it may seem fine today to recommend a more punitive approach to address the problem of sexual abuse, at the time that tactic would have been condemned as heartless and patently unfair. "Remediate and refresh," "rehabilitate and renew"—those were the strategies that were being sold at the time. Almost everyone bought into them. It is easy today, of course, to say that therapy was an inadequate response, but that is what the bishops and the school superintendents and everyone else were instructed to do. That would account for why those who were "treated" were reassigned to a new parish or school. Mistakes were made, but the motives were not bad.

It is also important to realize that every priest who ever

sinned against a minor violated the teachings of the Catholic Church. Had these priests kept their vows, instead of following their id, there would have been no problem. In other words, not only is there nothing wrong with Church teachings; the cause of the scandal was the abandonment of these teachings. Similarly, we know from authoritative Church reports that the bishops who did the most damage—transferring miscreant priests instead of dealing seriously with them—acted against canon law. Had they followed canon law, putting aside other considerations, they would not have become enablers. But a perverse interest in "not damaging the Church's reputation" skewed their judgment.

As the late Father Richard John Neuhaus often said, the answer to this problem on the part of priests and bishops is "fidelity, fidelity, fidelity." Had they remained faithful to the Church's teachings on sexual ethics, the entire problem would have been checked. So on what moral grounds does the Church say that chastity is right and promiscuity is wrong? On the grounds of Scripture and Tradition. The answers have always been there. It was not the teachings that failed us; it was the teachers. The way to resolve any sinful behavior, sexual or otherwise, lies in the faithful application of the Church's teachings. In other words, the prescription is right, even if some of those who should have followed it are seriously flawed.

Humanae Vitae *and Its Progeny*

Mention the encyclical *Humanae Vitae* to many Catholics, as well as to anyone else who has heard of it, and the likely result will be a sigh of regret. Ask how many have actually read it and watch the reaction: "I may not have read it, but I know what it's about—it's against contraception." There is a reason that this conclusion is wholly inadequate; even a cursory read would yield a more mindful response.

Those who have read *Humanae Vitae* know that is a positive statement on human sexuality; those who have not see it in a negative light. What they have missed, for instance, is Pope Paul VI's emphasis on the "unitive significance and the procreative significance" of the marriage act. "[T]he fundamental nature of the marriage act," he writes, "while uniting husband and wife in the closest intimacy, also renders them capable of generating new life—and this as a result of laws written in the actual nature of man and of woman."[16]

The encyclical portrays marital relations as an expression of love and as a means toward the propagation of the human race. The intention is not to condemn sexuality. To be sure, *Humanae Vitae* discusses, with astounding insight, the consequences of promiscuity, but it does so in a way that highlights the healthy and love-affirming beauty of sexual relations between husband and wife. Paul VI also showed himself to be ahead of the curve in addressing the rights of women. One of the first things he asks us to consider is "a new understanding of the dignity of woman and her place in society, of the value of conjugal love in marriage and the relationship of conjugal acts to this love."[17] This is not the voice of someone with an animus toward sexual matters.

The objections Paul VI raised to abortion, contraception, and sterilization are made in service to the fulfillment of the marital act and to the cause of human life. It is generally acknowledged, the pope indicates, that sex cannot be imposed on our spouse, for doing so defies love. But there is something else, not well understood, that remains a problem. He is speaking about "an act of mutual love which impairs the capacity to transmit life." Such acts frustrate God's design by contradicting "the will of the Author of life." This teaching, which counsels against abortion, contraception, and sterilization, is admittedly controversial, but it isn't anything new: right up until the twentieth century, all Christian denominations accepted this tenet as an article of faith.

Humanae Vitae spelled out, in brilliant detail, what happens when the traditional Christian understanding of human sexuality is jettisoned. The use of artificial birth control, Paul VI said, paves the way for "marital infidelity and a general lowering of moral standards." It also allows young men to "forget the reverence due to a woman, and, disregarding her physical and emotional equilibrium, reduce her to being a mere instrument for the satisfaction of his own desires, no longer considering her as a partner whom he should surround with care and affection." Finally, it allows the agents of government to adopt reproductive measures that "attempt to resolve the problems affecting an entire country." All of these predictions have come true.

No one seriously doubts that contraception has lowered moral standards and made infidelity more commonplace. In fact, those who tout the wonders of the sexual revolution have always insisted on maximum sexual liberty, never looking back to weigh such matters as infidelity. For the more radical among them, marital fidelity has long been seen as a problem anyway. But then technology set them free. The availability of the pill, which became commercially available in 1960, did more to upend traditional standards of sexual morality than any other single factor. It also dramatically transformed sexual relations between men and women: it achieved equality between men and women, making women more promiscuous like men. If there are any winners, it is hard to find them.

What Pope Paul VI said about men objectifying women reads like a feminist manifesto right out of the 1960s. Who can seriously deny that he was right? These days, from the Internet to musical videos, women are portrayed as objects to be disposed of. The commodification of sexuality has created a nightmare for girls and young women, but not for the guys; the irresponsible young turks get what they have always wanted: sex without responsibilities. Even better, they get what they want in the name of women's rights. Think about it. Read any survey; there is a reason that young men have always been the biggest champions of abortion rights.

Pope Paul's third prediction has also yielded ugly fruit. Governments are using reproductive technologies to control their subjects. In China, government officials have long monitored the menstrual cycle of women, carefully checking for unauthorized pregnancies. In other nations the monitoring is less systematized, but no less worrisome. Moreover, population control is not something confined to despotic nations; for ages it has attracted the attention of the elites in the democracies. Those drawn to eugenic policies, and to utopian ideals in general, have had an enduring appetite for limitations on population growth, as well as for filtering various racial, ethnic, and religious strains. "Not all are welcome" has been their unstated motto.

In 2010, on the fiftieth anniversary of the introduction of the pill, Catholic theologian Janet Smith noted, "Contracepted acts of sexual intercourse are inherently ephemeral; they have no ordination to the future. They express simply the desire of the partners to share a great pleasure."[18] Some might object: what's wrong with this outcome? For starters, sexuality practiced in this way works to undermine what it takes to forge a marital bond, and that is not something society can take lightly. By appealing to the here and now, and by celebrating instant gratification, these short-sighted sexual encounters encourage us to think in the present, casting future concerns as social baggage. It is not a good sign when future responsibilities are seen as a nuisance to worry about down the road.

You don't have to be Catholic to appreciate these insights. In 1998 the Jewish intellectual Irving Kristol observed that Pope Paul VI was "absolutely right" to contend that "once you cut the link between sex and reproduction and permit sexual activity to become a pleasurable end in itself, all sorts of ghastly things will happen to your society."[19] And what has happened is not pretty. Just consider one aspect. If it is important for the good society to encourage men and women to "focus on the other," then how can celebrations of sexual rights without responsibilities be constructive to that end? Such cultural phenomena form a continuous thread. What many seem to be saying, however, is nothing if not immature: we want to enjoy sexual liberation from social norms while we're single, but we want to summon self-restraint when we decide to marry. But a culture, and the character of its members, is not like a spigot that can be turned on and off at will. We are what we nourish.

This is why Pope John Paul II, in *Evangelium Vitae*, admonished us to guard against "the contraceptive mentality." He was not being alarmist; he was simply speaking the truth. This mentality invites us to trumpet self-indulgent behavior, portraying commitment to spouses and children as more burdensome than it need be. By trampling on the virtue of temperance, "the contraceptive mentality" lets sail our most debased appetites, hardly a recipe for the good society. "A freedom which claims to be absolute ends up treating the human body as a raw datum," John Paul II told us in *Veritatis Splendor*, "devoid of any meaning and moral values until freedom has shaped it in accordance with its design." This concern with the sanctity of the human body was something he had explored earlier when he developed his "theology of the body."

Between 1979 and 1984 John Paul II gave 130 public addresses explaining what he meant by a "theology of the body." In sharp contrast to the prevailing preoccupation with the self, he offered a socially positive view of sexuality, one that put a premium on "self-giving." The theology he developed directly challenged the popular zeitgeist: the only sexual expression worthy of human beings, he argued, is one that is based on self-giving love, not self-indulgence. Profoundly countercultural, he beckoned us to see how continence was the friend of marital sexual satisfaction, not its nemesis. Just as Saint Paul understood before him, self-mastery facilitates true freedom, just as surely as intemperance works against it.

Again, the emphasis on self-mastery and its ties to freedom is not limited to Catholic thought. Although Durkheim was not discussing sexuality but the more general relationship between liberty and moral authority, what he said bears application: "Liberty is the daughter of authority properly understood. For to be free is not to do what one pleases; it is to be master of oneself, it is to know how to act with reason and to do one's duty."[20] When applied to sexual relations, this very Catholic thought, expressed by a Jewish nonbeliever, carries extra weight; it underscores how debilitating promiscuity can be. Similarly, we see in the Pauline letters the recognition that temperance sets us free. "You were called to freedom, brethren. Only do not use your freedom as an opportunity for the flesh."[21] What John Paul said about self-giving, then, makes great sense: by practicing temperance we are able to genuinely give of ourselves to others, and, most important, to our marital partner.

The Causes of the Sexual Revolution

Here's a thought experiment. Let's turn the clock back to the 1950s. It was a time when out-of-wedlock births, abortion, cohabitation, divorce, and sexually transmitted diseases were rare. So was sex education in the schools. Moreover, the pill didn't exist. Now let's think of ways to undo all of this: think of ways we could increase illegitimacy, abortion, cohabitation, divorce, and venereal diseases. What would you recommend? What kinds of changes in social policy and in the culture would you suggest if the goal were to disable the family?

Wouldn't you want to abolish the penalties for sexual misconduct? Wouldn't you want to encourage sexual experimentation? Wouldn't you want to make it easier to get divorced?

Wouldn't you want to be "nonjudgmental" and "tolerant" of illegitimacy and abortion? Wouldn't you want to increase funding for a cure for sexually transmitted diseases, without calling for a change in the behaviors that cause them? Wouldn't you want to develop and sell a pill that allowed for sexual rights without responsibilities? Wouldn't you want to teach children, in the name of sex education, how to enjoy sex, independent of social context?

Welcome to the 1960s. That's exactly what we did. In the matter of one decade we junked traditional morality and adopted the "progressive" agenda. Only the consequences were anything but progressive; we went backward. Now we have learned, after much chaos, that it is so much easier to upend a stable culture than it is to repair it. Keep in mind that no one deliberately set out to rip the culture apart; no one wanted to see an increase in all these undesirable behaviors. So if the intent was not to disable the family, how in the world did that happen? After all, we could not have done a better job of wrecking things if we tried.

Let there be no mistake about it, the change happened because we abandoned the principles of natural law, ignored some hard realities of human nature, and treated temperance as if it were a vice. We acted as if Catholicism didn't matter. It does, and not just for Catholics.

The sexual revolution had many causes, ten of which need to be discussed. As sociologist Robert Nisbet has pointed out, there is no greater instigator of social change than war.[22] It changes everything. World War I and World War II brought women into the workplace, replacing men serving overseas. They also brought about the Roaring Twenties and the wild

Sixties, as newly liberated men and women—away from the grip of family life—expressed themselves without reservation.

Technology played a role as well. The pill and other contraceptive devices radically changed sexual behavior. It was now possible to have sex without consequences, the consequences being children. Once sex was separated from reproduction, an increase in promiscuity was inevitable. A third factor that facilitated this trend was an increase in tolerance for sexual experimentation and its consequences; it was considered taboo to sit in judgment on how others conducted their sexual affairs. Accompanying this leniency, indeed driving it, was a marked decline in religiosity. For example, attendance at religious services quickly dropped off, and when that happened people abandoned the moral strictures that used to govern behavior. Fifth, there were wholesale changes in the schools: prayer was banned, discipline was not enforced, students were implored to express themselves, morally neutral instruction in "values clarification" replaced traditional ethics, and sex education—progressively understood—was widely implemented.

Changes in the media constituted a sixth change. Gone were the days when TV shows refused to show a married couple sharing the same bed; now men and women were shown jumping from one bed to another. Movies changed dramatically as well. Gone were basic standards of decency; obscenity in words and deeds were no longer censored—they became part of the mainstream. Another change was seen in demographics. Most baby boomers came of age in the 1960s, overwhelming every other age group. Young people, historians well know, have always been the greatest risk takers, the ones most likely to challenge the social order. They certainly did so in the sixties.

This was also a decade of tremendous economic prosperity, accounting for an eighth factor. Times of affluence are almost always accompanied by a loosening of moral constraints, and the sixties was no exception. Changes in social policy, especially welfare, literally rewarded unwed motherhood, creating an ethic of entitlement. Finally, the rights revolution took hold, yielding a preoccupation with individual rights and a concomitant loss of interest in individual responsibilities.

All ten of these factors put together explain how the war on temperance took hold. While the sexual revolution of the 1960s seems a long time ago, its effects are still with us. All of us, to some extent, are a product of our environment, and when that environment sanctions sexual recklessness, it should come as no surprise that what you see is what you get. In actual fact, the sexual revolution never ended; it just bled into the dominant culture. While calls for temperance have been emanating from important places, and some of the rates of family decline have been arrested, those who drive our culture, namely the elites, are as deeply committed to trashing temperance as ever before. Here are a few examples.

Researchers at the University of Pittsburgh disclosed in 2009 that students aged fifteen to sixteen who were highly exposed to sexually aggressive lyrics were significantly more likely to engage in sexual intercourse than those who were the least exposed. How can songs influence behavior? "These lyrics frequently portray aggressive males subduing submissive females, which may lead adolescents to incorporate this 'script' for sexual experience into their world view," the study reported.[23] We also know from an earlier study conducted by the Rand Corporation that teens exposed to high levels of sexual content on television were twice as likely to be involved in a pregnancy in the following three years as teens with limited exposure.[24] None of this should be surprising; if we create a milieu saturated with hypersexualized messages, those adolescents who regularly partake in what the media have to offer are the most likely to succumb to these messages.

While the media and the entertainment industry have certainly contributed to the war on temperance, it is too easy to blame them. What about our culture's teachers, the intellectuals who craft our values? After all, the kinds of conduct they sanction radiate throughout society.

Sexual Recklessness

James Miller, the author of *The Passion of Michel Foucault*, does not exaggerate when he says of his subject, "At the time of his death on June 25, 1984, at the age of fifty-seven, Michel Foucault was perhaps the most famous intellectual in the world. His books, essays, and interviews had been translated into sixteen languages. Social critics treated his work as a touchstone." Not only that: "In France, he was regarded as a kind of national treasure."[25] So who was this powerhouse? He was a man so narcissistically driven, so full of himself, so expressly defiant of nature and natural law that he died thinking that the AIDS he had worked so hard to acquire was merely a social construct. He may have been an inspiring writer, but he had about as much common sense as a man suffering from dementia. More important, what he inspired was moral and physical death.

Foucault matters not only because he infected many people with his poisonous writings, but because he provides a textbook case of what happens when someone holds to beliefs, and acts on them as well, that are in direct contradiction to everything Catholicism teaches. Appropriately dubbed "the French Nietzsche," he not only declared God to be dead, he said that "man is dead" too. He seriously believed that there was no such thing as truth or moral absolutes. In fact, talk of intrinsically evil acts struck him as mad. According to him there are no "facts," just interpretations of reality. Everything that exists is just a social construct. He lived for pleasure, declaring absolutely nothing to be out of bounds. He was so intoxicated with sex that he even justified rape.

Foucault was also a dreamer. In his utopia, there would be no God, no commandments—just free love and communes. Because there would also be places where drugs were plentiful, new forms of consciousness would continuously be emerging. When he finally "came out," this drug-addicted intellectual giant admitted to having had sex with boy lovers. More than that, he confessed that he cruised the gay scene in San Francisco intentionally hoping to infect as many young boys as he could with the AIDS virus. He did this because "sex is worth dying for." In fact, he openly bragged, "to die for the love of boys: what could be more beautiful?"

Although Foucault was warned over and over to practice "safe sex" and to stay out of the bathhouses, he refused to do so. His real love was sadomasochistic eroticism; he saw in it "the real creation of new possibilities of pleasure, which people had no idea about previously." The year before he died, Miller writes, "[Foucault] joined again in the orgies of torture, trembling with 'the most exquisite agonies,' voluntarily effacing himself, exploding the limits of consciousness, letting real, corporeal pain insensibly melt into pleasure through the alchemy of eroticism."

In the end, Foucault died of self-inflicted causes, never figuring out why he died prematurely. He treated his body like a human garbage can, dumping everything into it from drugs to sexual stimulants of the sickest kind. His life and death were surely a monument to intemperance. Unfortunately, he was more than self-destructive; he took young boys down with him. Although this is an extreme case, that's the way it usually works out: there is no such thing as purely self-destructive behavior; others are inevitably affected.

French intellectuals, in particular, have a long record of pushing to normalize sexual recklessness. In 1977, in addition to Foucault, a number of intellectuals signed a petition seeking to throw out all the laws on sex between adults and minors; among the names were Jacques Derrida, Louis Althusser, Jean-Paul Sartre, Simone de Beauvoir, André Glucksmann, Roland Barthes, and many others. Six years later, gay leader Andy Humm asked the New York City Council to consider treating pedophiles as persons deserving new rights.

None of this is new. Kinsey justified pedophilia, claiming "the current hysteria over sex offenders" was detrimental to the sexual development of children. Over the years, those who have expressed tolerance for pedophilia include feminist Kate Millett, gay activist Larry Kramer, lesbian polemicist Camille Paglia, homosexual writer Allen Ginsberg, and sexologist John Money. By the mid-1990s, an astute student of this subject, Mary Eberstadt, said that the push for treating pedophilia as a victimless crime had become so popular that it had acquired the status of "pedophilia chic." It didn't take long before the term *pedophilia* became unpopular. In the fields of the behavioral and social sciences, it is now common-place to call pedophiles "minor-attracted people," or simply "BLs." For the uninitiated, "BLs" stands for "Boy Lovers."

The Consequences of the Sexual Revolution

The war on temperance, waged in the name of sexual libera-tion, has had many consequences, none of which are healthy. Especially hard hit have been young women. In the United States approximately 40 percent of all births are to unwed mothers; the figure among African American women is 73 per-cent. We know from a mountain of data that the life chances of these women, and their children, are dramatically dimin-ished. They are more likely to live in poverty, more likely to drop out of school, more likely to commit crimes, more likely to take drugs, and more likely to spawn another generation of dysfunctional adults and children.

That's what happens when society decides to lessen the penal-ties for illegitimacy. There is no denying that when the stigma attached to illegitimacy was severe, the rates were low. What so many of us want, of course, is a society with no stigma and low rates. But this overlooks some stubborn facts, such as human nature. It is a function of human nature to respond predict-ably to reward and punishment. What this means is that if we want more of something, it makes sense to subsidize it or otherwise make it attractive; if we want less of something, we attach negative sanctions to it. We have decided we want less stigma, but we are not happy with the logical results. It is this kind of immaturity, thinking we can have our cake and eat it too, that is responsible for the negative consequences of the sexual revolution.

Here's another example. Everyone knows that promiscuous sex leads to a host of venereal diseases, some of which are deadly. But the rates keep climbing. So why are so many infected? It was reported in 2010 that one in six Americans aged fourteen to forty-nine are infected with genital herpes; half of all black women are infected.[26] The age of people contracting sexually transmitted diseases has dipped so low that health departments are now offering nine-year-olds vaccines. Nobody wants these diseases, so why do so many contract them? A simple cost-benefit analysis answers the question: for some, the benefits of having promiscuous sex outweigh the costs of contracting a disease. These people are not acting rationally; it is not rational to expose oneself to a disease that can linger for years, or worse, in exchange for a sexual encounter; but the fact that so many people are willing to accept the risk tells us that something invidious has happened to our culture.

Promiscuity is the result when people don't use their brakes. For the brakes to work—it's called our conscience—requires the recognition that to accelerate when faced with precarious conditions is risky, even foolish. Many opt out from using their brakes because curbing themselves seems inhibiting. So they accelerate when they're not supposed to, and then they crash. Most of us don't need better brakes, just the common sense to use the ones we have. But that requires practicing temperance, and our culture urges us to do just the opposite; it teaches the value of intemperance. And if we follow that path we're on a collision course with nature, and nature never loses. Nature's God has seen to that.

It is often said that the Catholic Church is too strict, too unyielding in its teachings on sexuality. But just as with the issue of wayward priests, the Church can either lower the bar, and thereby make it easier to clear it, or it can keep the bar where it is while extending a helping hand to those having difficulty getting over it. Such a stance may be unpopular, but the Catholic Church never entered a popularity contest. It is involved in the only contest that matters—the pursuit of truth.

No segment of the population has been more devastated by their refusal to step on their brakes than homosexual men. Unlike lesbians, who are usually monogamous, the vast majority of gay men are promiscuous. In the United States, the rate of AIDS among gay men is more than 50 percent greater than among everyone else;[27] in Mexico, gays are 109 times more likely to contract HIV.[28] Though HIV/AIDS is not easy to get, those who practice promiscuous anal sex find it easy to acquire.

Gay students, it was reported in 2010, are more than twice as likely to have been sexually abused as children; they are three times as likely to have been the victim of dating violence; they are four times as likely to have been the victim of forced sex; and, surprisingly, they are three times as likely to be involved in a pregnancy. The majority use drugs and their suicide rate is four times greater than among heterosexual kids.[29] It is not homophobia that accounts for the high rate of suicide (if that were the case, then the rates should be declining); the statistic is explained by the same factor that causes all the other problems: intemperate behavior. By treating calls for self-restraint as if they were calls for slavery, the gay community has been devastated by disease and violence. And it's not just AIDS that gays are fighting; the rates of syphilis, chlamydia, and gonorrhea are out of control among gays as well.

It's sad. Sexually transmitted diseases are behaviorally induced maladies, quite unlike hereditary diseases. They can be avoided, with the exercise of temperance, but for many, the temptation to experience sexual freedom, defined as genital liberation, is too much to resist. When hard drugs are added to the equation, the lure of self-destructive behavior often proves irresistible. Take Mauro Ruiz.

Mauro grew up in Mexico where he was shunned for being a homosexual. He fled when he got older and moved to San Diego. In his thirties he made a lot more money there than he ever could have back home; he also escaped the stigma attached to homosexuals. Indeed, he was welcomed in the gay community, so much so that his friends introduced him to crystal methamphetamine and gay bathhouses. He contracted full-blown AIDS in 2008. He had to wonder whether the freedom he bought was worth it in the end.

From a Catholic perspective, Mauro didn't buy freedom, but the corruption of it. If anything, his fate illustrates what happens when the teachings of the Catholic Church are not applied. What happened to him in Mexico—being rejected for who he is—is in direct violation of what the Catholic

Church teaches regarding homosexuality. Homosexuals are as equal as anyone else in the eyes of God; they possess the identical dignity afforded heterosexuals. There is positively nothing in the moral teachings of Catholicism that sanctions treating homosexuals as outcasts, as pariahs to be shunned or punished. That there are Catholics who twist Church teachings to justify gay bashing is not in dispute. But it cannot be said too strongly that those who condemn homosexuals are sinners in the eyes of the Church. Regrettably, the way Mauro conducted himself in California was also in direct violation of the Church's moral teachings. The point should be clear: just as there is nothing in Catholic thought that condones promiscuity; nowhere does the Church approve of mistreating homosexuals.

This has to be said because the Catholic Church is often unfairly depicted in the media as being anti-gay. But if the Church is anti-gay because it rejects sodomy, then it must be anti-straight because it rejects adultery. But no one believes this. The Church opposes nonmarital sex, which includes fornication, sodomy, and adultery. As such, it objects to certain forms of conduct, not certain statuses. To be a homosexual is fine; to practice anal sex is not. To be a heterosexual is fine; to have sex outside marriage is not. The idea that sex should be the preserve of a man and a woman joined in matrimony may be a tall order in a society bordering on libertinism, but that is no excuse for misrepresenting the tenets of Catholicism.

It's not just that the Church's teachings are frequently distorted; too often the good work the Church does is not reported. Mother Teresa, for instance, established the first hospice in Greenwich Village for AIDS patients. In 1989, the same year a radical gay group interrupted Mass at St. Patrick's Cathedral, the Archdiocese of New York established the first AIDS nursing home in New York City; the archdiocese gives more money to fight AIDS than any other private institution in the New York area. Worldwide the Catholic Church provides 27 percent of all the HIV/AIDS services. Just as important, Catholic caregivers provide home-based services to those with HIV/AIDS, and as the United Nations pointed out, such care is the gold standard by which other services are measured.

There is one consequence of the sexual revolution that rarely catches the attention of the media, and that is the marked decline in shame. Walter Berns, one of the most perceptive social scientists in the past half century, addressed this issue some forty years ago. Unlike many in his field who assumed that shame was a learned characteristic, he made the case that it is shamelessness which is culturally acquired.[30] If shame is a natural impulse, then attempts to neutralize it must be taken seriously.

Berns understood the value of teaching, and internalizing, the virtue of temperance because he saw temperance as indispensable to the harnessing of our passions. "To live together requires rules and a governing of the passions, and those who are without shame will be unruly and unrulable," he said. Worse, he warned, "having lost the ability to restrain themselves by observing the rules they collectively give themselves, they will have to be ruled by others." His conclusion cannot be rebutted: "Tyranny is the natural and inevitable mode of government for the shameless and self-indulgent who have carried liberty beyond any restraint, natural and conventional."[31] The link between temperance and self-governing individuals and self-government cannot be better expressed.

Marriage and the Family

It may sound pedestrian to say that marriage and the family are universal institutions, but what it suggests is actually quite profound. Given the wide diversity of cultures throughout history, any human institution that exists universally must speak to something deep in the human condition. Moreover, social institutions are richly textured systems with norms, values, and defined roles and responsibilities; they are not a mere collection of individuals. So, to say that marriage and the family are universal institutions is to say that they are a defining characteristic of man and society. If they are that important, then anything that threatens their vitality needs to be taken seriously.

Cardinal Justin Rigali, formerly of the Archdiocese of Philadelphia, nicely captures the Catholic perspective on marriage: "The true great goods of marriage—the unitive and the procreative goods—are inextricably bound together such that the complementarity of husband and wife is of the essence of marital communion." From this teaching, certain related matters follow. He continues, "Sexual relations outside the marital bond are contrary not only to the will of God but to the good of man. Indeed, they are contrary to the will of God precisely because they are against the good of men." The social glue that keeps the marital bond intact is temperance, the willingness of men and women to practice self-restraint by channeling the sexual appetite toward each other. When that glues comes undone, many suffer.

In its most ideal state, marriage institutionalizes Catholicism's "focus on the other." In other words, it succeeds best when husband and wife practice self-giving, focusing not on their own interests, but on the interests of their spouse. Since self-interest comes naturally to us, needing no social tutor, "focusing on the other" requires discipline. In fact, it requires the very stuff that temperance is made of. Temperance is a vehicle that facilitates our efforts to "focus on the other," its highest expression being love. That is why the inculcation of temperance in children is so vital: it helps them to love their parents.

Aristotle famously predicted that if children did not love their parents and siblings, they would love no one but themselves. That is not an outcome that bodes well for either the individual or society, and when narcissism replaces the love of family members, it undermines political, as well as social, prosperity. For when individuals habitually put their own interests and desires above all else, they are rendered impotent in carrying out their duties as citizens. The decline of temperance as a virtue, then, has dire consequences, vitiating the building of the good society. That brings us back to marriage and the family; that's where it all begins. To the extent that marriages and families are strong, social problems are mitigated. Because the converse is also true, it means that social forces that derail marriage and the family must be taken with the utmost seriousness.

Survey data on marriage are not encouraging. In 2011 it was found that about half of all adults in the United States were married, down from 72 percent in 1960. Worse, four in ten considered marriage to be obsolete.[32] Divorce and cohabitation explain much of the disillusionment, and no segment of the population is more disheartened than the young: they have witnessed, if not experienced, the effects of marital instability. Indeed, only 26 percent of those in their twenties were married in 2008, while a stunning 68 percent of people in their twenties were married in 1960.

It is not a coincidence that the divorce rate first began to skyrocket in the mid-1960s. The sexual revolution had begun, and with it the celebration of radical autonomy. This was reflected in family law. Breaking with tradition, unilateral divorce became the norm; it took only one partner to sever the marriage. As expected, these changes had a dramatic effect on the divorce rate: it more than doubled between 1960 and 2000; it has leveled off more recently. The social consequences for children vary depending on the degree of marital discord and the reasons for the divorce, but it is not uncommon for discipline problems and emotional difficulties to surface.

While most people understand that divorce is a social problem, the views on cohabitation are much more laid-back. Oftentimes we hear that it is nobody's business what two adults decide to do. This assumes, incorrectly, that cohabitation is without social effects. We know, for example, that couples who live together before they get married are less likely to stay married; this is true in both North America and Europe. This should not be surprising: cohabitation is based on convenience; marriage is based on commitment. The kinds of virtues that make for commitment, for example, temperance, are not likely to be nourished in a living arrangement with an opt-out clause. Moreover, when children are born into cohabiting couples, the majority of these relationships end in breakup. It thus makes no sense to say that cohabitation has no social effects that need concern others. When nearly two-thirds of young men say, "It is OK for an unmarried female to have a child," we have more than one social problem to worry about.

Cohabitation was initially touted by feminists as a triumph of women's liberation. By the mid-1980s, however, social observer Midge Decter was wondering who was really liberated. In cohabiting unions, she noticed, the big winners were the men: they got to split the rent while typically earning more; they also got to enjoy sexual relations without making a commitment.[33]

Cohabitation also affects the way men and women think about children. Except for couples who are engaged when they decide to live together, cohabitation generally engenders the attitude that children are unwelcome baggage. This viewpoint is particularly prevalent among feminists. In a recent book detailing women's achievements in modern times, *New York Times* columnist Gail Collins spent nearly five hundred pages recounting women's triumphs, saying next to nothing about children.[34] In fact, those women who marry and have children are often spoken of with derision; they are called "breeders." In this regard, it is not surprising that in many urban centers, dogs have become ersatz children for young women. This is not exactly the kind of fertile soil upon which to sow a "focus on the other" mentality.

Same-Sex Marriage

While divorce and cohabitation have long posed a threat to marriage, the push for same-sex marriage is relatively new. Never before, in all of history, has it been regarded as proper for two men to marry. While the gay community is itself split on this issue, those activists who promote same-sex marriage have been met with some resistance. Most Americans are fully on board with the goal of equal rights for gays; they balk when it comes to redefining marriage. One thing is for sure: same-sex marriage is emerging as a crucial social issue, one that is likely to be resolved either by the U.S. Supreme Court or by a constitutional amendment. Having won tolerance, homosexuals have set their sights higher: they want social affirmation, and many seem to think they can get it if society confers a marital status on their relations. The Catholic Church, like many other religions, is steadfastly opposed to redefining marriage.

Jonathan Rauch is a gay writer who believes same-sex marriage will actually strengthen marriage. He thinks it will do so by (a) making it more universal, (b) making it more appealing in contrast to civil unions, and (c) making the institution of marriage more just.[35]

Making a status more universal does not, however, strengthen the status; it may actually weaken it. By extending veterans' benefits to non-veterans, we have weakened the status of those who have earned the benefits. Indeed, there can be no benefits to one particular group if those same benefits are made available to everyone. It is true that the line between marriage and non-marriage alternatives would be clearer if civil unions and domestic partnerships became moot, but that hardly makes the case for redefining the most basic institution in society. Finally, a strong case can be made that justice demands that society confer a privileged position on marriage traditionally defined; no context better serves the well-being of children than to have them raised by their father and mother.

Rauch, at least, is careful in making his pitch for gay marriage. Others seem conflicted. Take the Catholic gay writer Andrew Sullivan. In 1997 he said that same-sex marriage would weaken the institution of marriage; in 1998 he said he didn't know whether it would strengthen gay relationships; and in 2001 he was convinced that same-sex marriage was good for everyone. But he also said that year that he personally valued the sexual freedom of remaining single. Three years later two things happened: he started a relationship with a man whom he would later "marry," while boasting that he liked the "spiritual value" of anonymous sex. To be taken seriously, gay proponents of same-sex marriage need to come to terms with what it is they are buying into, and what it is they are selling to the rest of us.

Evan Wolfson is one of the leading proponents of gay marriage. What he is buying into is not what most people would be comfortable with: not only does he object to the idea that sexual activity should be "orderly and socially accountable"; he goes further by labeling this Judeo-Christian precept "totalitarian."[36] Once again, the specter of radical autonomy is raised in a very disturbing way. Here's another example. In 2002 the *New York Times* made a decision to include public commitments by gay and lesbian couples in its Sunday "wedding pages." On the "Comment" pages of *The New Yorker*,

Rebecca Mead addressed this new development when she wrote, "Gay marriage is the ultimate celebration of individualism."[37] It is hard to top this enthusiastic embrace of radical autonomy. More important, radical autonomy is the very antithesis of what the institution of marriage delivers.

To discuss marriage in terms of how it satisfies the interests of the individuals involved effectively dismisses the interests of children. Many gay marriage advocates will admit to as much. Rauch, for instance, thinks it is possible to leave children out of the definition of marriage; he thinks raising children can be separated from marriage as a care-giving institution. Some gay writers concede that gay marriage will not generally involve children, and they even go so far as to say that if society wants to ban gays from adopting children as a condition of approving same-sex marriage, that would be okay. But that is not the way the courts interpret rights. If gays have a right to marry, then laws that prohibit them from adopting children will be struck down. No matter, the key concession being granted is that children are not central to the cause of gay marriage. It doesn't seem to have dawned on them that this viewpoint undermines their case for making marriage more inclusive.

The problem with radical individualism is that it puts the focus on oneself, turning the Catholic view on its head. It is unfortunate that this perspective generally marks the gay approach to social issues. As such, it works to disqualify the credibility of gay activists on the subject of marriage. If marriage is a "celebration of individualism," then it cannot function as the kind of social anchor it is intended to be. Marriage cannot be about individualism and commitment at the same time; the two attributes are polar opposites; commitment means the willingness to subordinate one's own interests for the sake of the union.

The idea that two people of the same sex ought to marry is one of the most foreign notions in Western civilization. Prior to Judaism, admittedly, there were few prohibitions on sexuality, but things changed with the advent of the Hebrew Bible. "The revolutionary nature of Judaism's prohibiting all forms of non-marital sex was nowhere more radical, more challenging to the prevailing assumptions of mankind, than with regard to homosexuality," writes Dennis Prager. "Indeed," he says, "for all intents and purposes, Judaism may be said to have invented the notion of homosexuality, for in the ancient world sexuality was not divided between heterosexuality and homosexuality. That division was the Bible's doing."[38] Christianity, of course, later built on this tradition of sexual restraint.

In secular thought, homosexuality was also taboo. "Males coming together with males, and females with females," said Plato in his *Laws*, "seems against nature, and the daring of those who first did it seems to have arisen from lack of self-restraint with regard to pleasure."[39] Homosexual sodomy was a capital crime under Roman law, and Thomas Jefferson made homosexuality a felony. The English Reformation criminalized homosexuality, as did English common law; eventually, these legal prohibitions were encoded in the statutes of the colonies. Such laws were passed not to persecute a minority, but to protect marriage from all competing forms of sexual expression.

The central problem with homosexuality, says Harry Jaffa, is that it is against the natural law. "Of all the distinctions in nature from which morality can be inferred," he says, "nothing is more profound than the distinction between male and female."[40] Although it is obvious that it takes a man and a woman to make a family—not two men or two women—the fact that this must be said in defense of marriage, traditionally defined, shows how far we have strayed as a culture from taking our cues from nature. Kinship, which not only defines society but is constitutive of it, is the natural preserve of a man and a woman, and their children, and their children's children. Since two people of the same sex are disqualified by nature from participating in this process, it should not be controversial to disqualify them from marriage. The fact that it is controversial today demonstrates how considerations of nature have been dismissed as irrelevant to the debate.

Proponents of same-sex marriage like to point out that because infertile couples are not prohibited from marrying, neither should homosexuals. But in the Christian tradition, and in Western law, the reason that infertile couples have not been forbidden to marry is because man and woman, the masculine and feminine, can still fulfill the biblical imperative of becoming one flesh. There is another, more practical, social concern: infertile men and women who are married can still function as surrogate parents for children who have lost their natural parents. Importantly, they constitute a ready reserve, providing backup support, when necessary. Unlike two men or two women, they can function as father and mother.

When nature is excluded from the conversation, certain realities follow. Instead of having the words *father* and *mother* on a birth certificate, gay parents are demanding *Parent A* and *Parent B*. In 2011 the gay community scored a big victory:

the State Department removed the words *mother* and *father* from U.S. passport applications, replacing them with *parent one* and *parent two*. In some cases allowance is made for listing three parents, as in the case of a sperm donor in a lesbian "marriage." Rock star Elton John's "children" have four parents: the egg donor, the surrogate mom, and the two homosexual "fathers," John being one of them.

This raises another issue: How do children who have two mothers celebrate Father's Day? How do children with two fathers celebrate Mother's Day? The celebration of these days has literally been banned at some elite New York City private schools, but in doing so the authorities have only underscored the need to deny nature. What happens when there is a father-daughter dance? And does anyone really believe that when one "married" lesbian calls her partner her "husband" that this is anything other than a fiction? "Once marriage has been detached from the natural, complementary teleology of the sexes," writes social critic Bill Bennett, "it becomes nothing more than what each of us makes it."[41]

In 2009 a number of Orthodox, Catholic, and Protestant writers and public figures, led by Charles Colson, Robert George, and Timothy George, signed a document titled the "Manhattan Declaration: A Call of Christian Conscience." The issues discussed in the document, which I signed, were life, marriage, religious liberty, and the threats to them. Regarding marriage, the statement stressed that "holy matrimony" was an institution ordained by God, one made possible because of the "sexual complementarity of man and woman." But besides using nature-based arguments, the document addressed forthrightly the contention of gay activists that marriage is a right.

"No one has a right to have a non-marital relationship treated as marriage," the document said. "Marriage is an objective reality—a covenantal union of husband and wife—that is the duty of the law to recognize and support for the sake of justice and the common good."[42] Notice that there is no reference to marriage as a "celebration of individualism."

The appeal to rights, though, is a very powerful one: equal rights are at the core of the American creed. In particular, gay activists maintain that just as it was once wrong to forbid interracial marriages, it is wrong today to deny same-sex marriages. But the prohibition of miscegenation was prompted by racism; it had nothing to do with any realistic concern over the welfare of marriage as a social institution. Furthermore, allowing blacks and whites to marry had absolutely no effect on marriage as an institution. The same cannot be said about gay marriage; it fundamentally changes the governing rules of marriage. Interestingly, no segment of the population is less supportive of gays marrying than the African American community.[43]

Beyond Marriage

The premium that Catholic social teaching places on fidelity in marriage between a husband and wife is being tested today more than ever before. In the third millennium, challenges to the wisdom of the Church will continue, affecting the very essence of society. The choices are real: we can continue down the path of rubber-stamping intemperance and moral relativism in law, or we can return to more tried and true ways of living. There may be a moral smorgasbord to choose from, but not all the pickings are equal. It is the mark of a mature society that it settles on what works best, and what works best cannot be judged purely from the perspective of adults; children matter.

The challenges to the Judeo-Christian tradition on sexual matters are being fought on the level of law and culture. In 2003 the U.S. Supreme Court struck down the sodomy statutes in Texas and in doing so opened the door for more novelties. Although the sodomy laws were rarely enforced, they provided a basis upon which to forbid such things as incest and polygamy. It was not long before Allen and Patricia Muth, brother and sister, had their case tried in federal court. Leaning on the logic of *Lawrence v. Texas*, they claimed their incestuous "marriage" should be legal.[44] Similarly, three adults from Utah also brought their case to the courts, maintaining that if it was unconstitutional to ban homosexual sodomy, it was equally unconstitutional to ban polygamy.[45] Although incest and polygamy are still unlawful, the will to strike down statutes that ban them is strong. More important, as a result of *Lawrence v. Texas*, such appeals are bound to be given a more receptive hearing.

In 2006 hundreds of prominent professors, lawyers, writers, and activists signed a statement that was, without doubt, the most radical assault on marriage ever promoted. "Beyond Same-Sex Marriage: A New Strategic Vision for All Our Families and Relationships" accurately shows the trajectory of this issue. The "new vision" was all-encompassing. It declared that the very term "family" should have "no borders," meaning that all relationships should be treated as equal by society and in law. "To have our government define as 'legitimate families' only those households with couples in conjugal relationships does a tremendous disservice to the many ways in which people actually construct their families, kinship networks, households, and relationships," the document said.[46]

So what is to be included in this new vision of relationships? Not only should gays be allowed to marry; gay couples should be allowed to raise children along with other gay couples, even if they don't live together. To be exact, "Queer couples and siblings who decide to jointly create and raise a child with another queer person or couple, in two households"[47] should be afforded the same status in society and in law as a man and wife who marry and have children. It is important to note that those who buy into this "vision" do not want to allow private institutions to opt out; they want to force their program on them. They say explicitly that their goal is "securing governmental and *private institutional recognition* of diverse kinds of partnerships, households, kinship relationships, and families" (my italics).[48] Even churches may not be exempt. One of the leading promoters of this statement, Judith Stacey, openly admits that her goal is to deinstitutionalize marriage. This explains her enthusiasm for divorce, cohabitation, and unwed motherhood.[49]

The ultimate goal of the "beyond marriage" advocates is a completely polyamorous society, a sort of free-for-all where everything goes and no one form of sexual expression or union is given a privileged position. But free-for-all societies have a way of self-destructing, leaving behind a trail of misery that burdens children more than others. This is not a matter of speculation; there is a reason that departures from the traditional, much maligned nuclear family are called dysfunctional: they tend to produce dysfunctional individuals. And when the numbers multiply, society itself becomes dysfunctional.

The Road to Recovery

A society that prizes self-indulgence is bound to be plagued by a range of personal and social disorders. While certain unalienable rights must be guaranteed, celebrations of individualism only guarantee havoc, for both the celebrants and society in general. The only medicine that works is self-restraint, or the cardinal virtue of temperance. Harry Jaffa is proof that one does not have to be Catholic to understand. "In truth," he says, "all normal people have within themselves, at one time or another, desires which they know they ought not to gratify. The difference—by and large—between those who live moral and those who live immoral lives, is that the former refuse to indulge their passions merely because they have them."[50] Practice makes perfect, he suggests, and he beckons us to consider "what moral education is all about."

Surely one way to achieve a good moral education is to steep oneself in the Catholic tradition. It can be said with confidence that those who learn and internalize Catholic moral teachings are well suited to act as guides for those on the road to recovery. Such people value precautionary measures, such as regulating activities that give expression to the passions. Prostitution and pornography, for instance, work against a "focus on the other," as do gambling and narcotics use; checking their prevalence through legislation makes sense.

Moral education also inculcates the wisdom of making the right "value judgments," not pretending that all values are of equal moral import. Sex education that is void of any discussion of the centrality of love in relationships is hollow. Furthermore, when it merely instructs on the methods of preventing pregnancy, without addressing the wrongness of relying on technology to resolve problems, it is itself immoral. To wit: if the pill were the answer to abortion, then abortion rates should have declined markedly, but just the opposite has happened. Similarly, if condoms were the answer to sexually transmitted diseases, infection rates should have decreased precipitously, but just the opposite has happened.

One major reason that out-of-wedlock births, abortion, and sexually transmitted diseases continue to wreak havoc is because those in a position to affect thinking and behavior have decided not to treat the issue of sexual experimentation with the same degree of fortitude that has been evident in the war against smoking. The reason that smoking has declined sharply is because of the all-out assault on it; from Hollywood to the academy, it is treated as taboo. The days of adults smoking on TV shows and movies are largely over, as are the days when smoking was treated as a leisurely exercise in health classes. From kindergarten through college, students are warned not to smoke. But there is no similar effort when it comes to sexuality. In fact, young people are inundated with sexual imagery and hypersexualized messages. They are taught abstinence when it comes to smoking, but they are told to dutifully follow the fifteen approved steps on the proper application of a condom as outlined by the Centers for Disease Control. In other words, we have created a cultural environment that gives a red light to smoking and a green light to sexual expression. We should not be surprised by the results.

The road to recovery must begin with a new appreciation of the family. Strong families, as Confucius instructed, beget a strong society. What constitutes a strong family may be debated among partisans, but the hard evidence does not support all ideological preferences. To be sure, it is important to acknowledge that there are strong single-parent families, but the social science data show that in general the best family structure is the intact family. What is encouraging in this regard is the extent to which the data coincide nicely with the teachings of the Catholic Church on this subject. In other words, the attributes that make for strong families find expression in Catholic social thought. Some scholars have shown the utility of applying Aquinas's theory of virtues to marriage and the family.

David Popenoe is one of America's most influential students of the family. The Rutgers sociologist has concluded, "The family began to weaken significantly beginning in the late 1960s."[51] He cites the drop in the marriage rate, the increase in divorce, and the increase in the out-of-wedlock birthrate as evidence. What struck him most about these developments was the almost complete denial on the part of social scientists of what was happening. They said the family was simply changing. Yes, but changing to what? Was it getting healthier or sicker? Given the strong feminist influence at the time, it was "academically incorrect" to talk about the family getting sicker. So the refrain on family change took root. The good news is that by the 1990s the ideological cloud had begun to lift, and social scientists began to pay more attention to the evidence. The evidence, of course, showed that scholars like Popenoe had been right all along. By 2000 he had been vindicated.

The 1950s, Popenoe says, was the decade that witnessed the family as "a major social achievement." He observes that "greater family stability was achieved in the fifties than at probably any other time in history, with high marriage rates, low unwed birthrates, and low death rates not yet offset by sky-high divorce rates."[52] That all changed with the advent of the birth control pill, the relaxation of sexual norms, and the increase in the welfare state. As the penalties for aberrant behavior and sexual experimentation dropped, their prevalence soared. That development coupled with welfare rules that gave men an incentive to abandon their family resulted in social chaos. It was as if the culture and social policy had conspired to declare war on temperance.

Popenoe stresses the need for men to get married and stay married. Marriage is a civilizing force for men: it keeps them in check, placing new burdens on them. When they are released from their commitments and responsibilities, social problems mount. Furthermore, children badly need their fathers. Popenoe stresses that "the main reason children are being hurt is because fathers are more and more absent from their children's lives, with children being raised instead by lone mothers." Society must find ways to bring them back, and the one proven way, he says, is to strengthen the institution of marriage. The good news is that most social scientists today are willing to concede that "two married, biological parents are the gold standard for childrearing." He emphasizes the term *biological parents*, maintaining that "sex differences are biologically programmed in various ways."

The role of religion in building healthy families is clearly acknowledged in Catholic social thought, but it is not always given its due by social scientists. Popenoe admits to being a "reluctant secular humanist," but he readily concedes that "religion is so intricately connected with the family that the decline of religion and the decline of the family seem to be going hand-in-hand. The more secular the culture, the weaker the family."[53] Indeed, the secularization of Western nations has meant the triumph of radical autonomy. What kept individualism at bay, namely temperance, has largely collapsed. It is only by recapturing this virtue that we can proceed along the road to recovery.

If it is now acknowledged that there is no substitute for the intact family, then social policy should confer on it a privileged status. There are many competing lifestyles, ranging from cohabitation to same-sex unions, but there is only one structure that is the "gold standard," and that is the traditional nuclear family. This being so, all competing lifestyles must be given a subordinate status. If the intact family is special, then it should be treated as special in law; attempts to relativize its competitors must therefore be resisted. By analogy, if society wishes to confer special status and benefits on senior citizens, then proposals to award these benefits to non-seniors must be rejected.

The good society must be founded on good families, and good families are a reflection of good marriages. Practicing the virtue of temperance facilitates the building of good marriages, making it easier to "focus on the other." We should therefore nurture the development of this virtue instead of treating it as the enemy of freedom and good living. As we make our way through the third millennium, the virtue of temperance will become an even larger issue: we can either continue down the path of radical autonomy, paying an increasingly big social bill, or we can turn back to Catholic moral teachings, allowing temperance to play its role in restoring cultural equilibrium. This demands that the Catholic voice be given a fair hearing. If this is allowed to happen, then it will be clear to everyone why Catholicism matters.

FOR DISCUSSION

As a Catholic, I treasure how the Church's teachings provide the best road map to salvation ever written. As a sociologist, I appreciate how those teachings provide the makings of the good society. This book addresses the latter issue.

If the Church's teachings are a tonic to our social ills, then should not everyone follow them? Ideally, yes. However, I hasten to add, they need to be embraced without coercion. The Catholic Church, as Pope John Paul II said many times, is here to propose—it is not here to impose. But, yes, if everyone chose to follow the precepts of Catholicism, we would approximate the good society.

What makes the teachings of the Catholic Church so suitable to good living are its abiding principles: natural law, natural rights, human dignity, subsidiarity, as well as its overarching focus on the other. These are the elements that make Catholicism special. The Golden Rule teaches that we should treat others the way we want others to treat us. This is true, but it is a platitude. Catholicism provides the meat on the bones—it offers a more exacting guide to the attainment of the good society.

In writing this book, I kept in mind how students might react to it. Clarity is important, as is honesty. The Catholic Church has had its ugly chapters, but it is important to acknowledge that every member of the clergy, religious, and laity who tarnished the Church's record did so by flouting its teachings. The converse is also true: those heroic sons and daughters of the Church who make us so proud did so by scrupulously following the Church's teachings.

There is a lot of information in this book. But while historical facts, quotes, data, and the like are central to the book's credibility, at the end of the day what matters most is what the reader takes away from it. To help guide the reader in this regard, I have prepared ten discussion items. It is my hope that in the course of answering these questions, students can come to a greater appreciation of the role that Catholicism plays in the making of the good society.

1. Explain why the pursuit of the good society is predicated on a realistic understanding of human nature.

2. Discuss why a free society rests on strong marriages and strong families.

3. Discuss why prudence is integral to justice, fortitude, and temperance.

4. Why is the Catholic response to the dispossessed more efficacious than the secular response?

5. Compare and contrast the way Pope Pius XII responded to fascism with the way Pope John Paul II responded to communism.

6.   Discuss the negative stereotypes regarding the Catholic Church's view of science, as well as its role in the Crusades and the Inquisition, and why the conventional view is flawed.

7.   Explain the relationship between temperance and liberty.

8.   Discuss the role that natural law played in the Church's approach to slavery.

9.   Explain how the nuns put the Church's principle of subsidiarity into operation.

10.   Explain why abortion should be considered a civil rights issue.

Acknowledgments

No book is written without the support of loved ones, and in my case this means Valerie, Caryn, Caitlin, and Tara. My mentor, Father Philip Eichner, to whom this book is dedicated, has been a source of reliable advice for decades. No person influenced my professional career more than Irving Louis Horowitz, the founder of Transaction Publishers; St. Irv passed away on March 21, 2012.

The idea for this book belongs to Trace Murphy, and while I accept all responsibility for its contents, without his initial input this book may not have been written. Trace passed the baton to Gary Jansen, who has been an absolute joy to work with. The Image team: Jennifer Puglisi, Cindy Brovsky, Johanna Inwood, and Carie Freimuth have done a splendid job; the advice of Maggie Carr proved inestimable. As always, my agent, Loretta Barrett, has been an invaluable resource.

Finally, I would like to thank all of my Catholic League members, as well as my staff. Their dedication, encouragement, and overall level of enthusiasm is what drives me to excel. Their support is deeply appreciated.

It is my hope that this book will trigger a new sense of pride in practicing Catholics, and that it may act as a catalyst for renewal within the ranks of those who have fallen away. To those who are not Catholic, may it inspire a fresh look at the noble legacy of the Catholic Church.

NOTES

Introduction

1. Robert Nisbet, *Prejudices* (Cambridge: Harvard University Press, 1982), p. 46.
2. Ibid., p. 47.
3. Ibid., p. 41.
4. Thomas E. Woods, *How the Catholic Church Built Western Civilization* (Washington, D.C.: Regnery, 2005), pp. 47–57.
5. James J. Walsh, *The World's Debt to the Catholic Church* (Boston: The Stratford Co., 1924), p. 55.
6. Elisabetta Povoledo, "Two Rebel Figures, One Traditional Painting," *New York Times*, June 8, 2011.
7. Walsh, *The World's Debt to the Catholic Church*, p. 18.
8. Pope Benedict XVI, *Great Teachers* (Huntington, Indiana: Our Sunday Visitor), p. 25.
9. Ibid., p, 27.
10. Will Durant, *The Age of Faith* (New York: Simon and Schuster, 1950), p. 856.
11. Pope Benedict XVI, *Great Teachers*, p. 27.
12. Charles David Eldridge, *Christianity's Contributions to Civilization* (Nashville, Tennessee: Cokesbury Press, 1928), p. 135.
13. Ian Marcus Corbin, " 'Great Art Survives,' " *Commonweal*, February 27, 2009.
14. Michael Novak, "How Christianity Created Capitalism," *AEI Online*, January 1, 2000.
15. Ibid.
16. Charles Murray, "Human Accomplishment," *AEI Bradley Lecture*, March 9, 1998.
17. David Kelley, "An Interview with Charles Murray," www.objectivist center.org.
18. Rodney Stark, "Catholicism and Science," www.catholicleague.org, September 2004.
19. David Klinghoffer, "Breaking Cease-Fire Between Science and Religion," *Forward*, July 17, 2009.
20. Stark, "Catholicism and Science."
21. James Hannam, *The Genesis of Science* (Washington, D.C.: Regnery, 2011), p. 347.

22. Jerome Christenson, "Vatican Astronomer: Science, Religion Not Enemies," www.lacrossetribune.com, February 15, 2011.

23. Profile, "Georges Lemaître, Father of the Big Bang," www.amnh.org.

24. Mark Midbon, "'A Day Without Yesterday': Georges Lamaître & the Big Bang," www.catholiceducation.org.

25. Ibid.

26. Rodney Stark, *The Victory of Reason* (New York: Random House, 2005), p. x.

27. Ibid., p. 233.

28. Pope Benedict XVI, *Caritas in Veritate*, June 29, 2009, at 53.

29. Cindy Wooden, "Selfishness, Lack of Respect for Life Lead to Destruction, Pope Says," www.catholicnews.com, January 11, 2010.

30. Ibid.

31. Thomas McKenna, Interview with Harry Jaffa, "Morality Is Absolute," www.tfp.org.

32. Gene Edward Veith, "Golding's Anniversary," *World Magazine*, June 5, 2004.

33. Steven Pinker, *The Blank Slate* (New York: Penguin Books, 2002), p. 139.

34. William D. Gairdner, *The Book of Absolutes* (Montreal, Canada: McGill–Queen's University Press, 2008), p. 66.

35. Nicholas Wade, "Is 'Do unto Others' Written into Our Genes?" *New York Times*, September 18, 2007, Section F, p. 1.

36. Donald E. Brown, *Human Universals* (New York: McGraw-Hill, 1991).

37. Robert B. Edgerton, *Sick Societies: Challenging the Myth of Primitive Harmony* (New York: Free Press, 1992).

38. Jonathan Haidt, *The Happiness Hypothesis* (New York: Basic Books), p. 167.

39. William C. Mattison III, *Introducing Moral Theology* (Grand Rapids, Michigan: Brazos Press, 2008), p. 61.

40. Michael P. Foley, "The Catholic Contribution to Western Law," St. Thomas More Society, Diocese of Dallas, May 7, 2009.

41. Benedict Groeschel, *The Virtue Driven Life* (Huntington, Indiana: Our Sunday Visitor, 2006), p. 49.

42. Mattison, *Introducing Moral Theology*, p. 181.

43. Josef Pieper, *The Four Cardinal Virtues* (Notre Dame, Indiana: Notre Dame Press, 1966).

44. Groeschel, *The Virtue Driven Life*, p. 86.

Prudence

1. Fareed Zakaria, *The Future of Freedom* (New York: W. W. Norton & Co., 2003), pp. 30–34.

2. Orlando Patterson, *Freedom, Vol 1: Freedom in the Making of Western Culture* (New York: Basic Books, 1991), p. x.

3. Rodney Stark, *The Victory of Reason* (New York: Random House, 2005), p. 31.

4. Patterson, *Freedom, Vol. 1*, p. 403.

5. "Pundits and Editorials," *The National Journal*, April 18, 2008.
6. The Universal Declaration of Human Rights was adopted by the General Assembly of the United Nations in Paris on December 10, 1948.
7. Mary Ann Glendon, "Rights Babel: The Universal Rights Idea at the Dawn of the Third Millennium," *Gregorianum* 79/4, 1998, p. 623.
8. Thomas D. Williams, *Who Is My Neighbor?* (Washington, D.C.: The Catholic University Press of America, 2005), p. xv.
9. Pope John Paul II address to the diplomatic corps accredited to the Holy See, January 9, 1989.
10. Thomas S. Kidd, *God of Liberty* (New York, Basic Books, 2010).
11. William D. Gairdner, *The Book of Absolutes* (Montreal, Canada: McGill–Queen's Press, 2008), p. 183.
12. Walter Berns, *The First Amendment and the Future of American Democracy* (New York: Basic Books, 1976), p. 13.
13. Michael W. McConnell, "Trashing Natural Law," *New York Times*, August 16, 1991.
14. For an interesting op-ed on this subject, see Jerome J. Shestack, "There's Nothing Alien About Natural Law," *Wall Street Journal*, September 6, 1991.
15. Charles E. Rice, *50 Questions on the Natural Law* (San Francisco: Ignatius Press, 1993), p. 26.
16. Fred Stopsky, *Bartolomé de las Casas* (Lowell, Massachusetts: Discovery Enterprises, 1992).
17. Fred Stopsky, *Catholicism and Slavery* (New York: Catholic League publication, 1999).
18. Stopsky, *Bartolomé de las Casas*, p. 14.
19. Joel S. Panzer, *The Popes and Slavery* (New York: Alba House, 1997), p. 16.
20. Stopsky, *Bartolomé de las Casas*, p. 39.
21. Ibid., p. 42.
22. Hadley Arkes, "Our Natural Rights: Speaking Prose All Our Lives," *The Heritage Lectures*, December 11, 1991.
23. Thomas G. West, "The Theology of the United States," www.insidecatholic.com, March 4, 2009.
24. John T. Noonan, *The Church That Can and Cannot Change* (Notre Dame, Indiana: Notre Dame Press, 2005), p. 32.
25. Shestack, "There's Nothing Alien About Natural Rights."
26. "The Legacy of Dr. Martin Luther King," www.voanews.com, January 18, 2010.
27. Rice, *50 Questions on the Natural Law*, p. 28.
28. Edmund Burke, in Ross J. S. Hoffman and Paul Levack, eds., *Burke's Politics* (New York: Knopf, 1967), p. 285.
29. "Jerry Springer Dirties Carnegie Hall's Reputation," www.catholicleague.org, March 24, 2008.
30. "Myers Desecrates the Eucharist," www.catholicleague.org, July 24, 2008.

31. James Q. Wilson, *The Moral Sense* (New York: Free Press, 1993), p. 5.
32. Dennis Prager, "No Act Is Always Wrong," *Ultimate Issues*, January–March 1991.
33. George Washington, "Letter to Roman Catholics," March 1790, www.teachingamericanhistory.org.
34. Dennis McManus, "Looking at the World in a Theological Way," *The Catholic World*, November 1, 1994.
35. Williams, *Who Is My Neighbor?*, p. 35.
36. Ibid.
37. Pope John Paul II, *The Gospel of Life* (Boston: Pauline Books and Media, 1995), at 19, p. 37.
38. Pope John Paul II, *The Splendor of Truth* (Boston: Pauline Books and Media, 1993), at 73, pp. 92–93.
39. Ibid., at 96, p. 118.
40. Ibid., at 17, p. 30.
41. Ibid., at 13, p. 25.
42. Ibid., at 32, p. 48.
43. Pope Benedict XVI, *Caritas in Veritate*, at 78.
44. "Benedict XVI: Freedom Is in the 'Yes,'" www.zenit.org, June 25, 2008.
45. Pope Benedict XVI, *Spe Salvi*, November 30, 2007, at 25.
46. Pope Benedict XVI, *Caritas in Veritate*, at 43.
47. See "Religious Freedom Is the Path to Peace, Pope Says," www.asianews.org, December 16, 2010.
48. Pope Benedict XVI, "Address of His Holiness Benedict XVI to the Bishops of the United States of America on Their 'Ad Limina' Visit," January 19, 2012.
49. Pope Benedict XVI, "Address of His Holiness Benedict XVI to the Participants in the Ecclesial Diocesan Convention in Rome," June 6, 2005.
50. Pope Benedict XVI, *Caritas in Veritate*, at 9.
51. Williams, *Who Is My Neighbor?*, p. 147.
52. Richard John Neuhaus, "The Politics of Bioethics," *First Things*, November 1, 2007.
53. Steven Pinker, "The Stupidity of Dignity," *The New Republic*, May 28, 2008.
54. Pope John Paul II, *The Splendor of Truth*, p. 24.
55. Richard John Neuhaus, "One May Be Opposed to the Use of the Death Penalty and Still Not Terribly Cheered by the Vote of the United Nations General Assembly in Favor of a Global Moratorium Against It," *First Things*, March 1, 2008.
56. Leon R. Kass, "The Meaning of Life—in the Laboratory," *The Public Interest*, Winter 2002.
57. Ibid.
58. Robert P. George, "Embryo Ethics," *Daedalus*, Winter 2008.
59. Malcolm Ritter, "Adult Stem Cell Research Far Ahead of Embryonic," Associated Press Online, August 2, 2010.

60. Michael Fumento, "The Great Stem-Cell-Research Scam," *New York Post*, July 15, 2009.

61. Serrin M. Foster, "How Men Convinced Women to Be Pro-Abortion," *Our Sunday Visitor*, March 23, 1997, p. 17.

62. Ibid.

63. John T. Noonan, *The Morality of Abortion* (Cambridge: Harvard University Press, 1970), p. 5.

64. Pope John Paul II, *The Gospel of Life*, at 54, p. 89.

65. Pope John Paul II, *The Gospel of Life*, at 20, p. 39.

66. "Mother Teresa Quotes," www.brainyquote.com.

67. Pope John Paul II, *The Gospel of Life*, at 2, pp. 12–13.

68. Ruth Padawer, "Unnatural Selection," *New York Times Magazine*, August 14, 2011, p. 22.

69. Pope John Paul II, *The Gospel of Life*, at 99, p. 157.

70. Mary Meehan, "Why Prolifers Won't Quit: The Children," *National Catholic Register*, January 17, 1988, p. 5.

71. Ray Kerrison, "Stop Jack the Dripper Before Life Becomes Worthless," *New York Post*, August 27, 1996.

72. Joyce Price, "Kevorkian Attacks the AMA, the Media; Anger Also Aimed at Religious Foes," *Washington Times*, July 30, 1996, p. A6.

73. Mary Eberstadt, "Pro-Animal, Pro-Life," *First Things*, June/July 2009, p. 15.

74. Pope John Paul II, *The Gospel of Life*, at 72, p. 119.

75. See Robert Jay Lifton, "German Doctors and the Final Solution," *New York Times*, September 21, 1986; Harold O. J. Brown, "Euthanasia: Strange Bedfellow," *The Religion and Society Report*, April 1996; Miguel A. Faria, Jr., M.D., "Euthanasia, Medical Science and the Road to Genocide," www.jpands.org.

Justice

1. The National Council of Catholic Bishops (NCCB, later renamed the United States Conference of Catholic Bishops, USCCB) released their pastoral letter *Economic Justice for All* in 1986.

2. Dan Lynch, "Dorothy Day's Pro-Life Memories," www.catholiceducation.org.

3. Pope Leo XIII, "On Capital and Labor," May 15, 1981, at 6.

4. Ibid., at 3.

5. Ibid., at 42.

6. Pope Pius XI, "On Reconstruction of the Social Order," May 15, 1931, at 46.

7. Ibid., at 80.

8. Pope Leo XIII, "On Capital and Labor," at 30.

9. Brad Miner, "Subsidiarity: A Primer," www.catholiceducation.org.

10. Pope John XXIII, "On Christianity and Social Progress," May 15, 1961, at 68.

11. Pope Paul VI, "On the Development of Peoples," March 26, 1967, at 77.
12. Pope John Paul II, *Centesimus Annus*, January 5, 1991, at 13.
13. Ibid., at 48.
14. Pope Benedict XVI, *Caritas in Veritate*, July 7, 2009, at 57.
15. Charles Murray, "The Coming of Custodial Democracy," *Commentary*, September 1988.
16. Alexis de Tocqueville's *Memoir on Pauperism*, translated by Seymour Drescher (London: Civitas, 1997).
17. Ibid.
18. Charles Murray, *Losing Ground* (New York: Basic Books, 1984).
19. Thomas Sowell, "Preserving a Vision," *New York Post*, June 3, 2006, p. 19.
20. Richard Cloward and Frances Fox Piven, "A Strategy to End Poverty," *Nation*, May 2, 1966, pp. 510–517.
21. William Donohue, "Beware the 'Friends of the Poor,'" 2001, www.catholicleague.org.
22. William Donohue, "Charitable Giving: Stereotypes Exploded," 2007, www.catholicleague.org.
23. Richard Greene and Eric Marrapodi, "Religion Is Good for America, Authors Argue," www.religion.blogs.cnn, December 17, 2010.
24. Donohue, "Charitable Giving: Stereotypes Exploded."
25. "Catholic and Other Church-Owned Health Systems Deliver Better Quality Care, According to Thomson Reuters Study," PR Newswire, August 9, 2010.
26. Charles J. Chaput, "A Charitable Endeavor," *First Things*, November 2009.
27. Jean Maalouf, "Teresa of Calcutta, Blessed (1910–1997), *Encyclopedia of Catholic Social Thought, Social Science, and Social Policy*, eds. Michael L. Coulter, Stephen M. Krason, Richard S. Myers, Joseph A. Varacalli (Lanham, Maryland: The Scarecrow Press, 2007), p. 1056.
28. Father Brian Kolodiejchuk, *Mother Teresa: Come Be My Light* (New York: Doubleday, 2007), p. ix.
29. "Mother Teresa Quotes," www.brainyquote.com.
30. Carol K. Coburn and Martha Smith, *Spirited Lives* (Chapel Hill, North Carolina: University of North Carolina Press, 1999), p. 101.
31. Maureen Fitzgerald, *Habits of Compassion* (Urbana and Chicago: University of Illinois Press, 2006), p. 4.
32. Timothy M. Dolan, "The Catholic Schools We Need," *America*, September 13, 2010.
33. Ibid.
34. Ibid.
35. William Donohue, "Father Rick: Haitian Hero," *Catalyst*, April 2010, www.catholicleague.org.
36. Ibid.

37. William Donohue, "What Inspires Father Rick," *Catalyst*, May 2010, www.catholicleague.org.
38. Ibid.
39. Ibid.
40. Ibid.
41. Ibid.
42. Mother Frances X. Cabrini, "The Sweetness of a Sunday Gathering," *Catholics in New York: Society, Culture, and Politics, 1808–1946*, ed. Terry Golway (New York: Fordham University Press and Museum of the City of New York, 2008), p. 81.
43. "The Hispanic Presence: Challenge and Commitment," Pastoral Letter of the United States Bishops, 1984.
44. "Strangers No Longer: Together on the Journey of Hope," A Pastoral Letter Concerning Migration from the Catholic Bishops of Mexico and the United States, 2003.
45. "Forming Consciences for Faithful Citizenship," United States Conference of Catholic Bishops, Washington, D.C., 2007.
46. "Answering Tough Questions About Immigration," *Our Sunday Visitor*, May 16, 2010.
47. Gerald Renner, "The Legacy of a Workers' Champion," *National Catholic Reporter*, May 10, 2002.

Fortitude

1. Pope John Paul II, *Veritatis Splendor*, at 92–93, pp. 114–15.
2. Robert Royal, *The Catholic Martyrs of the Twentieth Century* (New York: Crossroad, 2000), p. 1.
3. Pope Benedict XVI, "Faith, Reason and the University: Memories and Reflections," University of Regensburg, September 12, 2006.
4. Pope Benedict XVI, World Peace Day Message 2010.
5. "Pope Supporters Speak Up," www.catholicleague.org.
6. Ibid.
7. Ibid.
8. Thomas F. Madden, *The New Concise History of the Crusades* (Lanham, Maryland: Rowman and Littlefield, 2005), p. 217.
9. Ibid., p. 218.
10. Ibid.
11. Thomas F. Madden, "Inventing the Crusades," *First Things*, June/July 2009.
12. Robert Spencer, *Islam Unveiled* (New York: Encounter Books, 2002), p. 138.
13. Madden, "Inventing the Crusades."
14. Thomas F. Madden, "The Truth About the Spanish Inquisition," *Crisis*, September 2003.
15. Henry Kamen, *The Spanish Inquisition: A Historical Revision* (New Haven: Yale University Press, 1998).

16. Madden, "The Truth About the Spanish Inquisition."

17. Ibid.

18. Ibid.

19. Ibid.

20. William D. Rubinstein, *Genocide: A History* (Harlow, England: Pearson Longman, 2004), p. 34.

21. Daniel Bell, "Ethics and Evil: Frameworks for Twenty-First-Century Culture," *The Antioch Review*, March 22, 2005.

22. See Henry Kamen, *The Disinherited: Exile and the Making of Spanish Culture 1942–1975*, and the review by Mark Falcoff, "At War with Itself," *The Weekly Standard*, August 11/August 18, 2008, pp. 42–44.

23. David Horowitz, *The Politics of Bad Faith* (New York: Simon and Schuster, 1998), p. 108.

24. Eugene V. Rostow, "The Role of the Vatican in the Modern World," at a Boston College conference on "The Vatican and Peace," March 27, 1968.

25. See R. J. Rummel's several books on this subject, *Death by Government* (New Brunswick, New Jersey: Transaction Books, 1994) and *China's Bloody Century* (also by Transaction, 1991).

26. Daniel Johnson reviews *Mao: The Untold Story* by Jung Chang and Jon Halliday in *The American Spectator*, February 2006.

27. Pope John Paul II, *The Splendor of Truth*, 1993, at 101, and *Centesimus Annus*, 1991, at 46.

28. Ibid.

29. Waller R. Newell, "It's the Ideology, Stupid," *The Weekly Standard*, August 16, 2010, pp. 27–29.

30. Paul Johnson, *Modern Times* (New York: Harper and Row, 1983), p. 261.

31. Ibid., p. 689.

32. Ibid., p. 296.

33. "Playboy Interview: Albert Speer," *Playboy*, June 1971, p. 72.

34. Ed Koch, *New York Daily News*, March 27, 1998. See "The Vatican and the Holocaust: Responses to 'We Remember: A Reflection on the Shoah,'" www.catholicleague.org.

35. Sr. Margherita Marchione, "Three Jews and a Pope," June 2006, www.catholicleague.org.

36. Marc Saperstein made his remarks in the *Washington Post*, April 1, 1998, and is available at "The Vatican and the Holocaust," www.catholicleague.org.

37. See chapter 16, "The Play and the KGB Plot," Ronald Rychlak, *Hitler, the War and the Pope* (Huntington, Indiana: Our Sunday Visitor, 2010).

38. Ibid., p. 288.

39. David Dalin, *The Myth of Hitler's Pope* (Washington, D.C.: Regnery, 2005).

40. Ibid., pp. 2–3.

41. Ibid., p. 4.

42. Ronald Rychlak, "At Cross Purposes," *Washington Post*, February 12, 2001, p. C3.

43. William Rubinstein, *The Myth of Rescue* (New York: Routledge, 1997), p. 101.

44. Dan Kurzman, "Hitler's Plan to Kidnap the Pope," *Catalyst*, June 2007, www.catholicleague.org.

45. Ibid.

46. William Donohue, letter to the editor, *Commentary*, January 2002. My letter was a response to an article in the October 2001 *Commentary* by Kevin Madigan, "What the Vatican Knew About the Holocaust, and When."

47. Ibid.

48. Ibid.

49. William Donohue, "War on Pius XII Hits a New Low," www.catholicleague.org.

50. Dalin, *The Myth of Hitler's Pope.*

51. Bill Doino reviewed Dalin's book in *The Weekly Standard*, June 12, 2006. See also Doino, "Pius the Good: The Brief for a Much-Maligned Pope," www.catholicleague.org.

52. Ralph McInerny, *The Defamation of Pius XII* (South Bend, Indiana: St. Augustine Press, 2001), p. 26.

53. Sr. Margherita Marchione, *Consensus and Controversy: Defending Pope Pius XII* (Mahweh, New Jersey: Paulist Press, 2002), pp. 30–31.

54. Sr. Margherita Marchione, *Yours Is a Precious Witness* (Mahweh, New Jersey: Paulist Press, 1997), p. 53.

55. Doino, "Pius the Good."

56. Msgr. Stephen M. DiGiovanni, "Pius XII and the Jews: The War Years" (as reported by the *New York Times*, March 31, 2000), www.catholicleague.org.

57. Martin Gilbert reviews Dalin's book, "Once Again, Hitler's Pope?," *The American Spectator*, July/August 2006.

58. DiGiovanni, "Pius XII and the Jews."

59. Gilbert, "Once Again, Hitler's Pope?"

60. DiGiovanni, "Pius XII and the Jews."

61. James Bogle, "The Real Story of Pius XII and the Jews," *Salisbury Review*, Spring 1996. It is available at www.catholicleague.org.

62. "The Pope's Verdict," *New York Times*, December 25, 1942. It is available at www.catholicleague.org.

63. This was cited in a *New York Times* ad placed by the Catholic League on April 10, 2001.

64. Sr. Margherita Marchione, "New Vatican Archival Evidence Vindicates Pope Pius XII," *Catalyst*, November 2003, www.catholicleague.org.

65. Sr. Marchione, *Consensus and Controversy*, p. 51–52.

66. William Rubinstein reviews John Cornwell's *Hitler's Pope* in *First Things*, January 2000.

67. Jeno Levai, *Hungarian Jewry and the Papacy* (London: Sands and Co., 1968), pp. 54–98.
68. Royal, *The Catholic Martyrs of the Twentieth Century*, p. 133.
69. Edward Krause, "Catholic Resistance in Nazi Germany," *Homiletic & Pastoral Review*, April 1991, p. 30.
70. Sr. Marchione, "Three Jews and a Pope."
71. Doino, "Pius the Good."
72. John Toland, *Adolf Hitler* (New York: Anchor Books, 1992), p. 760.
73. Gilbert, "Once Again, Hitler's Pope?"
74. Sr. Marchione, "New Vatican Archival Evidence Vindicates Pope Pius XII."
75. Bogle, "The Real Story of Pius XII and the Jews."
76. Ibid.
77. David Dalin, "A Righteous Gentile: Pope Pius XII and the Jews," February 26, 2001, www.catholicleague.org.
78. Sr. Margherita Marchione, "The Truth about Pope Pius XII," March 27, 2000, www.catholicleague.org.
79. Rubinstein, *First Things*, January 2000.
80. Bogle, "The Real Story of Pius XII and the Jews."
81. Sr. Marchione, "Three Jews and a Pope."
82. *New York Times*, July 27, 1944; it was published in the *Times* ad by the Catholic League on April 10, 2001, and is available at www.catholicleague.org.
83. Eugenio Zolli, *Why I Became a Catholic* (Fort Collins, Colorado: Roman Catholic Books, 1996), p. 187.
84. Gilbert, "Once Again, Hitler's Pope?"
85. Bogle, "The Real Story of Pius XII and the Jews."
86. Dalin, "A Righteous Gentile."
87. "Communion and Liberation Meeting Sees Record Numbers," August 25, 2009, catholiconline.org.
88. Royal, *The Catholic Martyrs of the Twentieth Century*, p. 44.
89. George Weigel, *The Final Revolution* (New York: Oxford University Press, 1992), p. 123.
90. John O'Sullivan, *The President, the Pope, and the Prime Minister* (Washington, D.C.: Regnery, 2006), p. 14.
91. Weigel, *The Final Revolution*, p. 125.
92. Joan Frawley Desmond, "Witness to Hope: George Weigel Writes a Sequel to John Paul II's Biography," *National Catholic Register*, September 12–25, 2010.
93. George Weigel, *Witness to Hope* (New York: HarperCollins, 1999), p. 320.
94. Richard Bernstein, "Did John Paul Help Win the Cold War? Just Ask the Poles," *New York Times*, April 6, 2005.
95. O'Sullivan, *The President, the Pope, and the Prime Minister*, p. 111.
96. Michael Hastings, "A Pontiff for the Ages," *Newsweek*, April 11, 2005.
97. Weigel, *Witness to Hope*, p. 402.

98. "Italian Commission: Soviet Union Ordered Pope John Paul II's Shooting," Associated Press, March 3, 2006.

99. Andrew Nagorski, "The Life of a Pope," *Newsweek*, April 2, 2005.

100. O'Sullivan, *The President, the Pope, and the Prime Minister*, p. 133.

101. Franklyn J. Balasundaram, ed., "Martyrs in the History of Christianity," chapter 13: The Martyrdom of Fr. Jerzy Popieluszko by G.J.B. Theophilus, www.religion-online.org.

102. Jane Barnes and Helen Whitney, "John Paul II and the Fall of Communism," Frontline, www.pbs.org.

103. CBC News Indepth: "Pope John Paul II Stared Down Communism in Homeland—and Won," CBC News Online, April 2005, www.cbs.ca.news.

104. George Weigel, *The End and the Beginning* (New York: Doubleday, 2010), p. 186.

Temperance

1. Alexander Hamilton, James Madison, and John Jay, *The Federalist Papers*. The quote is from Madison, No. 63.

2. Walter Berns, *The First Amendment and the Future of American Democracy* (New York: Basic Books, 1976), p. 13.

3. Richard John Neuhaus, *The Naked Public Square* (Grand Rapids, Michigan: William Eerdmans, 1984), p. 95.

4. Alexis de Tocqueville, *Democracy in America*, J. P. Mayer, ed. (New York: Harper and Row, 1969), p. 294.

5. Aleksandr I. Solzhenitsyn, *East and West* (New York: Harper and Row, 1980), p. 48.

6. Ibid., pp. 64–66.

7. *Planned Parenthood v. Casey*, 112 S.Ct. 2791 (1992).

8. Joseph Pronechen, "Spreading True Tolerance," *National Catholic Register*, October 24–November 6, 2010, p. B1.

9. Lisa L. Thompson, "Faces of Prostitution: Portraits of Exploitation," August 4, 2006, www.iast.net/documents/Facesofprostitutionlanguage.

10. Mary Eberstadt and Mary Ann Layden, eds., *The Social Costs of Pornography: A Statement of Findings and Recommendations* (Princeton, New Jersey: The Witherspoon Institute, 2010).

11. Ibid., p. 23.

12. Ibid., p. 42.

13. Dennis Prager, "Judaism's Sexual Revolution," *Ultimate Issues*, April–June 1990, p. 2.

14. Pope Benedict XVI, "Pastoral Letter of the Holy Father to the Catholics of Ireland," March 19, 2010.

15. Philip Jenkins, "Myth of a Catholic Crisis," *American Conservative*, June 2010.

16. Pope Paul VI, *Humanae Vitae*, July 25, 1968, at 12.

17. Ibid., at 2.

18. Janet E. Smith, "In Focus: Uncovering a String of Lies," May 2, 2010, www.osv.com

19. Patrick G. D. Riley, "Contraception: A Worldwide Calamity?" *The Catholic Social Science Review*, 2005, p. 320.

20. The quote is from Durkheim's *Education and Society*, pp. 89–90. See Jeff Weintraub, "Durkheim and Weber on Moral Autonomy," jeffweintraub.blogspot.com/1990/02/durkheim-weber-on-moral-autonomy.

21. Pope John Paul II, *The Splendor of Truth* (Boston: Pauline Books and Media, 1993), at 66.

22. Robert Nisbet, *The Twilight of Authority* (New York: Oxford University Press, 1975).

23. "Explicit Lyrics Linked to Sex Among Teens: Scientists," www.breitbart.com, March 5, 2009.

24. Laura T. Coffey, "Sexy TV Shows Tied to Teen Pregnancies," www.msnbc.com, November 3, 2008.

25. James Miller, *The Passion of Michel Foucault* (Cambridge, Massachusetts: Harvard University Press, 1993), p. 13.

26. Roni Caryn Rabin, "Hazards: Report Finds High Rate of Herpes in U.S.," *New York Times*, March 16, 2010, Section D, p. 6.

27. Walt Senterfitt, "AIDS 50 Times Higher in Gay/Bi-Men Than Other Groups," www.realitycheck.org, August 25, 2009.

28. Ceci Connolly, "As Latin Nations Treat Gays Better, Asylum Is Elusive," *Washington Post*, August 12, 2008, p. A3.

29. Maggie Gallagher, "Does Gay Marriage Prevent Gay Teen Suicide?" wvvw.townhall.com, October 20, 2010.

30. Walter Berns, "Pornography vs. Democracy: The Case for Censorship," *The Public Interest*, Winter 1991, p. 11.

31. Ibid., p. 13.

32. "Barely Half of U.S. Adults Are Married—A Record Low," Pew Research Center: Social and Demographic Trends, December 14, 2011.

33. Midge Decter, "Liberating Women: Who Benefits?" *Commentary*, March 1984.

34. Gail Collins, *When Everything Changed* (New York: Little Brown and Company, 2009).

35. Jonathan Rauch, *Gay Marriage* (New York: Henry Holt, 2004).

36. Evan Wolfson, *Why Marriage Matters* (New York: Simon and Schuster, 2004).

37. "State of the Unions," *Commonweal*, September 27, 2002, p. 5.

38. Dennis Prager, "Judaism's Sexual Revolution," pp. 3–4.

39. "What Plato Said," *Catholic Dossier*, September–October 1995, p. 26.

40. Thomas McKenna, Interview with Harry Jaffa, "Morality Is Absolute: Equal Protection Clause Has Nothing to Do with Same-Sex Marriage," April 27, 2004, www.tfp.org.

41. George Sim Johnston, "Open Fire," *Crisis*, March 2002.

42. "Manhattan Declaration: A Call of Christian Conscience," November 20, 2009.

43. Frank Bruni, "Race, Religion, and Same-Sex Marriage," *New York Times*, October 31, 2011.

44. Matthew J. Franck, "Kissing Sibs," August 4, 2005, www.national review.com.

45. Kay S. Hymowitz, "I Wed Thee ... and Thee ... and Thee," October 18, 2004, online.wsj.com.

46. "Beyond Same-Sex Marriage," July 26, 2006, www.beyondmarriage .org.

47. Ibid.

48. Ibid.

49. David Blankenhorn, *The Future of Marriage* (New York: Encounter Books, 2007), p. 134.

50. Harry V. Jaffa, letter to the editor, *Collage*, November 14, 1989.

51. Carol Iannone, "Family Matters: A Conversation with David Popenoe," *Academic Questions*, Winter 2008–2009, p. 12.

52. Ibid., pp. 20–21.

53. Ibid., p. 31.

Printed in the United States
by Baker & Taylor Publisher Services